I WANTED THE WORLD

I WANTED THE WORLD

The story of Joshua Hui

as told to

David Porter

HODDER AND STOUGHTON
London   Sydney   Auckland   Toronto

Scriptural quotations are reproduced from the New International Version by permission

British Library Cataloguing in Publication Data
Hui, Joshua
  I wanted the world
  1. Christian life – biographies
  I. Title II. Porter, David 1945–
  248.4092
ISBN 0–340–52459–6

Published by Hodder and Stoughton, a division of Hodder and Stoughton Ltd., Mill Road, Dunton Green, Sevenoaks, Kent TN13 2YA. Editorial Office: 47 Bedford Square, London WC1B 3DP

Photoset by Chippendale Type Ltd., Otley, West Yorkshire.

Printed in Great Britain by Cox & Wyman Ltd., Reading.

CONTENTS

PREFACE

The names of all characters apart from immediate family and spiritual advisers have been changed to names in common use. No reference whatsoever is intended to any individuals who might happen to bear these names.

The words of Triad rituals quoted in this book have all appeared in print before in other books. The name of Joshua's Triad and several details have also been altered.

In working with Joshua on his story I have been given a great deal of help by many people and organisations. From a long list I would particularly thank The Verne Prison administration for permission to work with Joshua on prison premises; Rev. Derek Cordell and Rev. John Bloomfield, successive Chaplains at The Verne; and representatives of Prison Christian Fellowship, Overseas Missionary Fellowship, and Emmaus Bible College. The organisations represented above do not, of course, necessarily endorse all the opinions and statements in the book.

Joshua learned a great deal from Annette Harris and Melvin Dunk, and so have I, over and above their great help in contributing their own recollections and information. I am also grateful to Rita Nightingale for assistance in a number of ways, and to Edward England who, by encouraging Joshua and myself, was largely responsible for the book being written.

I am also grateful to my wife, Tricia, and my daughters Eleanor and Lauren, who have allowed 'The Joshua Book' space in our crowded home and have contributed in countless ways.

David Porter

ACKNOWLEDGMENTS

My gratitude to many people who have helped me will I hope be clear from the book. I would like to acknowledge here some who have not been mentioned by name but who were very important in my time in England.

In addition to the prison administration at The Verne, my thanks to Physical Education Department Senior Officer Mr D. Grey for allowing me to work on the book when my duties permitted, and the Education Department staff for their helpful advice. I am also grateful to my Senior Probation Officer Mr G. Cowley and his wife, who have supported the project with prayer, and Rosemary, who visited me regularly with Grace Walker; both of them encouraged and helped me. Pauline, Heather and their friends were also regular visitors, praying and sharing fellowship with me.

My closest friends in The Verne, Allan Gay and Steve Spencer, have been a marvellous support to me, and there are Christians all over the world whom I have never met, who have read my testimony and pray for me.

I am grateful to many individuals and organisations in Malaysia who have taken an interest in my situation and planned to care for me on my return home, and to Bishop Ban It Chiu who put me in touch with people in Malaysia who have prayed for me and offered help. And a special thank-you to Reservoir Garden Baptist Church, Penang, whose members have visited my mother and shared the joy of the Gospel with her.

Joshua Hui

1

PROLOGUE

I was born Chan Hop Hui.

As Chinese names go it is not unusual. In English it means 'good-looking, carefree, fighter for justice'. In Malaysia there are many Chans and many Huis.

Yet the name of Chan Hop Hui became well known. In my home town of Georgetown, capital of Penang Island, many people knew it. Football fans and sports spectators shouted for Hui; girls talked about me, men secretly envied my expensive clothes and luxurious lifestyle.

I grew older. My name and reputation spread further afield. Now people asked for Hui in hotels and airports, and knew my name in exclusive night-clubs and dance halls, where my mere initials secured me credit.

And my name was known in other places. In dark alleys and secret dens, in betting shops and illegal gambling saloons people knew who Chan Hop Hui was. In back rooms where heroin was carefully packaged and repackaged, my name whispered at the door was enough to gain me entrance.

In Amsterdam and London, Hui was known. In a Penang food market, in a waxworks museum in Amsterdam, in hotels in London, people knew my name: Chan Hop Hui, the man who sold drugs.

Though I did not realise it my name was already written down in official places. Chan Hop Hui was in many files. At passport checkpoints customs officers unobtrusively looked for me on their lists and sent messages that I was in town.

Eventually I heard my name spoken by police as they came to arrest me at Heathrow Airport, London. At my trial the witnesses who had been watching me condemned me by name, though few of them knew the right way to pronounce Chan Hop Hui.

In prison Chan Hop Hui became a number. Back in the East fewer people knew me, and other names became well known in their turn. Hui lost his power to frighten and control. How could it be otherwise? My empire had stretched from Malaysia to Thailand and Singapore, down through Djakarta and on to Europe and London. Sometimes I had circled half the globe in hours, at other times hiding in up-country villages. But now my home was a cell a few feet wide, and the men I lived with had reputations of their own.

In Georgetown, Bangkok and all my old haunts people thought Chan Hop Hui was finished. Mine was a name that belonged to the past. And they were right, though not in the way they thought.

Chan Hop Hui had ceased to exist.

This is the story of how I came to change my name.

2

MR BHANG

The small grey fishing boat rocked gently in the water as the men on board hauled in their nets. Nobody spoke, apart from grunts and curses as the thick, slippery rope with a life of its own snaked this way and that, and the gleaming fish leapt around the deck in a shower of scales. The men worked clumsily, occasionally looking fearfully over their shoulders; skilled operators with too little time to do the job as well as they knew how.

Far below in the clear water, fish swam lazily, nibbling at the anchor rope, their shadows flecking the sea bed with a pattern of leaf-like shadows. Above them, out to the horizon, islands lay like black lily-pads on the sparkling sea. In other fishing vessels here and there, occasionally casting glances at the grey boat, men were minding their own business.

The afternoon wore on. Sometimes a diver slid into the water with a muted splash. Snatches of conversation, laughter and sometimes muttered song drifted towards the silent, hurrying men. But far away on the shore no sounds carried from the wealthy house and outbuildings, though people were at work there too, trimming Bhang's lawns, exercising Bhang's horses, cleaning Bhang's cars, or doing one of the many other tasks that his large estate demanded. From the grey boat Bhang's staff appeared as small, animated dolls in the distance. But nobody on the boat was watching. If they looked up at all from their straining nets, it was to scan the sea with troubled eyes.

＊   ＊   ＊

When the roar of the gun-boat shattered the uneasy silence, it was as if everybody had been expecting it.

It rounded the nearest island at speed, slicing through the water in a curtain of spray. A short, wiry man had the grey boat in the sights of a lethal M-16 machine-gun mounted in the bows. His companion stood at the wheel. They were headed straight for the fishing vessel. As they approached the gunman opened fire.

The fishermen dived for safety, hitting the water like sacks of wet grain, thrashing in the widening wake of the gun-boat. The gunman ignored their flailing bodies as his boat pulled up alongside. Leaping on board he looped a rope round the mast, tossed the other end to his partner and jumped back.

The fishermen in the distance watched sullenly as the power-boat towed its prize away. As the noise of the motor dulled in the distance they returned to their work as if nothing had happened.

Nobody would ever find out who had reported the trespassers to Bhang. Nobody would bother to ask; such murders happened regularly. The trespassers had been lucky. Not all Bhang's enemies were killed so cleanly. Some died roped together, huddled in their cabins, the doors nailed shut, the boat drifting out to sea with gaping holes hacked below the waterline. Nobody crossed Bhang and lived.

Mr Bhang lived on the tip of Arang Province, one of the rural west coast provinces of Thailand, in a house on a peninsula looking out to the Andaman Sea. Hundreds of tiny islands dotted the sparkling waters. Among them, negotiating narrow channels between rocky prominences rearing sheer out of the crystal depths, Bhang's workers toiled.

He had made his fortune from the sea, and he lived well. He was respected in the community. His generosity to charities made him popular. He was a leader in community politics and claimed friendship with members of the Thai royal family. Everybody knew him.

But behind the affluent, benevolent image Mr Bhang was a powerful and feared underworld giant. He kept an iron control over the coastal waters. That part of the sea, reaching to the boundary with Malaysia, was one of the richest fishing grounds in South-East Asia. He forbade any boats but his own to enter it. Anyone who tried was soon spotted by one of Bhang's high-speed boat patrols. Punishment was immediate.

Mr Bhang was a man whose hands were red with blood. Everybody knew it; most people chose to ignore it.

Mr Bhang loved me like one of his own sons.

Death was cheap in Thailand. You could hire an assassin for between £50 and £100. Guns were plentiful, everything from 0·38 hand-guns to M-16s could be easily obtained, and there was no government control. The police tended to turn a blind eye on street murders and gang killings. Usually there were powerful people behind them whom it would be unwise to annoy.

My involvement with Mr Bhang was not as an assassin but as a hired extortionist. Like most of my best jobs it came about because I spoke several languages and knew my way round the Far East.

A friend from my home state of Penang was illegally exporting and importing goods from Burma. Burma is a country tightly controlled by a socialist government, and many Burmese, particularly in the southern provinces, live in extreme poverty. The country possesses large natural resources – valuable minerals and easily-processed rubber. Many people risk everything to smuggle such items to sell in Penang, and to buy luxury goods such as radios to take back to Burma where they make a huge profit on the black market.

The only way to Penang was by sea. It was a well-established route plied by fishing boats loaded with contraband, battering their way across high seas and often continuing south through calmer waters to Singapore. Yet the chief danger did not lie in the stormy waters but in the presence of the Thai navy patrol boats, and the sea pirates controlled by Bhang.

The Penang operators knew that the only way to be sure their consignments would get through was to make their peace with Bhang. For a substantial bribe he would make a deal with the Thai navy guaranteeing a safe passage. It was a protection racket used by many small-time smugglers. Bhang's control of the sea was complete, so they had little choice.

My knowledge of the Thai, Chinese and Malay languages, and the fact that I knew many people in Penang and Thailand, made me the obvious person to act as go-between in the negotiations. I was young and reckless, had big ambitions, and could see the opportunities for wealth and influence in the situation. I said I wanted to talk to Mr Bhang. In no time I had talked myself into the job of being his agent.

It was an easy way to make money. The harbour-master in Penang was a friend of mine. It was a simple matter to find out from him how many Burmese boats had arrived, and to which agents they had delivered their cargo. Every month I arrived from Thailand and went on my rounds, collecting from each merchant the agreed payment due to Mr Bhang.

I never stole from him. It would have been crazy. He would have found out sooner or later and would have had no mercy. I saw too many people killed in Thailand to have any illusions about what would happen to me if I tried anything like that. So I was scrupulous and Bhang regarded me as trustworthy and paid me accordingly. In his own way he was kind to me and treated me as a special favourite.

So my reputation as the associate of a powerful underworld figure grew. People gave me respect, and many were frightened of me. A word to Bhang could cause them real trouble. I began to acquire my own glamour. Important and wealthy people sought me out and bought me presents.

I enjoyed it all. I had money, and not for the first or last time in my life I discovered that money buys friends. And I had power, because I was the trusted agent of Mr Bhang. People who wanted to get to Bhang had to come through me. Life was the way I liked it.

To most people Mr Bhang was a hard master, cruel and merciless. A tall, clean-shaven giant of a man, he was muscular and swarthy like a fisherman. The noise of gunfire often echoed round his estate – he had his regular shooting practice and rarely went anywhere unarmed. He wore shirts with four pockets, each packed with cigarettes; and under his shirt, tucked into the back of his belt, he carried a Colt 0·45 hand-gun.

He loved me, but he was no fool.

My new lifestyle was leading me astray, and Bhang knew it. I was becoming wild and undisciplined. I was drinking heavily. In my frequent bouts of drunkenness I did crazy things. I was often involved in fights or street brawls, or just in making an exhibition of myself in public. My friends regularly brought me home unconscious.

Bhang began to take action. At first I did not notice what was happening, but then I realised I was not being sent on important errands as often as before. When I went to collect the monthly payments there would sometimes be another of Bhang's men to accompany me. It was always amicable. Nobody said I was being disciplined or that my authority and standing were being curtailed, but they did not have to. Soon everyone could see it. I was still prosperous and a friend and agent of Mr Bhang, but things were changed. Bhang had taken away some of my power. And that hurt.

For a while I did try half-heartedly to drink less and behave correctly in public; but I was not strong enough to change my style. I was too fond of being surrounded by admirers and hangers-on. But I longed for Bhang's admiration too. I wanted him to love me as before, to put me in charge of his most important business, the way it used to be. And I knew that the clock could not be turned back. In the end, a full year after he had first shown signs of losing confidence in me, I went to see him.

'Mr Bhang,' I said, 'it has been very good to work for you.'

Bhang nodded. He was gently stroking his ring, a large gold band set with a green jade stone. That was a bad sign; he was displeased.

'Yes,' he said, in the soft voice that is considered the courteous way to speak in Thailand.

I took a deep breath, 'I am looking for another job, Mr Bhang. I need a change.'

Bhang showed no surprise. It was as if he had been waiting for the announcement, which he may well have been. He was a shrewd judge of personality and had his wits about him.

Sitting in his expensive room that day he was a symbol of a lifestyle on which I had come to depend. He was wearing his usual jewellery: the thick gold chain round his neck, dangling with clusters of Buddhist pendants; the heavy gold Rolex watch on his wrist; the opulent gold ring. *How can I leave him*, I thought. *This man has given me a good life*. But I knew I could not turn back now.

Bhang was biting his lip, saying nothing. He was staring at me as if he could read my thoughts. His own features remained unreadable. He toyed with his ring, waiting. After what seemed an age he spoke again, still in that polite, quiet voice.

'Go then, Hui. I wish you well.'

And so I left his service.

I found another job quickly. My contacts were good and I had my ability in languages. I became a tour operator for a travel agent in Haadyai, a town in southern Thailand about 250 kilometres from Bhang's village. My departure from his employment was not bitter. We remained friends and I was pleased; he was not somebody to make an enemy of. He often came to Haadyai and we usually went to a restaurant and had a meal together.

One evening we were walking back from the restaurant to his hotel through the busy town centre. Haadyai is famous for its shops and its exotic night life. Thousands of tourists and local residents were out in the streets enjoying the sights and the fresh air. Seeing a Malaysian friend among them, I stopped to exchange a few words. Bhang walked on. By the time I turned to rejoin him he was twenty yards ahead. When the gunshots came they sounded oddly flat, more like somebody bursting three large paper bags in slow succession. Mr Bhang collapsed, clasping his head. Blood poured between his fingers.

I was shocked and terrified. I hung back, frightened to approach. Passers-by who knew Bhang rushed over to help him. Somebody sent for an ambulance. But it was no use. By the time he arrived at the hospital he was dead. He had been hit by two bullets in the head and another in the chest.

Although I did not know why he was murdered I had half-expected it for a long time. Bhang had had many rivals in his legal and illegal business activities, and had ruled his empire with a vice-like grip. It was a dangerous way of life, and too many people had reason to hate him for Bhang to be lucky for ever.

News of his death travelled fast. The response from his family and associates was immediate and frightening. Thirty vans set out from Bhang's village in convoy to Haadyai carrying a huge armoury of guns, and hundreds of people determined to find the killer and wreak vengeance. When the news reached Haadyai the police and the mayor called in the army to intercept them and plead for patience until the results of the police investigation were known. An uneasy agreement was reached, but the atmosphere in Haadyai remained tense.

As information filtered through the underworld network I began to piece together what had happened. Mr Bhang, it seemed, had sent his bodyguard on a mission a few days earlier to murder a business rival living near Haadyai. The victim, like Bhang, was a powerful man, well respected in the community and loved by his followers. The family retaliated by dispatching their own killer in search of Bhang, whose regular visits to the town were well known.

The vendetta boiled to fever pitch. I went to pay my respects to Bhang's grieving family. I did not need to fake my own grief; Bhang had been good to me and if I had had more control over my own behaviour I would never have left his employment. I went to the temple in Haadyai where his body lay, brought by his family the day after the shooting. In the large hall set aside for funeral preparations monks were praying for the dead man every hour of the day and night; and relatives and friends stood in sober groups. From the field outside the soundtrack of a Thai epic filtered into the cool interior; as was the custom, a huge cinema screen had been erected to entertain the mourners waiting to enter the temple.

In death the hard, unemotional face had relaxed its severity, and the eyelids were closed. The bleak stare that had wielded a savage authority over his territory was for ever extinguished.

Bhang's family received me well. I said all the proper things that should be said at such a time. As I was preparing to leave one of his sons took me aside.

'There is something you can do,' he said quietly.

I tried to control an ominous prickle of fear.

'Anything,' I replied automatically, hoping the family had not chosen me as the next executioner in the chain of revenge.

'We know who killed my father. So do you. And we know where he lives. We want you to go there.'

'Of course,' I said. My mouth was dry.

'Wear Malaysian clothes. Pretend you can't speak a word of Thai. Pass yourself off as an innocent tourist. Hang around the usual places, listen to people talking, spend money. Stay close to where they're keeping the body of my father's enemy. Come back with evidence. Find out all you can.'

'I'll be glad to do it.'

I was relieved nothing more was asked of me. I didn't want to get involved, but I could hardly say no. It would have been so serious an insult that my own life would have been in danger.

I booked into a hotel for a few days near where the man lived. Soon I had made friends among the hotel staff. In the local bars and clubs I rapidly became known as a talkative and generous tourist. But before I could unearth trustworthy information I heard that the police had arrested the man. He was a Thai police officer from another district, betrothed to the daughter of Mr Bhang's victim. Feelings were running so high that the police had to escort the suspect into hiding and then fly him to prison in Bangkok. If he had been kept in a cell in the police station Bhang's followers would almost certainly have broken in and killed him. Not to be thwarted, they planned a massacre at the funeral of Bhang's victim. But the police heard of it and issued a public warning.

They told Bhang's family also to arrange for the monks and mourners to take the body for secret burial. As a final precaution an army escort was allocated to the procession.

But when the time came for Bhang's own burial, the authorities refused to allow his body to be carried by road; an army helicopter took it home to his village. So Bhang was buried in sight of the sparkling waters over which he had once been king.

And I was left with my life in ruins.

Bhang's murder was the most violent, horrific spectacle I had ever witnessed, let alone been involved in. While working for him I had witnessed many killings. They had not worried me; I was in the care of my protector. But now my peace of mind was gone. Every unfamiliar face belonged to a possible assassin sent by Bhang's enemies. How many people knew how close I had been to him? I remembered how incautiously I had boasted of my high standing with him, and bitterly regretted doing so.

On the other hand I was not free to leave Haadyai to seek safety further afield. To leave now would look like running away. Bhang's family would be suspicious. They might think my disappearance meant a guilty conscience, perhaps that I had betrayed Bhang, that I had been bribed by his enemies. I remembered miserably that I had been several yards behind him when he was shot, and they might think it was deliberate, that I knew what was going to happen; and they might come for me too.

So I stayed in Haadyai. I stopped sleeping at night, imagining every creaking timber signified an assassin waiting to strike. My hard drinking returned. I spent days in muddled drunkenness.

My girlfriend, a Thai singer in a night club, couldn't help me. She was terrified too; we didn't talk to each other any more and our old friends and acquaintances saw little of us. Our relationship never recovered from the experience and we broke up not long after. It was not unusual for me. None of my relationships with women lasted long. I was always looking for the next conquest.

The downward spiral continued. I who was respected and feared in the old days was a drunk nobody thought anything of. Physically, stress and alcohol were beginning to push me towards a breakdown.

I'd lost face, and that hurt. I'd lost power and influence. What money I had made from the job was lost too, on drink and wild behaviour. But I had lost something else: the man who had loved me and trusted me like a son. He had been everything I admired, and now he was dead, gunned down in the street like a nobody. He had been my hero, my father in crime. Now he was not there any more.

Sometimes in the long hazy nights, fuddled with drink and with nerves gone to pieces, childhood memories flooded back. I'd come a long way to Haadyai. Once things had been simple. This was not the first time I had lost a father.

3

CHILDHOOD

After all these years what I remember most of all are the chains. In the hot nights they became hot themselves, rubbing painfully when I tried to move. The links bit into each ankle, and blood seeped through, warm and sticky against the metal. Every time I stretched myself, trying to ease the weight of the heavy chain round my neck, spasms of pain shot through my feet. My father had shackled my legs and my neck together with dog-chains. It was a punishment for persistent truancy. I was twelve years old. My punishment lasted for several months.

Dad was an unusually tall Chinese, about six feet and heavily built, and terrifying when angry – which he often was when I misbehaved at school. His ambitions for me included a good education, and he was determined I should not run away from school again.

When he was asleep my mother came and bathed my cuts. I turned away from her, cold and unforgiving, hunched against the wall. She wept as she tended me.

'Chan Hop ... Chan Hop ... Turn around, let me hold you ...'

I never moved towards her, even when I felt her soothing nurse's hands, skilled and careful, swabbing my legs. In my pain I saw her only as part of the enemy, one of the adults, all-powerful, who could bend you to their will and enforce obedience by hurting you. Lying rigid, I ignored her, staring bleakly at the wall until she went away.

Ambition and achievement were the driving factors in my
father's life. His name was Shee Woo Yoong, but that was
not the name my grandfather gave him at birth. Shee Woo
Yoong was the name my father took for himself. It means
'battle for glory' or 'equip yourselves to achieve renown in
life'. He chose the name with care, and lived up to it.

Most of the Chinese in Malaysia came, as my father did, as
refugees. When the Communists seized power in mainland
China after the Second World War he was serving with the
Nationalist Army and my mother was working as a nurse.
Together they fled to Malaya and managed to find teaching
jobs in a Chinese primary school in Penang. A year later, in
1947, I was born, and my sisters Angela and Joyce in 1948
and 1949. My younger brother Woo was born in 1953.

It was not easy being the eldest. My father demanded
the highest standards of achievement, and declared his
expectations in the name he chose for me: Chan Hop,
'good-looking, carefree, fighter for justice'. He was apply-
ing to me the same rigorous single-mindedness that he
possessed himself. He was the fifth son of a poor paddy-
farmer living in a rural village in the province of Canton,
and his seven brothers all left school in their early teens
to help work the fields. But my father broke with family
tradition. He refused to work on the land with the others,
and spent all his time studying. He was so anxious to prove
himself that he left home at fifteen, went to the city, and
found employment as a boy servant to a wealthy family,
while continuing his education.

Often as he told me about those early struggles tears
welled up in his eyes. It was a story to be proud of. He
worked his way through junior school and high school
and eventually graduated from university. At twenty-four
he was commissioned in the army but gave it up to follow
his first love, writing. When the Second World War broke
out he became a war correspondent, and went to the front
line where he was wounded by the Japanese, leaving him
with a scar he bore for the rest of his life.

He and my mother worked strenuously to support their children, but their wages were small and my father had to take part-time work as well. He decided to make use of his talent for writing. He wrote short stories and a column for the local newspaper; and some of his stories were dramatised for the stage. He was accepted into literary circles, and was popular and well-liked. That is my happiest memory of my father: sitting with his friends in our home, his rich voice booming out; relaxing after a hard day's teaching, his belly quivering as his huge frame shook with laughter, the sweet smell of the cigarettes he chain-smoked drifting in the air.

'Writing is an art,' explained Dad, 'just like painting is. See, this is how you hold the brush.' He made a precise, carefully-judged stroke down the centre of the clay tile held on his knee. 'Now, you can try it.'

I looked at the confident, graceful line already drying on the porous clay, picked up the brush, and tried to imitate it.

'*No!*' Dad's hand grasped mine, forcing it to make the stroke again. Anger made his voice loud; I could feel his bulky body trembling with fury. 'How many times do I have to tell you? It is simple, you only need to learn it once. Why are you so stupid?'

I was four years old. Dad taught me to write and read before I started school. By the time I was eight I could write Chinese script better than any of my classmates, and I was winning school prizes for calligraphy. But my father still insisted on perfection. When I made mistakes he beat me. He never allowed any misdemeanour to go unpunished. When I pleaded for pardon he was inflexible.

'Look what I went through,' he said. 'Look at what I have achieved. Do you think it was easy? Do you think you will succeed at anything, if you are allowed to go unpunished and do what you want?'

His hand would reach out for the cane or the belt as I braced myself for the beating that always followed.

Looking back, the harshness and the beatings seem, in a strange way, an expression of his love for me. He had known poverty and had fought his way to a worthwhile future. He believed that the only path to success lay in iron discipline and enormous effort. He wanted me to be successful, so he pushed me hard and refused to tolerate weakness.

I was a bright child and a quick learner, and for the first few years of my schooldays Dad's strict discipline had some effect.

Until I was eleven years old we lived in the teachers' quarters in the school compound. Outside our windows was the school sports field. In the afternoon and evening the boys and girls arrived to play basketball and other games. I longed to join in, but Dad forbade it. Instead he drew up a timetable of study and made us go to our rooms each evening to work.

'You can't make a living playing games,' he told us. 'Get on with your study. When you can stand on your own two feet without me to support you – then you can play all the games you want.'

It was hard to watch other boys and girls of my age playing while I was locked away. The other children laughed at us. They laughed at my father too, behind his back. They called him 'Teacher Fatso', and made fun of us because of him. I couldn't concentrate on my studies anyway. I stared frustratedly out of the window. When I heard my father's footsteps outside the door I fell to writing furiously. If my parents went out for the evening I sometimes forced the door open and sneaked out of the house to play with the others. I often forgot to watch out for their return and was flogged for my disobedience. Those were the times that I nursed my secret ambition: one day I was going to prove my father wrong. I was going to be a famous sportsman and have lots of friends, great wealth and enormous power and influence.

When I was eleven Dad had saved enough money to buy a home of his own and we moved from the school accommodation to a house with six bedrooms. It was a two-storey, semi-detached property with large grounds in the most beautiful district of Penang Island. For my father it was the symbol of success, something that his years of toiling and saving had produced. Rich and famous people lived in the same street, and three exclusive schools were within walking distance. Standing at the foot of Penang Hill, the house was near major tourist attractions such as the racecourse and the Buddhist pagoda temple, and there was a bustling market nearby.

Dad took great pleasure in settling into the new home, choosing the best place for each item of furniture and arranging his large collection of books. He was an avid reader whose library ranged from political textbooks to wildlife handbooks. Every month we children had to dust them all.

For my mother the new house was the end of years of work, worry and illness in which every spare penny was saved for the children's education and the house that was now ours. She was – and is – a woman with a great love for her family. Every day she left home to work in the school; and returned to begin the household chores of cooking, washing and looking after her four children. The years of struggle left her health permanently damaged. I never saw her occupied in a hobby or interest of any kind inside or outside the home. She wore the same style of clothes for forty years. The pupils at the school gave my father nicknames because he was so fat; but when they left school they remembered my mother because she always wore the same clothes.

She was very kind-hearted, never meddled in other people's business and I never heard her say a bad word about a neighbour. I have no doubt that she loved me. Many mothers whose children misbehaved as I did threw them out of the family home. But she refused to give up loving me, even though my disobedience often meant times of tension and unhappiness at home.

I never saw her cry for herself, though she was often ill and life was an unending struggle for most of my childhood. But she often cried when she came to me after Dad had punished me. She pleaded with me to make an effort to change my ways and please my father. 'It will work out good for you in the end,' she urged. She even tried to encourage me to work by scraping together extra pocket money as a reward for good behaviour. How she managed to save anything out of the meagre amount with which she had to feed and clothe the household, I cannot imagine. My mother was an educated, intelligent woman when she married my father. She tried to help me in my schoolwork, and educated me in countless ways. Nobody could have loved me more.

Perhaps it was the memory of my parents' struggles, the long years of childhood cooped in while other children were playing, and the absence of luxuries in our family that made me long to be rich. Perhaps it was my father's iron discipline and the rigorous study that turned me into a rebel. Maybe it was merely the fact that I was the schoolmaster's son that made me think it was desperately important to be seen as someone who was not a model pupil. Whatever the reason, from the age of ten I knew that I wanted the good life. And I set out to prove myself.

Whenever there was trouble in school I was one of the ring-leaders. If there was a disturbance or a riot or a fight, when the teachers broke it up I would be found in the centre of it. I was the culprit so often that I was blamed for things I'd not done, which made me even more rebellious. The teachers did not know how to make me obey them, and I refused to submit to their authority. They talked to my father about me. It was agreed that some of the teachers should be detailed to keep a special watch on me, to take an interest in my problems and give me any special help I needed. But I managed to evade them easily, and carried on exactly as I wanted to.

Dad was furious. The education he had worked to provide for me, the discipline, the long hours of study I had been forced to endure were all being wasted. He threatened to disown me, but I didn't care.

When I was twelve the school accepted the inevitable. I was expelled for continuous bad behaviour. By the time they managed to tell my father I had already gone home, collected a few belongings and run away.

In my wild escapades at school I had got to know some small-time gangsters in town who were friends or relatives of my classmates. Now I went to them and asked if I could stay. They let me sleep on the floor. I lived with them for several weeks. They didn't ask me to do anything for them.

Among the younger members of the gang was Roger, a schoolboy like myself. He was a year older than me and taller, thickly set and extremely fit, though I hardly ever saw him without a cigarette in his mouth. I liked him and envied his strength and style; he was one of the fighters, somebody the gang would send to put pressure on a stall-holder or shopkeeper who was falling behind with his protection payments. After a visit from Roger few caused trouble again. We spent hours together talking. He was ready to start an argument about anything. Only politics and religion bored him. They bored me too. Religion especially played no part in my life; it was a crutch that other people used. I despised religious experiences and was repelled by rites and ceremonies. When I saw Hindu mystics piercing themselves with nails and twisting their bodies into tortuous shapes I ran past laughing. In Penang there was a Chinese temple dedicated to the goddess of mercy. Worshippers brought food to the altar and left it there. I and my friends often crept into the temple unobserved and stole the chicken and fruit. Because of my education and the country in which I lived, I grew up with a token understanding that there were spiritual beings outside my immediate experience. But I wanted to know nothing about them, and if they existed – which I doubted – they did not seem interested in me.

'Have you thought about initiation?'

The question came from a tall, good-looking Chinese who was one of my particular heroes in the gang. I knew exactly what he meant. Though they are secret societies, you cannot live in South-East Asia without being aware of the Triads, the brotherhood that runs organised crime in the region. The name is taken from the triangular symbol which represents the threefold union of heaven, earth and man, and membership is by a secret initiation ritual. The Triads demand complete loyalty and courage from their members, and their secrecy is emphasised in the initiation and the secret signs, such as the complex system of handshakes. Today some of the secrecy is gone and many branches have discarded the initiation rituals; but the power of the Triads remains very strong.[1] I knew the leaders of the gang were Triad members because I often saw them exchanging secret signs and passwords, or huddled in conversations that came to an end as I approached. They were the ones who had influence, who could make things happen as they wished.

The origins of the Triads lie centuries back, in the days of the dynasties in mainland China. In Penang strong links with the mainland in the eighteenth and nineteenth centuries brought Chinese secret societies to the island. In 1867 British rule was threatened by ten days of rioting, which began as a fight between two Triads and ended with a massive death-toll. In Malacca, Singapore and every part of the Far East, the Triads were to be found. At

---

[1] A description of Triad activity in Hong Kong from the point of view of a missionary working in the Walled City is given in Jackie Pullinger, *Crack in the Wall* (Hodder & Stoughton, 1989). Sean O'Callaghan, *The Triads: the illustrated inside story of the Chinese Mafia* (W. H. Allen/Star, 1978), gives detailed information; I am indebted to his descriptions of Triad procedures and activities.

first they confined themselves to exploiting impoverished labourers, but before long they expanded their criminal interests. Today they dominate crime in the region and there is increasing concern about their control of the drug market. In 1975 a major police offensive against the Triads in Malaysia scored some major victories but failed to break their power.

I grew up knowing something of this, in much the same way as most Westerners know the Mafia exists. Most of my contemporaries knew individual members. I knew that the leaders of my gang belonged to the House of Fragrant Blossoms, a branch of the powerful 14K Triad active in Hong Kong and all over the Far East. The very name, and the history that went with it, exerted a magical appeal to me.

'Have you thought about initiation?' The question was repeated with a slight edge of irritation.

I shook my head. It was a lie. I had often thought about it.

'Uh-huh,' I replied casually. 'Maybe later. When I'm older.' I felt very cool and sophisticated.

He stared at me for a moment through narrowed eyes. 'OK, not to worry.' He turned away.

I played it wrong, I told myself angrily. I knew I had missed a chance that might not come again for a long time, if ever.

So I determined to prove to the gang that I was as hard as they were, that I could do anything they could do. Though they didn't involve me in their criminal activities, I went off on my own looking for trouble, beating up any kids I met who were on their own. I prowled the streets, a twelve-year-old gangster. I was as hard as nails and ready for anything.

But one evening several weeks after I went to live with them my parents caught me as I was walking in the road. Back at home, Dad flogged me until I bled. My mother was in anguish; I think she felt more pain than I did. I remained like a rock in my mind.

That was how I came to be locked up in dog-chains, heavy shackles round my neck and feet that clanked as I moved.

Nothing, not even the long months in chains and the brutal beatings, altered my determination. I had failed to escape this time, but there would be others. Sooner or later I was going to leave home and live as far away from Penang as I could.

4

THE GOOD LIFE

There were no more attempts to run away. Instead I made plans. Lots of plans. Next time I was going to do things properly. That meant I was going to need money. My dream of riches became suddenly urgent. I wanted the world.

Dad managed to find a school willing to overlook my record, and I set out to achieve my ambition. With a good deal of natural ability and a talent for picking up facts and figures easily, I began to do quite well at my lessons. But I found the work boring and was soon back in my old ways. I ignored my classmates, preferring to hang around the playground with older boys, watching the world go by and looking for opportunities to get into trouble. Gradually reports of my bad behaviour began to reach my parents. The beatings began again.

Yet if Dad could only have realised it, I was actually achieving something. My driving ambition was to be the leader in everything I did. I was not satisfied with being just good: I had to be the best. In the old days I'd watched other children playing games and competing in sports; now I blossomed. I discovered I was a very good sportsman. I also became a Boy Scout and did well at that too; when I was seventeen I gained the Queen's Scout award. I loved the outdoor life and the opportunities to exercise leadership over other people.

In sport I became a successful and popular figure. For two years I was captain of the school team, and acted as a football coach for my old school. As a pupil there I had never been allowed to play: now my skills were admired and everybody wanted to be like me.

From the age of sixteen to nineteen I was a member of the Penang Combined Schools football team, competing for the Inter-States Schoolboys' Championship. We won inter-school and inter-state championships, and I was picked to be a striker for the Penang Youth Team regulars.

Eventually even my father's severity began to thaw. He was still suspicious; to him sport was a career with few financial prospects, and he was desperately anxious that his children should not have struggles like his own. But both he and my mother were proud that I was achieving something, that I had got somewhere by hard work and ability. I was in bed early every night, and was working hard at my studies and spending a good deal of time training.

If they had only known the whole story! Nothing had changed deep inside me. I was still rebellious, still planning to make my fortune one day and live in luxury somewhere far from Penang. My success at school only made me hanker even more for that good life which would give me credibility in the eyes of the gangsters and petty criminals I admired.

My football heroes were Pele and George Best. During my teens I followed every game in which Best played for Manchester United. I wanted to wear number 7 because it was his favourite number; I copied his playing style, memorised his tactics and pored over every newspaper account of his drinking and womanising. He was everything I admired and envied. I wanted to live as he did, and I didn't care how I managed it. I was prepared to take every opportunity, legal or not, to make money or increase my prestige.

My reformation didn't last long.

At the end of my high school career I was a celebrity. Footballers in Penang are almost like film stars. It didn't bring me the vast amounts of money I craved, but I was tasting glamour, power and influence. Success went to my head. I was invited to wild parties, so my early nights had to go; I began to smoke heavily, so my fitness dropped; I was surrounded by beautiful girls and went from relationship to relationship not caring who I hurt; and I began to mix with gamblers and hard drinkers. The last of my self-discipline disappeared.

After I left school my involvement with the gang increased. My popularity as a footballer gave me prestige with its members. If I wanted to do something I could count on their support. Often I called on them when fighting people with whom I had scores to settle.

We were one of several gangs operating in different parts of Georgetown, each with its own gathering-place. Our gang met in a market on the edge of town which stayed open all night. People thronged to buy the food piled in colourful heaps on barrows, and met in the coffee shop. I thought it was the most glamorous place I had ever seen. Rich and poor, the well-dressed and the ragged came to the market from the city and surrounding countryside. The aroma of my favourite spicy foods hung over the barrows, and prostitutes hovered watchfully among the crowds. But I had no need of them; I was a glamorous figure myself, a sporting hero and a rising gangster. I always had beautiful girls around me.

Lounging in the hubbub of the market, we kept our ears open for opportunities. Businessmen often came to us asking for our services – usually to help a deal along with extortion or threats, or sometimes to recover bad debts. If the money was right we agreed to do what they asked. For really important discussions we moved to a nearby children's playground, deserted at night, and youngsters from the gang kept guard as we fixed the deal.

We had a hand in drugs, illegal betting, gambling of various kinds and extortion. I specialised in betting. I made money and spent it freely. I haunted night-clubs and gambling dens, and acquired expensive hobbies; a love for fast cars led to membership of the RAF and Penang motor clubs. Daredevil driving and skill brought prizes for scrambling and grass-track racing. I entered for the Penang

Grand Prix production class motor-cycle race, coming third
in the 250cc class. Another interest was go-karting, but
I couldn't afford to compete with the top machines; I
had to be content with just taking part, experiencing the
excitement of the track. I realised I had a long way to go
before achieving my dream of unlimited wealth, but I had
made a start. I was on the brink.

I discovered that being a popular footballer provided
excellent opportunities to acquire money. You could sup-
plement your income, for example, by 'fixing' a match.
Gamblers betting on the result would pay handsomely if
someone like me would persuade some of his team mates
to arrange a particular scoreline. As I fought my way into
the senior squad of the Penang football team, and also
became a Malaysian Youth player in the Asian Youth
competition, more and more opportunities for cheating
and swindling opened up.

It seemed as if everything I had longed for all my life
was there for the taking. Money, power, fame – a dizzying
prospect. All I had to do was to reach out and grasp it. So
when, shortly after my nineteenth birthday, the matter of
my Triad initiation was raised again I accepted.

'You've come as far as you can with us,' the leaders told
me. 'If you want to go further, you must be initiated.'

I didn't need persuading. Not only were Triad members
touched with the kind of glamour and power that I craved,
but it was also clear to me that the only way to acquire a
fortune was with the help and approval of the Triad.

5

INITIATION

Since the end of the Vietnam war there is evidence that large quantities of heroin are reaching the Triads in Malaysia . . . The Malayan Chinese are the best supplied and the most aggressive of the Triad Secret Societies now operating in the growing European market. (Sean O'Callaghan, *The Triads*)[1]

The man was dressed in ceremonial Chinese costume. It was difficult to see more than the outline of his face as his features were concealed behind a mask of make-up. He might have stepped out of a classical Chinese opera. The voice that emerged from his heavily-painted, concealed mouth was deep and serious.

'Why have you come here?'

An older boy in front of me replied, 'We have come to enlist and to obtain rations.'

'There are no rations for our army,' replied the man.

'We bring our own,' the boy responded.

'The red rice of our army contains sand and stones. We eat it.'

'If our brothers can eat it, so can we,' came the response.

The words tolled like sonorous bells in the shadows. Their gravity, the darkness of the midnight meeting-place, and the almost ludicrous effect of the caked make-up all combined to make an unforgettable impact.

---

[1] op. cit. pp. 59-60.

'If you have spoken truly, you are loyal and righteous. You may enter the city and swear allegiance.'

Excitement was making my heart race. *I'm going to join the family*, I thought.

I had been told to wait by one of the coffee stalls in the market an hour before midnight. Several other young men were there. Some I knew quite well, others I recognised. None of us said much. We tried to be casual but were all tense. At half past eleven two cars arrived. I squeezed with six others into the back seat of a battered Hillman saloon. We left the lights of Georgetown behind, and travelled in silence along a deserted road, across to the mainland and on into a rural area where there were no street lights. The headlamps picked out occasional trees and houses, but we had no idea where we were. Eventually we swung off the main road down a bumpy dirt-track into a rubber plantation, and came to a stop. I emerged cramped and stiff-legged outside a derelict pig-house, grotesque in the pale amber beams of the two cars. There was a small crowd of people already there, all young men like ourselves. The leader of our group approached the costumed man. For some reason the ornate costume and heavy make-up struck me as very funny. I turned away and stuffed my fist into my mouth, stifling a manic desire to giggle. The two greeted each other with the secret handshake. The sombre interrogation began.

'Why have you come here?'

After the declaration of loyalty and the invitation to 'enter the city', we were beckoned into the pig-house. My giggles subsided quickly. It was dark; candle-light flickered in the gap between two curtains hung inside the door. From behind the curtains appeared another richly-costumed man with a book, in which he wrote our names. Then he led us through the curtain.

'Take off your shirts.'

We did so. The sudden rush of cool air to my chest made me shiver. I looked round me. The flickering candles illuminated an extraordinary scene quite at odds with the tumble-down shack in which we were assembled. The interior was set out as a series of doorways, simple frames made of bamboo. Banners hung from the walls, and at the end of the series of bamboo doors was an altar piled with fruit. A large picture of Chinese warriors hung above it, and round it were gathered the Triad officials.

A man in his fifties, dressed in the same ancient Chinese costume and wearing a symbolic hat with a wide embroidered brim, stood in the shadows at the altar. He began to intone a litany to the gods. Then the ceremony began.

One at a time we progressed through the bamboo doors, answering the old man's questions and being prompted through a sequence of vows. Finally we were all assembled at the altar. The old man picked up a live chicken which had been lying with its legs tied together. He plucked some feathers from its neck, then slowly cut its throat with a large knife. The warm blood dripped into a large china bowl. The chicken's body relaxed and dangled limp in his hands.

'If you betray the Society, your fate will be like this chicken's fate,' he warned.

The last of the blood dripped into the bowl. Wine was added. The thirty-six oaths of the House of Fragrant Blossoms were recited; we repeated each one in chorus.

'Stretch out your hands.'

The old man moved along the line. When he came to me he grasped my hand. I felt a sharp knife stab my finger tip. Nothing would have persuaded me to flinch. I stood rigidly to attention as he squeezed a few drops of blood into the mixture in the bowl. When he reached the end of the line, we all drank from the bowl in turn.

Afterwards I could remember few of the details of that night. Some of it was to me mere play-acting, a childish pantomime that had to be complied with because it was the route to wealthy contacts and a position of power. When, during my initiation, I prayed to the Six Eternal Beings, the gods and goddesses to whom the House of Fragrant

Blossoms was dedicated, and vowed to serve them and consecrate my life to them, I thought nothing of it.

Other parts of the ceremony were more meaningful to me, and I took them seriously. Two of the oaths in particular became guiding principles of my life:

> I will assist and offer financial assistance to my sworn brothers when they are in trouble. If I pretend to have no knowledge of their troubles, I shall be killed by five thunderbolts.

> When brothers visit my house, I will provide them with board and lodging. If I treat them as strangers, I will be killed by myriads of knives.

'Myriads of knives' was a reference to the notorious death of a thousand cuts, which was part of the folklore of our gang. It was a method of execution in which the victim bled to death from numerous incisions in his body. Gang executions were not unknown, but the death of a thousand cuts was generally believed to have died out, though there were occasionally rumours of corpses found drained and torn. But it was not fear that made me keep the oaths. They seemed to me to express noble and selfless ideals, ideals I could live for. In the midst of my relentless search for power and money the unlikely world of the Triads brought me nearer to a religious commitment than anything I had yet found. In the archaic and bloodthirsty oaths I embraced a love and commitment to my fellow members; so I strove conscientiously to keep them, though I was a firm atheist and scorned even the gods and goddesses of the Triad rituals. As I grew older and began to take leadership I often negotiated with the local police when my Triad brothers got into trouble. I gave financial help when they needed it, and sometimes made myself responsible for the welfare of the family of a brother who had been sent to prison. I cared more for the Triad than for my own family.

❊ ❊ ❊

In 1969 when I was twenty-two years old it was discovered that Dad, at the age of forty-four, was suffering from nose cancer. He had previously been in reasonable health; a heavy chain-smoker in his early life, he had given it up when I was ten. He never drank alcohol, preferring his favourite green tea. He lived a moderate life. He did not gamble for money, content with an occasional round of mah-jong with his circle of friends.

He had a genuine desire to help others and interested himself in many charitable projects. Though the political situation made it impossible for him to visit his own family in China he regularly sent money and other necessities to his brothers. But he cared most for his children. Through the years of beatings and harsh discipline I never doubted that he thought it was best for me. The memory of his own struggles had left him with a fierce determination that none of his children would have to go through the same experiences. However, it was his strong ethical instincts that guided him rather than a belief in God.

'If you believe in God, God exists for you,' he told his children. 'But if you don't believe in him then he doesn't exist; and if you go looking for him, there's nothing to find.'

It therefore came as a surprise when Dad joined the local branch of the South-East Asia Society for Moral Uplifting. It was the closest he got to religious faith. The organisation was based on the belief that the five major religions (Confucianism, Taoism, Buddhism, Christianity and Islam) were all ways to reach God; it gave them equal respect and members were free to worship where they chose. Dad was elected a minister of the education department, a post he carried out successfully for seven years, resigning only when the diagnosis of cancer made it impossible for him to continue.

'Chan Hop—'

My father woke from a fitful doze. I was sitting by his bed staring at him. His face was bandaged after surgery; his breath came in slow, rasping sighs and his bedclothes were crumpled and sweaty. I thought of how he had looked in the old days, going out for the evening to the society or the literary circle, or off to a public speaking engagement, his coat carefully pressed by my mother, his bow tie immaculate. He had always taken a pride in his appearance. Now he looked a sick, tired old man, older than his forty-four years, his face lined from months of pain. I thought of the beatings and the discipline, and the way his voice had trembled with anger, and all I felt was pity.

'Chan Hop.' He looked at me with heavy-lidded eyes dulled by painkillers.

I moved closer to catch what he wanted to say. He pointed to my mother, sitting quietly nearby.

'Look after her. See that she wants for nothing.'

I nodded. I couldn't think what to say. He cleared his throat.

'Chan Hop, if I die, I'll have only one regret. Only one thing in my life I'll be sorry about.'

I looked back, dimly wondering what it must be like to have lived a life with only one thing in it to regret.

'I won't be here to see you get to the top. When you succeed, when you reach it, I won't be here. It's the one thing I regret. I regret it very much. I waited a long time for it.'

Something opened inside me, and I began to talk to my father in a way I never had before. I told him some of the successes I had had, little pieces of news he had not heard yet. I told him what the local newspapers had said about me recently, and the details of my winning performances and the progress of the Kedah State side, the football team I now played in. He listened carefully, his face occasionally lighting up in a pleased smile at some interesting tit-bit. He took particular pride in the fact that his son had been chosen to play football for Malaysia.

I didn't tell him why I had changed to the Kedah State team. I had been disciplined by the Penang Football Association for accepting bribes, and for breaking the strict code of conduct by being involved in an illegal betting syndicate.

Dad talked about the old days when his children were small, and his pleasure that things were now so much better. He was most insistent that I should remember that the honour of our family was something to be cherished and fought for.

'Remember, Chan Hop,' he urged gently, 'you carry the good name of our family with you. Whatever you do, you do as a representative. Remember that, and bring honour to our family in all you do.'

I thought of the various activities in which I was engaged: bullying small traders, frequenting gambling clubs and all-night parties where all sorts of things went on behind closed doors. I bowed my head, glad the room was so dim that Dad couldn't see my burning cheeks.

'I'll remember that, Dad.'

There was a tug at my sleeve. I turned to see my mother beside me. She beckoned me into the passageway and gave me a piece of paper.

'Take this to the society,' she said softly. 'Be quick. Seek God's help through them.'

When I got there Dad's old friends and colleagues were sympathetic and courteous. They offered words of religious comfort, and prayed for my father. They read my mother's note and went to an inner room, returning with a sealed container.

'It is blessed water,' they told me. 'Seven different flowers are infused into it, and the power of prayer, the blessing of God, and the virtues of the seven flowers – these will heal your father.'

I looked at the container doubtfully. They smiled reassuringly.

'Bathe him with this water,' they said. 'He will recover.'

At home we broke the seals and bathed Dad with the fragrant water. Over the next few days we waited to see what would happen; my mother with a desperate faith, I with a sympathetic yet angry scepticism. Dad got worse.

In his last weeks we spoke together about many things and achieved a closeness we had rarely experienced before. One day when he had become very weak he took my hand and looked at me intensely.

'Son, God can only help you if you want to help yourself.'

It was as if the effort of delivering that simple sentence exhausted him, and he fell into a light sleep. My mother indicated that I should leave him; she remained bowed over his bed in the dimmed room. Not long afterwards I heard her sobbing and went in. Dad had died.

In the weeks that followed there was much to be organised, and as the eldest son most of the responsibility fell to me. In the middle of all the practical decisions and duties I thought of my father's last words to me. Like most Chinese he had a strong sense of the father's role as moral instructor of his children, and must have given some thought to what his final exhortation should be. But what had made him speak of God's help? He had spent his life teaching me that what helped a man was hard work and discipline. In the end I put it down to the ramblings of a dying man, and got on with more important matters. Whatever God might be – if indeed he existed – I was getting on fine without his help.

After Dad died I met Helen and we decided to get married. We had a baby son, Joseph, and for a while I calmed down a little. I was now a father myself, and the influence of my father's example was strong. But my behaviour soon deteriorated. As footballing successes increased, my lifestyle became wilder. I was now playing for the Malaysian Football Association in internationals against Hong Kong Chinese and Singapore Chinese teams, which were major events in the football calendar. We also played friendly matches against Malaysian Indian and Malay sides. But after the matches fights usually broke out, and eventually the Malaysian government stopped the fixtures because of the racial unrest.

I was drinking and gambling more frequently. Soon I was heavily in debt. Periodically I confronted my mother with my problems and she paid my debts. For her it was an act of love; but it was not the right way to help me, for I simply assumed she'd unlimited resources and went on gambling. I knew how to manipulate my mother. Yet she did not have enough money to pay for the kind of lifestyle I wanted, and I was not prepared to work for it as my father had. So I plunged deeper into the criminal underworld, looking for more money.

Helen and I had a second child, Eunis. But by the time she was four months old I was gone. I deserted my wife and children, and in due course Helen divorced me.

There were limits to what Georgetown could provide for me. I had always vowed that one day I was going to get out; and so I began to travel around Malaysia with members of the gang, looking for new thrills. I stayed in one town for a while and then another; I would get to know the local underworld people, and after moving on we would often keep in touch.

The reason for travelling was mainly to follow the horse-racing circuit, which was based in four major areas from Singapore to Penang State. We slept by day and spent the nights drinking; we were looking out for jockeys with the purpose of making them drunk and getting information from them. If they refused to co-operate we beat them up and sometimes threatened to kill them as well. Usually they were under the protection of rival gangs, so we were often involved in street fights. Survival in the racing circuit meant knowing how to fight, and how to fight dirty.

A jockey who was a close friend told me privately to bet on him when he was going to fix the race. As a result my bank balance grew. But one day my friend fell from his horse and died in hospital. I hadn't got the sense to stop betting; greed was always my weakness. I bet heavily without inside information and ended a loser at most race meetings. Sometimes my luck let me down really badly. Once during a losing spell I was 'betting on credit'; having lost once I had no money to bet again but persuaded the bookmakers to take my bet, promising to repay the stake out of my next winnings. I didn't win all day. But I kept on betting. At the end of the day I owed a small fortune. I had no choice but to lie low and slowly raise the money to pay the bookmakers. They were out looking for me. They rang me constantly, and when they couldn't contact me they went to my mother's house and threatened her.

'If he's run away, you'll have to pay his debts,' they told her.

I was furious when I heard what they had done. It was one thing for me to ask my mother to pay my gambling debts; it was quite another for somebody else to do so. By then I had managed to collect the money I owed, so I went home. My mother greeted me with accusations and tears, but I ignored her. I had telephone calls to make.

One call was to the bookmakers. I told them to come and collect their money. They came to the house and I handed over the money and told them to get out. When they left the house my Triad friends were waiting for them. They beat the bookmakers up and then dragged them back into the house, where they forced them to apologise to my mother. In addition, following the underworld code of honour, they had to pay a sum of money to the gang as recompense for their insult.

'You see, these are my friends. They won't let you be insulted again,' I told my mother grandly. 'You can trust me. I will protect you, and so will my friends.'

She didn't reply but regarded me with a hunted, accusing look.

My mother was deeply worried about me, and tried to set me on the right path by encouraging me to find a job.

But I was not interested in any jobs she suggested; my only interest was in having a good time and becoming rich.

Eventually I found employment that suited me, smuggling rice and other food from towns on the Thailand–Malaysia border to inland Malaysia. I drove a powerful six-cylinder vehicle, often loaded to the roof with sacks of rice. I gloried in my new life. It had glamour, it had excitement, and it earned me a lot of money. The government anti-smuggling squad knew the routes well and often set up road blocks, but I thought nothing of driving the heavy vehicle right at them. When the government issued orders to shoot to kill if we refused to stop it made no difference to me; I learnt to arrange sacks of rice to form an impenetrable armour round the cab and we escaped the bullets.

Now I was making good money again and living the wild lifestyle I wanted I became arrogant and demanding. When drunk – which was often – I beat people up; sober, I sometimes found my victims looking for me in their turn. It was a miracle I was not murdered out of revenge; I'd had friends who had died that way. I also survived several road accidents caused by my reckless driving. When I escaped with superficial injuries my friends looked at me with amazement.

'God knows how you got away with it that time,' they would say.

I just laughed and carried on unheeding. But one day my luck ran out and I found myself being hunted by an enemy who was trying to kill me. I realised I would have to lie low for a while, so I went to Thailand and settled in Haadyai, in the south.

Haadyai was full of tourists and popular with Malaysians and Singaporeans, and with its well known shopping arcades, its prostitutes, expensive hotels and red light district it was an ideal place to hide. Making use of my wide circle of contacts, I quickly got to know the local criminals. Membership of the Triad opened doors; a secret

handshake or one of the secret signs we used could trans-
form an uncommunicative gangster into a mine of helpful
information. It was not long before I was introduced to
Mr Bhang and began to work for him as I have described,
overseeing the smuggling of rice, tin ore and vehicle spare
parts by sea into Malaysia and Singapore. That was how I
became his agent negotiating safe passage for the smugglers.
That was when he came to love and trust me; how I found
in him another father, who understood where my heart
was leading.

6

WIDENING HORIZONS

Haadyai, the commercial capital of south Thailand, is a growing city . . . Because prices of many items (including night life) are lower in Thailand than in Malaysia, Haadyai has become a shopping and sybaritic haven for Malaysians who pour across the harbour on buying sprees. (*Thailand*)[1]

The incident that decided me to leave Bhang's employment was a chance meeting with an old friend. It was pure coincidence that we met one day in Haadyai. Joe had been a neighbour of ours in Georgetown. He was about the same age as me and a quiet, well-mannered boy. We were friends in our schooldays; though we went to different schools we often met in the evenings to talk, usually ending up at the cinema.

Joe had done well for himself. He was a manager for a large travel company and was in town on business, visiting his Thai counterpart. We picked up our friendship again and spent a lot of time together eating in restaurants and enjoying the delights of Haadyai nightlife.

'And what are you doing, Hui?' he asked, as we sampled a particularly good curry.

I told him about Bhang.

'It's an executive job, really,' I explained. 'I handle the permits side for him. You know, cargoes in, cargoes out, they see me and I fix it.'

---

[1] Insight Guides, Apa Productions, 1982.

My friend smiled cynically.

I reddened. 'OK, it's a bit more than that. It's protection. Bit of extortion; we take a slice of the action. Nobody goes anywhere without Bhang says so.' I grinned defiantly, 'Not like Georgetown.'

'Sure, sounds a good set-up,' he said casually.

I swallowed a forkful of curry. It was red-hot, just as I liked it. Joe smiled as I reached for a glass of tepid water.

'Now our outfit,' he said thoughtfully, 'would suit you better. You know we've got an office here in Thailand. They're looking for somebody at the moment. You should think about it.'

I laughed out loud. The idea of sitting behind a desk, working in an office, turning up for work every day – I was looking for excitement, money and power. I said so.

Joe shook his head. 'It's not that kind of job. You'd be useful to us because you speak most of the languages. There isn't much desk work. You'd do a lot of travelling. Escort clients through customs, meet parties at the border, handle immigration formalities. It would help us a lot. We've been looking for somebody like you.' He winked. 'I would think you would be able to make use of the opportunities you'd have.'

As he told me more about the job, the more attractive it became. Even the office part of it sounded quite interesting, and I would have status in the company. I knew a little about tour couriers. I'd seen them in bars and night-clubs, poised and confident, on easy terms with the management and surrounded by wealthy tourists and their beautiful women. A job like that was sought after, and I knew I was lucky to be offered it. And if I couldn't use it to further my private ambitions, I wasn't the man I thought I was.

I threw myself into the new work with enthusiasm. I was given training as an assistant tour leader, and did well. The company was pleased with me; I was good at the office work and popular with the tourists. I enjoyed being seen in the most expensive clubs and bars, staying at good hotels, mixing with the rich and influential. One of the directors of the company was the deputy mayor of Haadyai, and so the company was in good standing with the border officials. They gave me every help and made many of the formalities very easy.

I could have done very well and earned a good living, but I wanted more. As fast as I earned money I spent it on good living and alcohol. Because I was fluent in several languages – I could tell jokes in Chinese, Thai, Malay and English – the tourists turned to me to sort out problems and give advice. In return they often bought me drinks and gave me handsome tips.

I was soon drinking heavily again. Restaurants, massage parlours and discothèques were where I could be found after office hours. Sometimes I was so drunk that my friends had to check me into a hotel to sober up. That made me worse; I decided I could drink as much as I liked. My friends would see me safely home.

The company let it be known that they were concerned about my behaviour, though they took no action because they were pleased with my work. But my problems were only beginning. Haadyai was full of people who were looking for somebody like me; a man well placed with the border officials, trusted by the authorities, willing to bend the rules to make quick money. Before long I was involved in smuggling again. I undertook to get illegal goods through the border, and in return I shared the profits. Sometimes I even carried the goods in the company coach.

But the big money was in a different sort of smuggling. In the mid-1970s heroin was becoming a hugely profitable business. The notorious Golden Triangle, the lonely mountainous area where the boundaries of Thailand, Laos and Burma meet, was world-famous for its only crop, and drugs grown there were finding a ready market in Europe. I'd heard of the vast fortunes to be made in drug dealing and wondered if I would ever be able to get into the action.

Until I did so I seemed further away from the big money than ever before.

Then things changed.

I was promoted and became responsible for tours in and out of Thailand and Malaysia. I met Chang, a young Singaporean, with whom I became very friendly. He wore expensive clothes and had an air of quiet authority that attracted me. He introduced me to his business associates, and soon I was regularly arranging flights for them to Bangkok and Europe. As I got to know them better they began to trust me. I discovered that the Singaporean had served a sentence in Europe for drug-smuggling and was now an influential and feared figure in South-East Asian crime. It was obvious that he and his associates were a drug syndicate and that their travels revolved around narcotics dealings.

When asked to use my own contacts with the customs posts and border guards to ensure safe passage for their cases I agreed willingly, knowing they contained drugs. Sometimes I accompanied their couriers from Haadyai to Bangkok, saw to the checking-in of their luggage, and made sure that they got away from Thailand safely. The airport officials knew me well, many of them were personal friends, and there was little risk. For this I was paid well, and I became popular with the syndicate. A year after my promotion to tour officer the syndicate asked if I would be interested in a trip to Europe. I agreed immediately and resigned from the travel company.

'Here are the bags.'

Chang pushed them across the table to me. The two suitcases were ordinary travel bags, neither brand-new nor travel-worn. He opened them. They contained neatly packed clothes and travel needs. He patted the lining. 'Take care,' he said lightly.

I smiled. He lit an expensive cigarette, and as he slipped the gold lighter back in his pocket a diamond ring sparkled on his finger. Inside the lining of the suitcases, I was well aware, were 10 kilograms of heroin packed in plastic bags and stuffed into a tiny space. The stitching had been well done.

'Understood.' I picked up the suitcases easily.

'And your tickets,' said Chang, handing me a fat envelope. 'You check in at Bangkok. The cases will be loaded on the plane. You won't have any worries there. You fly to Frankfurt. I've booked you on a flight that gets in before ten o'clock. That's important because there aren't many customs people working at that time of day. Then you take a connecting flight to Hamburg. That's why your cases have Hamburg labels. Do you know why we do it this way?'

I shook my head. 'Why not fly direct to Amsterdam?' I suggested.

'Because this way the trip is considered an internal flight, and you avoid international customs checks. You get to Hamburg at the weekend, there's hardly any customs staff on duty. Mostly they just wave you through the green channel.'

'And then?'

'Then you take a train to Brussels, and finally you go on to Amsterdam by road – a taxi or coach.'

It was a brilliant and much-used system. A few years later the governments involved realised the amount of drugs coming in by the Frankfurt route and increased the customs surveillance at the borders. But for me it meant that my first trip had a high chance of success.

Everything went like clockwork. The suitcases were nodded through cheerfully by customs officials I had got to know during the past months, and I arrived in Amsterdam exuberant. I emerged from my bus at Central Station into a bright morning. I walked with my suitcases past an organ-grinder, and on into the heart of the bustling Dutch capital. My heart was beating faster than at any point in the customs halls. I had made it! I'd finally found a way into the rich and powerful world of international smuggling. My teenage escapades of which I'd been so proud seemed very insignificant now. I looked at the map I'd been given and turned off the main shopping thoroughfare, plunging into a district of narrow streets lined with crumbling mansions, sex shops, seedy cinemas and run-down shops. Here and there women lounged in doorways, staring incuriously at me as I walked by. I had no trouble in recognising them as prostitutes. This was my kind of territory. I handed the suitcases to a syndicate member who took them without ceremony and handed me my return tickets to Bangkok. Within a few hours I was looking out of the plane window, watching the flat green fields and neat canals of Holland falling away as I headed for home.

If the murder of Mr Bhang had jolted me into awareness of what I was getting myself into in my pursuit of wealth, another such experience was the close shave I had with a prosperous Chinese Thai who appeared at my hotel not long after the Amsterdam trip. I knew Brother Lee by reputation. He was in the drug trade, and well respected by the Triads. His cover business was a large and prosperous distribution operation, transporting among other things rice. Many of the sacks that went out on Lee's trucks had plastic bags stuffed deep inside.

'You've got the contacts, you speak all the languages. And you're in the travel business. Couldn't be better, Mr Hui. How about it?' He beamed at me and sat back, waiting for my reply.

I thought carefully. Everybody who knew him said that Brother Lee was immensely greedy and interested only in his own welfare. He was somebody who regarded promises as meaningless, who was only waiting for a chance to turn on his friends and colleagues and take advantage of them. I decided I could handle Lee.

'What do you want me to do?'

Brother Lee smiled again, a slow, fat, sleepy smile. 'I want to set you up in business.'

My interest quickened. 'What do you mean?'

'I have some drugs, good expensive ones. In Europe they will make a great deal of money. I need couriers, people I can trust, who will take my drugs to Europe and sell them. Then they are to bring the money back to me.'

'So?'

I tried to keep the rising excitement out of my voice. This sounded like a big operation with real money to be made. I had thought the trip to Amsterdam for the syndicate had been profitable, but this was something else entirely.

Lee continued, still with his slow smile, 'So you find the couriers, and you make the arrangements. You make sure your people bring the money back. Maybe you travel with them. For this I will share my profit with you.'

'I'm interested.'

'Of course you are interested. And I will tell you why it is such a good deal for you, Hui. I don't want people to know that the drugs are mine. There are too many people in this town who would make trouble for me. You can tell the couriers that they are your drugs and that this is your operation.'

This was a highly attractive thought. In one leap I would be established as a drug dealer handling large quantities, with an empire of couriers. I agreed to take the job.

'The drugs are in two suitcases. I'll bring them to you.'

I assumed his reluctance to be identified with the trans-action was the fear that people would try to cheat him, because he was a big, powerful dealer. But as I was soon to discover, he had worked one of the oldest tricks in the drug-smuggling business. He had arranged to buy the drugs from someone who had stock, and asked to meet him at his hotel to check the product. Before payment was made the suit-cases were stolen. Brother Lee thought it unlikely he would be suspected; but he was unwilling to let it be known that he was trying to sell two cases of drugs, in case the dealer and his friends drew the correct conclusion. He approached me a fortnight after the theft. Before I could organise the couriers for Europe, however, I met Lee one evening to go

to a restaurant. My girlfriend who was with us wanted to
go back to our hotel to pick up something we'd forgotten;
and while we were away Brother Lee was gunned down.

The owner came to my hotel demanding to know where
the suitcases were. I told him the truth, that I had no
idea. Fortunately some members of his gang vouched for
me. I was believed – though reluctantly – and for weeks
afterwards I knew there were people watching my every
move. I was terrified. If Lee's killers changed their mind
and decided I had been involved in the theft after all, I
was as good as dead. I spent the next few months in a very
depressed state.

The payment for the trip to Amsterdam was about £10,000
– an astronomical sum by my reckoning. When I agreed to
make a second journey I was allowed to invest some of my
earnings in the new project, and so a quarter of the consignment was mine, as would be a quarter of the profits.

I followed the same route as before and had just as easy a
time. I relaxed and enjoyed the flight. At Hamburg I took a
taxi to the railway station to catch the slow train to Brussels,
not relishing the journey. *But it's the only way to the big
money*, I reminded myself. *I'll just have to put up with it.*
When I found I had to wait two and a half hours for the
Brussels train I was in a very bad mood. I put the suitcases
in a left-luggage locker.

It was cold and I didn't fancy exploring Hamburg, so
I wandered round the station shops and news-stands; I
was not interested in the souvenirs and fancy cakes on
sale, and I flicked through the newspapers and found
them boring. I had no interest in European books either,
and the only magazines I thought worth bothering with
were *Playboy*, *Hustler* and the rest, which were stacked
out of reach. Thoroughly bored, I headed for the station
bar. It was half-deserted. I bought a drink. A young
man in his late twenties began chatting to me. I was
ill-at-ease with him, and the long wait in the station was

getting on my nerves, but I felt quite relaxed about the drugs.

'Where's your home?' he asked, in a friendly way.

'Thailand,' I answered brusquely.

He smiled broadly. 'You're Chinese, aren't you? Thought so,' he added, as I nodded. 'Lot of Chinese in Thailand, I know that.'

'Where are you from?' I responded, not caring but unwilling to let him ask all the questions.

'I live here – European citizen!' he smiled.

He seemed to be somebody who smiled a lot, and as he smiled he looked right into my eyes. I couldn't stand it. Before I could make him tell me exactly where he came from, he was asking questions again.

'What business are you in?'

'Travel courier,' I said shortly.

'Been in Europe before?'

'No,' I lied.

He grinned. 'I knew it! I can tell by your clothes.'

I looked at my smart outfit, bought with money earned from my last trip, and scowled. The man was instantly apologetic.

'No, I mean you're dressed real smart – you look like it's a special outing.'

I was getting a bit worried by all the questions and decided to concoct a cover story to put him off.

'I'm in Europe on holiday,' I said. 'My dad was over here before the war. I'm seeing places he told me about.'

'That's interesting,' he said. 'What brought him to Hamburg?'

'Oh, business – and friends,' I said vaguely.

I kept a story going for a few minutes longer, but I was running out of ideas.

'Want a drink?' I said desperately.

He shook his head and looked at me thoughtfully.

'Maybe you need a Bible,' he said abruptly.

'What?'

'Maybe you need a Bible.'

I was completely taken aback. Was this man a preacher? I had been thinking he could be the police. He'd stayed silent about himself – name, nationality, job – everything I had asked him. What did he want with me? Suddenly I was really frightened.

'I'm Chinese, and I'm not interested in Western religion,' I said. 'I couldn't accept it. I've never read the Bible. I never will. Have *you* read Confucius? What are you, anyway? Are you a preacher?'

He didn't answer but changed the subject. I muttered an excuse and went over to a seat, but he pulled up another chair and sat down. *What the hell does he want?* I racked my brains to know what to do next. All the time he carried on his bright, inquisitive chatter. He seemed determined not to leave me on my own. Maybe he was the police after all. I thoughtfully fingered the razor-sharp knife I always kept in my pocket.

'You need a Bible.'

I came out of my thoughts. He was back on about the Bible again. *I've got to find out who this guy is*, I thought, and hit on a plan. I drew a deep breath.

'Give me a hand with my luggage?' I asked. 'It's in a locker. I've got to get it to the Brussels platform.'

'Sure.'

We walked together to the lockers and I collected the cases. I was ready for him if he showed any interest in them. I'd take him to the corner of the still-deserted platform and knife him. Opening one case, I pretended to rummage for cigarettes. I made sure he could see that the contents were only clothes. I stole a glance at him but he was gazing at adverts on the other side of the track. He showed no interest in the bags and asked no questions as he picked one up and carried it for me. In fact the bags were the only things he didn't ask questions about.

Relief flooded over me. Whatever he was, I was fairly sure it was not the police. We chatted about other things.

Then the train came and the young man shook hands and went away.

On the train I was still slightly worried about him. Who was he and why so insistent that I needed a Bible? To me a Bible meant only one thing: accept Western punishment, go to gaol, do time, do the right thing. I didn't need a Bible, I needed money and more money. That was the only thing that mattered to me.

As the train pulled into Brussels I gathered my luggage and dismissed him from my mind.

Go to hell with your stupid Bible, I thought viciously. *This is what I need. This is where I'm going.*

7

SHRINKING HORIZONS

'Mother!' My voice shook with barely suppressed excitement. I held out a bundle of banknotes. 'For you – here, take it; there's a lot more where that came from. Your money worries are over.'

She looked, not at the money but at me, taking in the new suit, the smart haircut and the jewellery.

'What's that chain round your neck?'

I stroked the heavy silver loops and the gold medallion hanging on my chest.

'Do you like it? I bought it. I can buy anything now, mother. You too, here, have this; go shopping.'

She turned away as if the sight of my new finery hurt her eyes. 'I don't want the money. Take it away.'

'You must take it.' I was hurt and angry. 'Are you saying you have all the money you want? That you're not hungry and not in need?'

She looked me in the eyes. 'Where did you get all this, Chan Hop?'

'It doesn't matter. I've got a job, I go to Europe, I do business. You know that, I told you.'

I flung the money down on the table in front of her.

There was a note of scorn in her voice, 'All your schooldays you ran away, worked when you wanted to, played games, got into trouble. And now you're a big business man. Now you're earning lots of money going to Europe. I don't believe you.'

She carefully gathered the notes together, stacked them in a neat pile, and pushed them firmly into my hands. There was enough money there to pay the whole household budget for a month.

'Take it, Chan Hop, I don't want it. I know how you got it. I know your friends. I know what you're doing. Nobody gets that rich so quick by keeping the law.'

As I slammed the door and stormed out of the house I saw she was crying. I didn't stop.

I had successfully completed two more trips within a month, and everything had worked perfectly. I came home to Penang a hero, at least in my own mind. The syndicate paid well – very well. I returned from my second trip with about £75,000 to my name. For the first time in my life I had all the money I needed and every opportunity to make more. My mother wanted me to settle down and get a proper job, but I laughed at her. Now I'd found wealth nothing was going to change my mind. I'd travelled round Europe before coming home, spending lavishly on clothes, jewellery and night life. I now had the appearance to go with it. I was on my way.

And the money kept rolling in. I was back in my old haunts, and in many places I'd never had the money to go to before. I spent recklessly on other people as well as myself – in bars, restaurants and gambling dens – and a crowd of hangers-on followed me around. It was known that Chan Hop Hui was spending money like water, and that those in his favour could count on some of it coming their way. In fact they did well out of me. I rented a house and my inner circle moved in with me. I also bought a few cars for them to use.

It was not long before the syndicate made it clear that they were not pleased with my lifestyle. They gave me several warnings. 'Your behaviour is drawing attention to yourself,' they said. 'The police are already taking an interest in you. If they start asking questions about you, they may start looking further.'

I ignored the warnings. I knew I was good, I was a daredevil who had taken millions of pounds worth of heroin into Europe. I was in no mood to be disciplined by anybody. I had a swollen head and great ambitions.

The syndicate did not disown me or hint that they no longer needed my services; but when I refused to listen to their warnings they took care to distance themselves in as many ways as possible. I knew my days with them were numbered. We were nominally friends, we exchanged Triad handshakes and swore eternal loyalty; but they stopped asking me to important meetings, and began to ask my friends to do jobs they used to offer to me.

As the syndicate's work decreased, others made use of my skills. There was always some smuggling work available and the money was good. More and more hangers-on followed me around. I became the big name in the local underworld that I had always wanted to be. The local police began to think of me as a dangerous character.

I travelled round Malaysia meeting local gang leaders and became friends with many of them. When I was in Thailand I invited them to visit me and negotiated co-operative drug deals.

For the next few years my life became better and better. I travelled throughout Europe and Asia. The richer I became, the wilder. My constant drunkenness and uncaring and boastful attitude earned me many enemies, so I employed some Thai hit-men as bodyguards who protected me and went everywhere I went.

I became an old hand at choosing the best routes. Some were more risky. For example, flying to Paris and going on by train to Amsterdam some couriers from Hong Kong had been arrested, and the police were extra-cautious. As the number of drug arrests increased in the early 1970s Frankfurt too became a place to avoid; the German authorities were suspicious of any Chinese travelling from Frankfurt to Hamburg, and it was safer to fly direct to Hamburg despite the risk of being searched at customs.

In fact, though my confidence remained high, increasing publicity and police activity caused occasional problems.

I had come through from Singapore to Hamburg. My suitcases were the last to come from the carousel, and I was one of the last to arrive at the customs hall. There were only two others, both Europeans. The customs officer looked at me curiously and beckoned me to his table. I had no choice; I took the suitcases over and put them down in front of him.

'*Bitte öffnen Sie diese Taschen,*' he said politely.

I stared at him blankly.

He tapped the cases, '*Anmeldefreie Waren, ja?*'

I had no idea what he was saying.

'*Ich verstehe nicht* (I don't understand),' I stammered, producing one of the sentences I had memorised. '*Ich bin nur auf der Durchreise* (I'm just passing through).'

Immediately he became suspicious. He undid the straps of the cases and removed the contents – European clothes which were bought specially to make the suitcases seem as normal as possible. He checked everything, running his fingers along seams, turning pockets inside out, and shaking out neatly-folded shirts. He inspected the base and lid of each case, where the drugs were stored. I watched with some concern, trying to appear outwardly calm. He pressed his palms against the lids, pursing his lips. He spent some time examining the bases, and stood the cases on end, shaking them. I began to sweat. Anybody who knew anything about luggage should be able to tell that the bases and lids were too thick and too well padded. I considered lighting a cigarette to calm me down, but I could not risk my hands shaking.

He seemed to be taking a long time. *Too long*, I thought. Longer than it needed to decide to slit the cases open and find the drugs. Then it hit me. *He's new on the job*, I decided exultantly. *He doesn't know what to do! He can't make up his mind!*

As I watched him fumbling with my luggage I was sure I was right. He was avoiding my eyes, trying to seem expert and authoritative, but he was only going through the motions. I began to feel amused and a little light-headed. Eventually he grinned at me and pushed the cases back.

'I am sorry to delay you,' he said in English. He looked around the deserted customs hall. 'Where do you go now?'

'Taxi,' I said, hoping he wasn't going to ask too many questions.

'I help you with these.' He picked up one of the cases and we walked to the taxi rank. I tried to work out what was going on. I'd never been given help like this before. Perhaps it was a trap. Perhaps another officer was tailing us. My shirt under my jacket was damp with perspiration. A taxi was waiting. *A police plant*, I wondered? I got in. He passed my cases in after me, and waved me off. As we pulled away from the kerb I looked back to see if any vehicle was following. Everything seemed to be all right. I grunted with relief.

'*Bahnhof, bitte*,' I said to the driver, in another of my rehearsed phrases. We drove to the railway station.

Such episodes as this were an occasional brake on my recklessness, but not for long. I was obsessed with the good life, and my rise in the underworld hierarchy continued. The bubble was bound to burst some time. My mother warned me, but of course I didn't listen, I was having too good a time. When the first signs came I didn't recognise them.

In 1977 a French woman was arrested in Georgetown and her case caused widespread public interest; if she was found guilty she would be the first woman to be hanged under the anti-drugs laws of Malaysia. Her story was a common one. She claimed she had been duped by a drug-smuggling ring, which had used her as an unwitting courier. For the woman I had little but contempt; she was a fool who ought to have been more careful. I was annoyed by the publicity, however, as it meant that I could not go home to Georgetown for a while. The police were suddenly alert to drug offences, and as someone known to move in underworld circles I would be watched every minute. So I decided to stay in Thailand until things calmed down.

One hot night I was in my hotel room, sitting near the open window and gazing idly at the crowded, noisy street outside. I became aware that more was going on at the hotel next door than usual. Several police cars were parked outside the main entrance, and uniformed men were positioned strategically nearby. I could hear voices raised and people running back and forth in the entrance foyer. Before long a member of the hotel staff who was one of my informers came to my room to tell me what was going on. An Englishwoman had been arrested on drugs charges. I was mildly interested, and went down to see what was happening. I didn't stay watching for long. It was only another stupid European woman thinking she was big enough to play the drugs game. Or maybe, I thought generously, she was just a user who had got herself caught. Either way I was not bothered. It was amateur stuff.

I was in a different league: I had my own informers at the airport; I knew within minutes whenever anything changed; I could alter my plans, stay ahead of the police, avoid capture. Europeans were losers; I was going to be a millionaire. These small-time operators were no threat to me.

I couldn't have been more wrong.

The next day the newspapers carried the story. The woman was Rita Nightingale, a British nurse who had been working in Hong Kong as a night-club hostess. She claimed her boyfriend had tricked her into carrying heroin through customs.

Silly little bitch. My reaction was immediately contemptuous. *That's what they all say. It's the oldest story in the book.* The police thought the same, and she was taken into custody. I didn't give much for her chances.

The next night I checked my sources of information and found that the arrest had not caused any apparent change of policy at airport customs. I was relieved because I had two Indonesians about to leave with a consignment of drugs for Paris. There seemed no reason why they should not go as planned. But my couriers let me down. Their heads were full of the newspaper stories and bar-room gossip about Rita Nightingale. When they arrived at the check-in desk they panicked. They left the two cases of drugs behind and took a different flight. The police investigated the suitcases and discovered the drugs. The story was a big news item in the local papers. The check-in staff remembered that the bags had been checked in by Indonesians, and immediately foreigners were suspect.

By then it was known that Rita Nightingale was insisting she was the innocent victim of Hong Kong Chinese. The police began checking hotels, looking for Chinese visitors. They already regarded me as a suspicious character. A link could be traced back to me from the suitcases if enough people gave in under interrogation. There was nothing for it but to move very carefully for a while and keep an extremely low profile.

As far as I was concerned the result was financial disaster. My new-found wealth began to disappear. Malaysia and Singapore were no longer good places for drug-trafficking. The authorities were clamping down at airports and the border customs posts. We would be recognised as frequent travellers and would therefore be under suspicion. If we didn't use the airports the long route into Malaysia by way of the border was equally risky. Like all of us involved in the drug trade, I was bitterly angry with Rita Nightingale. Her carelessness and naïve stupidity had caused endless problems. Even so it was still possible to operate, but only a handful of couriers dared go through Bangkok Airport. The syndicates and big barons of the underworld from whom I obtained supplies, and for whom I often ran drugs, began cutting back on their activities.

A few months later an international campaign on Rita Nightingale's behalf focused the world's attention on the Golden Triangle. The Thai government was under scrutiny, and the position of King Bhumipol too. On one hand campaigners were calling for Nightingale's release, and civil rights activists were deploring Thai justice and Thai prisons; on the other the king and government were under pressure from the world superpowers to be seen to be determined to stamp out the drug trade, and to be harsh to convicted drug offenders.

Airport security became stricter. There were more arrests. I hated hearing about each new police success because it meant more problems for me. At the same time security was even more vigilant owing to the widespread concern about aircraft hi-jacking.

We reluctantly abandoned any hope of using Bangkok Airport for the foreseeable future. Some smugglers tried to use Kuala Lumpur and two Singaporean couples were arrested there. There were no major arrests at Singapore Airport but that was not an attractive option: drugs would have to be brought through at least two checkpoints. It would be almost impossible to persuade couriers to take the risk; but if we did persuade them and they were arrested they were quite likely to give our names and details of the operation to the police.

For the next year and a half I saw my work dwindling, and also my money. But I refused to alter my lifestyle. One by one my luxuries were sold to finance my wild extravagances: some of the jewellery; the cars; and then the house I rented.

Several of my hangers-on saw what was happening and disappeared as suddenly as they had come. In the end I was borrowing money from what few remained, without a hope of paying it back. That led to bitter arguments and soon the last of them abandoned me. My old companions kept me at arm's length, quietly slipping away when they saw me coming.

Nobody had ever treated me like that before; but there was nothing I could do about it. The injustice of it burned away in my heart. Here was I, my livelihood taken away by other people's stupidity, and my so-called friends deserting me as soon as things got difficult. They had had accommodation, cars, gifts, everything they wanted from me when I had money; and where were they now?

I started to drink really heavily. Not beer; in the days of my prosperity I'd always despised it as unworthy to wash my teeth in. In those days I drank brandy – and Extra-Old at that, I never bothered with ordinary brandy, whisky or gin – but now I was penniless I had to make do with *makong*, the local Thai whisky. It was virtually undrinkable, but it was cheap. I was permanently drunk and didn't care any more. My health began to deteriorate.

'The spirit in the *makong* has killed many,' my Thai friends warned me. 'Soon it will kill you.'

I'd been proud of my possessions and my smart clothes. Now most of the possessions were gone and the clothes I wore were crumpled and unwashed. I was a lonely, bitter man, bankrupt and up to my eyes in debt. Sometimes I thought of Rita Nightingale who had started the whole thing and wrecked my business.

I found a place to stay: a foreign music group who had a job playing in a local hotel took me in and looked after me. In more sober moments I looked at my situation and was overwhelmed by self-pity. The musicians were having to care for me as if I were a baby. I had hit rock bottom. *You're really lost*, I wept. *It's going to be a long, hard climb back to the top.*

After about a year in this situation I met a Malaysian friend who had once worked for the syndicate. He looked at me and the way I was living, and drew his own conclusions.

'You've got to choose,' he said flatly. 'Either you go on like this – drink yourself to death or get shot up in some brawl or just go on dragging yourself lower and lower – or you get back on your feet again.'

I sneered at him. 'You've seen me. You know how it is. So what do you think I can do about it?'

He shrugged his shoulders. 'Come back to Penang.'

I considered the idea. I had thought about it before, but the Malaysian authorities were still very active against drugs.

'I can't risk it,' I said. 'I'd walk into trouble.'

'I don't mean drugs. Get into something legitimate.'

I laughed huskily. 'That's not going to make me rich.'

He swivelled round in his chair and thrust his face close to mine. 'Look, Hui, you'd better understand one thing. Your problem isn't how to get rich. Your problem is how to stay alive.' He clenched his fist in the familiar Triad salute. 'You can come back to Malaysia and work for me. I'll pay you a decent wage. I won't make you rich but you'll have a respectable income. You can get back on your feet.'

'I'll come,' I said.

I stuck it out in Malaysia with him for two or three months and made some sort of an effort to pull myself together; but I couldn't stand the life I was living. It was almost worse than the year of drunken stupor in Thailand. I lived in our family home, which was bad enough; but to be in my home town where I had once had a reputation and money, and to be just like everybody else who went to work each day and drew a pay packet, was impossible. *No matter what happens*, I vowed, *I'm going to get back to the top. I'm going back into the drug business. Even if they hang me*.

One problem had to be solved at the outset. I was penniless. The syndicate didn't want to know me. I was useless to the people hiring couriers; the last two years had destroyed my reputation. I needed money to buy drugs and take them to Europe. But where was I to find it? The answer, when I discovered it, was beautifully simple. Our family house was in a prosperous part of Georgetown, and my mother owned it and also had an income left her by my father. When she died her children would divide the inheritance.

I was the eldest son and my mother loved me more than any of the others. I would demand my inheritance now.

My mother was horrified. 'No, I will not do it, Chan Hop. No, no, no, no.'

'Don't you love me then? Don't you want me to make a success of my life? What sort of a mother are you?'

'If I thought that giving you money would make you change your life, Chan Hop, I would do it tomorrow. No, I would do it today. Even though it would make things hard for me and I would have to struggle to make ends meet. But you won't change your ways.'

I flew into a rage. 'That is not your problem. It's nothing to do with you at all. The money is mine, it is my inheritance. It is mine by right. I want it now.'

She shook her head sadly. 'It is not yours until I die, Chan Hop. And the way that you are talking now, that may not be a long time.'

'I hope it will be today!' I screamed.

I swore and shouted and stamped my feet; I raised my fist to her and came within an inch of hitting her. Then I turned and stumbled away, swearing over my shoulder as I went. The disappointment made me go on a massive drinking bout that lasted for several days. A few nights after I had first demanded the inheritance, I went back to my mother. This time I was roaring drunk.

'I want that money!' I screamed.

My mother's eyes were wide with fright, but she stood firm. I swore and raged and became hysterical. I flung myself to the ground and howled like an animal.

'I will kill you if you don't give it to me!'

Later I marvelled at how my mother stood up to me. When my father used to rage at me and sometimes at her, she was timid and frail. As a widow she seemed to have gained strength. But she couldn't stand up to me for long. I was naturally strong, having been a trained athlete; and in my drunken rage I was even more dangerous.

'I will give you the money,' she said eventually.

I calmed down once I had got my own way.

'Give it to me now, then,' I demanded.

She refused. 'I will give it to you in instalments. I cannot afford to do anything else. And if I give it to you over a period of time, it is possible that you will realise the wickedness of what you are doing.'

I blustered and raged but she would not change her mind. Even faced with the loss of part of her income and betrayal by a son she truly loved, she was determined that any possibility should be tried of persuading me to think again.

The first instalment was a larger sum of money than I had seen for a very long time. I looked at it and something snapped inside me. I had been penniless for so long; now I had money, proper money, the kind of money I could do things with. I headed straight for the bars and gambling dens.

It seemed that nothing was going to pull me back from my headlong path to destruction. Then I met Tracey. She was nineteen, quite tall, and had the looks and figure of a model. For the first time in my life I fell deeply, head over heels in love. I'd been fond of Helen, but this was wildly, entrancingly different.

We were an oddly-matched couple. She was everything I was not. She was highly educated; I had been more interested in sport than in study. Her personality was gentle and quiet and she preferred listening to speaking; I was full of boasting and bluster. She neither smoked nor drank; I did both. She was fond of reading; I liked pornographic magazines and a few sports papers. I was wild and reckless; but she loved me enough to believe that she could help me to change.

We were married in 1980 and lived with a friend who was kind enough to let us have the use of a room in his house outside Georgetown. Tracey's mother was appalled and thought I was the most unsuitable person imaginable for her daughter. This opinion was not changed by the fact that

I showed her no respect, having discovered she had been a night-club dancer in the past. She had tried to keep this a secret from me, and so I taunted her with it gleefully. In my circles night-club dancers were an inferior social class.

I tried to turn over a new leaf for a while, because I responded to Tracey's love for me. But alcohol once again destroyed what we had been building up. Every time I drank I turned into a different, frightening person and Tracey bore the brunt of my bitterness and frustration. I knew I couldn't handle drinking and that my life was going nowhere. Though I loved Tracey dearly, when I was drunk I blamed her for everything that was wrong with my life and beat her up for things that were all my own fault. When I was sober I knew that she was the best thing that had ever happened to me.

Miraculously she stayed with me. We talked about our relationship and the future and decided to move to Thailand and make a fresh start. For a few months I really believed I could do it. But then I was drinking heavily again, hanging round bars and gambling dens. One day Tracey announced that she was pregnant. I was delighted; I felt our relationship was complete and was proud that I was going to be a father again. But I couldn't handle the fact that a new child meant new responsibilities. I made no effort to look for a steady job to support my new family. The future loomed ahead, bleak and frightening, but drinking dulled my mind against it.

Our son Ryan was born and for a while I behaved well. I rejoiced with Tracey and spent hours playing with Ryan, entranced by the joys that new babies bring. Neither of us really believed I had changed deep down. It was a sadness to Tracey, but not a surprise, when I began to accept invitations to drinking parties in town. Nor was it out of character for me to start throwing money around, buying drinks for my drinking partners and even inviting them back to the house for more drinks. Before our second child Regina was born the last instalment had come from my mother. All the money was spent; I had squandered my inheritance. And I was still without a job, without security, and without any prospects of supporting my family. Sometimes I remembered my father and the sacrifices he had made to make sure that his wife and children had enough to eat. I wept with frustration, remembering the beatings and the anger and the long weeks in chains. What sort of a father had he been, to treat me like that? But part of me always responded: he was a father who loved you. He lived a disciplined and difficult life so that you could have a good education and a good start in life. *And what sort of a father are you?* asked the voices in my head, and they would not stop asking until I had drunk myself into unconsciousness.

'You can't possibly stay like this,' said my mother-in-law.

She looked disdainfully round our apartment. Tracey did her best to keep it neat and tidy, but with a young baby and a husband who was drunk for most of the time there was a limit to what she could do. The place looked a mess. Evidence of our lack of money was everywhere. Tracey's mother was on a visit to see our new daughter. She made no secret of her disapproval of me, but she was also anxious for her daughter and grandchildren.

'They need security and they need proper food and care. You can't do it on your own,' she said, looking at me pointedly.

'I'm not on my own,' said Tracey.

Her mother grimaced. 'You might as well be,' she retorted.

She turned to me. 'Well?'

'Well what?' I was sitting on the other side of the room, moodily smoking a cigarette.

'Will you pack – or shall I?'

'What do you mean?'

'You can all come back to Penang with me. You can stay in my house.'

I ground out the cigarette on the floor and stood up reluctantly.

'I'll pack,' I said.

Back in Penang we settled into Tracey's family home. Nothing was changed except that Tracey now had some security. At least she knew that there was no landlord ready to throw us out of our home. But I made no effort to find a job, and I didn't stop drinking. One night my mother-in-law demanded to speak to me on my own.

'This situation can't go on,' she said.

I remained silent.

'You are responsible for my daughter and for your children. It is your duty to provide for them. They are entitled to a secure home, to regular meals and money for necessary things. You are not giving them any of this.'

A memory of my father reminiscing about his early struggles drifted into my mind. I was becoming angry.

'I won't put up with this for much longer,' Tracey's mother continued. 'I'll put a stop to it. I'll make you leave this house and never see Tracey again. Or your children.'

I felt the familiar knot of tension building up in my skull as my anger mounted. Then suddenly my self-control disappeared and I was on my feet shouting at her.

'You are a stupid woman. You know nothing. You do not know what you are talking about. You're a crazy old bitch and I am going to kill you one day—'

The words poured out of my mouth, all at the same high-pitched, trembling intensity. I waved my hands and stamped my feet, standing close up to her so that she was forced to back away. As I screamed louder and louder I could hear Ryan and Regina crying in another room.

'You see?' shouted my mother-in-law. 'You're making them cry. You're a bad father, and you're no good for my daughter. I want you out of here.'

The argument raged until she twisted past me and fled out of the room. I sank into a chair, my breath heaving, and tried to calm myself. After half an hour the door opened and two men in uniform came in. Tracey's mother had called the police. I spent that night in a prison cell, bitterly protesting that it was a family matter and that the police had no right to be involved. I slept very little. Neither did anybody in the other cells. Next day I went back to her house. I stood in the garden with a pile of stones and smashed every window in the house. I shouted threats that I would burn the place down. She fled for safety with my wife and children and hid in a relative's house.

Next day she returned. She had asked some gangsters to protect her, and they spent the day repairing the windows. They sent word to me not to come back or there would be trouble. But I was much too proud to acknowledge defeat. I ignored the warning. The next night I got drunk and went to the house.

'Well – where is your trouble?' I howled from the garden.

The gang beat me up and left me battered and bleeding in the grounds while they called the police and had me arrested for disturbing the peace. Fortunately the officer who handled the case was an old friend of mine.

'I'm putting you on a good behaviour bond, Hui,' he explained. 'That means you don't go to prison. But you should clear out of town for at least three months. And don't start making plans to come back for revenge.'

I agreed to go. Before I left I traced the addresses of all the gangsters involved and vowed I would have my revenge at the appropriate time.

I didn't complete the three months. Whenever I drank, memories of the beating swam before my eyes. I became obsessed with the idea of revenge. I had lost face, I had run away. I would rather die at their hands than be humiliated. My shame could not go unavenged. I went back to Penang secretly and looked for them. I fully intended to kill them. I had the weapons, and I knew where my victims lived. Inexplicably they were nowhere to be found. I hung around their houses, ready to strike. I visited the clubs and bars where they were usually to be seen. I asked for them and looked for them all over Penang. But I never saw any of them again.

8

BACK IN BUSINESS

I tried to get in touch with Tracey again, but she made it clear that she would only consider a reconciliation if I proved that I had genuinely changed my whole way of life. Until that happened she didn't want to see me again, and didn't want me to visit her or have access to our children. I was shocked and hurt. I had grown used to Tracey's long-suffering readiness to forgive me every time I let her down. But now she had run out of patience. She would never have thrown me out, but since I'd left she wasn't going to let me back, not until a lot of things had changed.

For a while I considered trying to get custody of the children, but realised very quickly that it would be impossible. I missed them terribly, but they were too young to leave their mother, and my police record and the evidence from neighbours and my wife's family would kill any chance of custody. In any case I wanted our family to be back together again. I wanted it to be as it was at the beginning, when the children were really small and our troubles hadn't got out of hand.

I went back to Thailand. I didn't know how I was going to do it, but I knew that this time I was going to get back into the big money. I'd tried before, but this time I was going to succeed. Money was the only way I would ever be reunited with my wife and children.

This time I was going to do it.

In Thailand I tried to pick up the pieces with the friends and acquaintances who had abandoned me when

I drank myself into despair. It was a painful, frustrating time. Hardly anybody would talk to me, and those who did only wanted to pass the time of day. I found myself talking about nothing, with people who could have made it possible for me to have another chance of earning big money. They didn't want to. They had lost faith in me.

I made a few new acquaintances, people who had only recently come to Thailand or hadn't been part of my circle in the old days. I talked big, hinted at past exploits and waited for an opportunity to come along.

The opportunity arrived when I met Larp Chikrit.

Larp was a Thai businessman who let it be known that he had a great deal more money than his clothes, accommodation and leisure interests implied. He had similar tastes to my own; he liked gambling, drinking and having a good time. We became good friends.

I instinctively behaved myself when I was with Larp. Thailand was a lonely country for someone whose friends had abandoned him, and I didn't want to frighten off one of the few people willing to spend time with me. But also I wondered whether this wealthy man might not somehow be the answer to my biggest need: to get back into the drugs business. Before long the opening came. We were talking about the Thai and Malaysian governments' stringent penalties for drug dealing.

'Do you know anybody in that line of business?' asked Larp, watching me closely.

I evaded the question, but I knew I had dropped hints previously. Larp must have had some suspicions.

'No,' I lied. 'How about you?'

Larp shrugged. 'Oh, yes. I know quite a few. People have offered to supply me if I want to get involved in the trade.' He sipped his drink, and wiped his mouth fastidiously. 'But I'm a businessman, not a smuggler. I like things the way they are. I don't need that kind of money, so why take that kind of risk?'

'Why indeed,' I agreed. But my brain was working overtime.

A few days later I broached the subject again. I explained my situation to Larp, and told him everything that had happened to me.

'I need money to get my family together again,' I said. 'I'm desperate. I'll face the risks.'

Larp stared at me. 'Even the fact that if you get arrested in Thailand, Malaysia or Singapore you'll probably get the death penalty?'

'I told you. I'm ready to take the risks.'

'And you want me to come up with the money?'

I nodded. Larp drummed his fingers on the table. There was a long pause.

'I'll think about it,' he said finally.

After a week he contacted me.

'I can lend you the money to buy the drugs and get to Europe,' he said. 'But I don't want to know anything about it. If it works out, fine. If you get arrested, I don't know you. I never met you. OK?'

I thanked him gracefully and began to organise the trip.

My destination was London via Singapore. I arrived at Heathrow on a cold February morning and made my way to the customs hall. I followed the signs to the green channel and presented myself at the checking desk. The officer scanned my face briefly.

'Anything to declare? Are you carrying more than your duty-free entitlements . . . ?'

The familiar cross-examination pattered on. I shook my head.

'Nothing to declare,' I assured him, and even gestured towards opening my cases.

'All right,' he said, and waved me through.

All the way to the hotel where I was to sell the drugs my heart was pounding with excitement. I'd been calm and unruffled on the flight over; but now there was a huge sense of release and happiness. I almost skipped along the road, swinging my precious cargo. The contents of my luggage had a street value of several hundred thousand pounds.

The deal was made and I was a rich man again. I spent three nights in London enjoying myself, and then flew on to Amsterdam where I lost no time in setting up a second trip. My contacts in Amsterdam were willing to do business with me, and we arranged my next trip in two months' time, arriving in England on Easter day. I spent a further week in Amsterdam, spending money and revelling in my newfound freedom. Then I flew back to Bangkok and repaid Larp his loan.

Bangkok was a very different place now I had money. Some of my old friends reappeared, anxious to know me again. Most of them I allowed to hang around – it made me feel good. Some I gave presents to and treated well. They were the people who might be useful to me later.

I didn't visit my family. Some sixth sense told me to keep a low profile. If Tracey's family saw that I was suddenly wealthy they might easily become suspicious and inform the police. I had my own plans for my in-laws. After I had completed my next mission I'd show them what I was capable of. The shame of losing face at the hands of their hired gangsters would be well and truly wiped out.

I laid my plans for the next trip with great care. It would be a major operation. In Amsterdam any quantity of drugs could easily be sold. I was going to carry a large amount of heroin. I would need to divide the load and employ several couriers to take it into Holland. They had to be people I could trust, and I would have to travel with them.

Obtaining and preparing the drugs would take time. Also, when I tried to book flights in advance I found that the Easter period was already over-booked and there were no seats available. So I rang my Dutch partners and put back the date of the trip. I did what organising I could in Thailand and then took a short holiday in Singapore. Afterwards I travelled north overland to Penang and Georgetown, to begin the task of finding couriers.

I had known Roger since he was thirteen; he was big, tall and spoke excellent English. 'I'll pay you well,' I promised, 'and if we succeed, there'll be a big bonus for you.'

Roger agreed at once. I found two other young men, Paul and James, to help as couriers; and two more were recruited on my behalf by my contacts in Amsterdam, to help with selling the drugs.

The plan was straightforward. Roger and I were to take a British Airways flight from Singapore to Heathrow. James would go direct to Amsterdam on a Singapore Airlines flight. Paul would leave the day before Roger and me, travelling via Brussels, and would meet us at Heathrow.

Paul left as planned, and we heard nothing of any problems at the airport. Roger and I had booked into a hotel in Singapore the previous night, and our plane was due to leave at midnight.

We were relaxing in our hotel room when the telephone rang. We had the drugs packed in our luggage, and there was nothing to do but wait. It was the hottest part of the afternoon, and Roger was lounging on his bed, staring at the ceiling and smoking. He was playing with a matchbox, endlessly rolling it from one hand to the other. I was on edge too. This was the biggest operation I had ever planned, and the rewards were astronomical. So would the penalty be if we were caught.

'Room 49?' The woman's voice was insistent. I didn't recognise it. I assumed it was one of the hotel staff.

'Yes?'

'To whom am I speaking?'

'This is Hui.'

'Can you tell me where you have come from, and your destination?'

A tiny alarm bell began ringing somewhere in the back of my mind. I thought fast. *This could be trouble*. I glanced at Roger. He was still fiddling with the matchbox.

'I'm on my way back to England. To work. I've been staying here on holiday.'

At the other end of the line she was making notes; I heard her carefully repeating what I'd said.

'Look,' I suggested abruptly, 'why not come up to the room, if you need information?'

Roger stared at me and at our luggage, neatly piled against the wall.

'What are your planned movements this afternoon?'

'We'll be here.'

'Thank you, Mr Hui.'

There was a click and the line went dead. I replaced the receiver.

Roger was on his feet. 'What's happening? Who was it? What will we do?'

'I'm not sure,' I said slowly, and reached for the telephone again. 'Desk? I just took a call. Can you tell me, was it an internal call or an outside one?'

'Just one moment, please.' The anonymous voice at the other end was back in seconds. 'No outside calls have been received for you.'

'Who rang, then? Was it the hotel administration?'

'We have no record of any calls, Mr Hui. Would you like me to make enquiries?' The voice was calm, professionally helpful.

'No, I was just . . . no, it doesn't matter.'

I put the telephone down and looked at Roger. He was trembling.

'What's going on?'

'That's what I'm going to find out.' I pulled on my clothes quickly. 'If anybody comes, just be careful what you say. Say as little as possible.'

I took the lift to the ground floor. *Something's going wrong*, I thought. When I reached the lobby I became even more worried. I was a regular visitor to the hotel, the manager was a good friend of mine, I knew most of the staff. But there were people hanging round the lobby whom I didn't recognise, and I instinctively knew that they were plain-clothes police. I went to the coffee bar in a corner of the lobby and sat down with a cup of tea, straining my ears to catch fragments of conversation and find out what was going on. Nobody within earshot was saying anything I could make sense of. In the manager's office there was the same air of suppressed excitement.

'What's happening?' I asked the manager.

He spread his hands. 'Two Malaysians,' he said. 'They've been in some sort of trouble in the last few days and the police heard they were in the hotel. So now the place is being turned upside down. And I'm supposed to be running a hotel while all this is happening.'

'Any idea who the two are?' I asked carefully.

'No idea at all,' he said distractedly. 'I got to get on, Hui. Give me a break.'

There was an insistent hammering in my chest; I could feel the pulse drumming in my ears, and my back was clammy with sweat. *How long is all this going to take? And who are they after, anyway?*

I tried to think it through logically. I'd not been in any trouble for a while, and Roger had been out of town. There was no hint that Paul hadn't got away from Singapore safely. How could they be after us? *You've got a lot of enemies in Singapore*, a sharp voice inside my head reminded me. *Maybe somebody's sent word from Thailand too*. I went back to our room.

Roger was sitting looking out of the window at the street below. He turned nervously as I entered.

'Anybody been here?' I asked.

'No.' Beads of sweat stood on his forehead. He was trying to appear calm.

'Look,' I said. 'Here's what's happening. The place is full of police.' I told him what little I had been able to find out. 'I don't *think* they're after us. But they could possibly be. And anyway, if they start searching the rooms we're in trouble.'

Roger swallowed. 'So what do we do?'

'We sit tight and wait. That's all we can do. We can still make the midnight flight if they leave soon.'

I returned to the lobby and sat for several hours drinking beer and trying to find out more. By nine o'clock that evening the police were still in the hotel. I went back to Roger.

'We have to make a decision, and I've made one,' I announced. 'If we're going to check in at ten thirty for the flight, we'll need a taxi at ten. I'm going to call now and book it.'

Roger was clearly panicking. 'Why can't we just go on the next flight?'

I sat down on the bed. 'Look, Roger. You don't have to come. If you want to get out now, I'll fix you up in another hotel and I'll book you on a flight back to Georgetown tomorrow.'

He buried his face in his hands, 'I'd be letting you down.'

'Not so much as if you turned and ran at the airport.' I smiled, and put my arm round his shoulders, 'Come on, Roger, it's not so bad. We'd still be friends. Maybe another time.'

I got up. I felt good; I was calling the shots, I was in control. I was the one who had the power.

Roger remained deep in thought.

'I'll book the cab,' I said. 'Let me know what you want to do. I need to know in half an hour.'

Before the half-hour was up the hotel manager called.

'They got them, Hui. They're taking them to the police station. So I got all these people out of my lobby finally. No trouble. Good thing.' As he was about to ring off, he suddenly added: 'Hey, Hui, another thing. Those guys are in big trouble. You know what? They found drugs on them. Malaysian nationals too. That's real bad news for them. Real bad.'

We gathered our belongings together, and were soon in a taxi heading for the airport. By the time the plane took off the horrors of the afternoon were a distant memory. Only a lurking shiver of fear occasionally flickered across my mind as I thought of the consequences of being arrested.

I arranged and rearranged the magazines in front of me, watching the stewardess demonstrating the safety procedures, moving like a mechanical doll with a fixed, glacial smile. The 'No smoking' indicators blinked off and I unclipped my safety belt and lit a cigarette.

Roger was grasping his armrest so hard that his knuckles showed white. He looked like someone who was terrified of flying.

In thirty hours, I told myself, *you'll have made it. You'll be colossally rich.* Money and power, and the capability to end years of misery. Those who had beaten me up and humiliated me would find out what it meant to have Chan Hop Hui for an enemy. I planned violent and complicated revenge as the plane soared into the night, and the lights of Singapore disappeared beneath the clouds.

Dad was right, I decided. *God can only help you if you help yourself.* I smiled happily, made myself comfortable and fell asleep.

9

ARRESTED

I was asleep for most of the long flight to Europe. I woke from time to time, to see Roger leafing restlessly through magazines and smoking endless cigarettes, but I always drifted back to sleep. I was finally woken by the pilot's announcement that we were about to land at Heathrow. I stretched my stiff limbs and rubbed my bleary eyes. I went to the washroom and had a quick wash, then chatted to Roger, giving him last-minute advice on how to handle the immigration officer's questions. But before I could wish him a final 'Good luck', I had to turn away. I felt suddenly sick and scared. There was a strange feeling inside me.

I fell silent and wrestled with my feelings. *I must stop thinking negatively.* Had I ever been caught? I was never even scared before; every time I'd taken drugs through customs I was carefree and relaxed about it. Sometimes over-relaxed; there were times when I'd offered to turn my cases out on the officer's desk, knowing the packets of drugs would be found if I did so. It was a madness that sometimes made me do crazy things; but I was never caught, they always waved me through.

But this trip was different. There had already been the panic at the hotel. Now, bleary from a long sleep and full of unease, I was afraid. It was a new experience for me. I looked grimly through the window as the plane began its final descent, and found myself gripping the armrests as the undercarriage touched down bumpily on the runway.

The plane landed on a bright English morning. The London suburbs looked green and peaceful after the hot Penang weather. There was a long walk to the immigration lounge. As we crossed the tarmac my mind was racing. *It's not too late even now*, I told myself. *You don't have to collect your baggage. You can just walk away from the whole situation.* I sensed Roger behind me, nervous too. I had a dreadful feeling that things were about to go very wrong.

The immigration officer glanced at my passport. I was expecting some tough questions about my reasons for returning to England so soon after my previous visit, but he didn't raise the matter. He ran through the usual questions: what was I here for, how long was I staying, where would I be living during my stay. I gave him the story we'd planned beforehand, and he waved me through.

I went to the carousel and collected my cases. Roger was there too, collecting his; he'd got through immigration safely. I should have been relieved, but the dull ache of fear wouldn't go away.

The customs officer beckoned me to put my cases on his table. I did so.

'Anything to declare?' he asked. I shook my head.

'Open your cases, if you would, sir.' As I did so he searched the contents briskly and efficiently. There was nothing to be found; the drugs were concealed in the base and lid. He snapped the cases shut, and pushed them back to me. His hands rested for a moment on the suitcase lid. I thought about the heroin that was stuffed in the lining. His face betrayed nothing. 'All right, sir. Next!'

Roger had gone ahead of me and I passed him on my way out. My heart lurched as I saw him. His face had a grey pallor; his baggage was emptied out on the table, and two customs officers were examining the cases themselves, very suspiciously. As I stood and waited one of them looked over at me and frowned. I smiled vaguely at him and carried on towards the exit. I was yards away from freedom.

Meanwhile I had no idea what was happening to Roger.

'Will you come with me, please, sir. This way.'

When the officer stopped me, I was expecting it. This was what all the fear and premonition had been leading to. He took my luggage from me and guided me to a side door with a firm hand on my arm.

Possibilities raced through my mind. I could make a run for it – no, that would be stupid, an admission of guilt and guaranteed to land me in the worst possible trouble. Maybe I could do a deal with the customs officers. No, that was stupid too. I would just have to stay with my prepared story. I was taken to a small room with a desk and some chairs.

'What's happening?' I tried to be calm and friendly.

The officer was non-committal, 'You will have to answer some questions, sir. An officer will be coming shortly to interview you.'

He offered me a cigarette. I accepted. Too eager, I thought, and tried to smoke it as if I had no worries about anything. But my luggage was standing there on a table, holding plenty of damning evidence which they'd find if they spent five minutes looking. Part of me was cherishing a wistful hope that some emergency would happen; that they'd decide not to search it; that they'd suddenly come in and tell me that the whole thing was a misunderstanding.

Perhaps it *was* a misunderstanding, I told myself, and flushed with excitement at the thought. Maybe it was nothing to do with the luggage after all. Maybe . . .

The door opened. Another officer came in, and introduced himself as Mr Gauld and his colleague as Mr Richardson. The questions began.

'Where are you going to?'

I told them the name of the hotel.

'How long are you staying?'

'Two weeks.'

Gauld pointed to my luggage. 'What's in that case?'

'I don't know.' I slid into the prepared story. 'I just brought it for somebody. I got a free trip.'

'Who is meeting you here?'

'Nobody. They will contact us at the hotel.'

That part of it was true. The hotel was in Belgrave Road near Victoria Station. I stayed there on my previous trip.

'What's the name of your contact?'

'I don't know. He's supposed to contact me.'

'So how will he know you?'

'He knows my name.'

It was a classic picture I was painting, the sort of thing that happens all the time; an innocent traveller is persuaded to take luggage on a plane for somebody else to be collected at the destination. It is a way of getting drugs into a country without having to go through customs yourself. In case the person is caught and punished, you make sure as little as possible is known about you, so that you can't be traced back. The newspapers are full of stories like it. It was a good cover story, and I was hoping it would work. I also hoped that Roger had had the sense to tell it convincingly.

Mr Richardson was studying some papers. He joined in the questioning.

'When were you here before?'

'A month ago.'

'Where did you stay?'

I told him; the same hotel. It was a mistake. He spotted it immediately.

'So you *do* know the man's name.'

I thought fast. 'No. I just came for sightseeing. A tourist.'

The officers searched me, a strip search that was thorough and expert. They went through my pockets and examined my clothes carefully. My wallet and all my papers were spread on the table. I complained all the time they were doing it.

'What's going on?' I demanded. 'Why am I being held?'

But I knew what the answer would be even before they made the formal statement.

'Chan Hop Hui, you are under arrest on suspicion of importing dangerous drugs.'

10

BETRAYED

'Who were you supposed to be meeting?'

The questions went on and on. I was numb with frustration and despair.

'Nobody. You saw the papers in my pocket. I was going to the hotel.'

All this time I was wondering about Roger, and about Paul who was supposed to have met the plane at Heathrow that morning. James, hopefully, was safe in Amsterdam by now.

Mr Gauld sighed, 'We know you were going to meet somebody.'

He gave a signal to his colleague. Richardson opened the door and a number of plain-clothes officers came in.

'Take a good look at Mr Hui,' said Gauld. 'We don't want you to lose him.'

They each looked at me intently. I averted my eyes.

'Go and take up your positions, gentlemen,' said Gauld, and they left the room.

'Now, Hui. We want you to go to the public terminal with your cases, just as you were when we picked you up. Walk around for five minutes and then come back. Do you understand?'

I nodded sullenly and they escorted me to the terminal.

The bright lights and crowds were a stark contrast to the cell-like interview room. I looked across to the main terminal entrance. No hope now of making a run for it. All round the area I saw the plain-clothes men at their posts, observing me unobtrusively. Gauld and his colleague stood by the customs hall exit, watching carefully.

The trolley with my cases was unwieldy and seemed to have a life of its own. I pushed it towards a news stand. For a moment I stood looking at the magazine covers, and then moved in the direction of the coffee bar. I was determined to avoid the reception point, because that was where I had arranged to meet Paul. But it was no use. Barely a couple of minutes after I emerged from the customs hall, I saw Paul hurrying over to me.

I walked past him quickly, and gave him a warning look as I passed. He seemed astonished at my behaviour. He watched me go by, then turned and followed me, gesticulating. I slowed down, and he tried to speak to me. I shouted at him in Chinese, telling him to get away from me. I used our special code words, but none of it was any use. After passing me the second time he stood in amazement and watched me go on, signalling our relationship to all the watching officers as clearly as if he had made a public announcement. I saw a plain-clothes man leave his post and start shadowing Paul, and knew that Paul was in deep trouble too.

I walked around for the five minutes, and then Mr Gauld appeared at my side and led me back to the interview room. He seemed very confident.

'Who was he?' demanded Gauld, looking at me fixedly.

'I don't know who you're talking about.' I looked back defiantly.

There was nothing left for me now. The only thing I could do was to make sure that Roger, Paul and James got off. At least I knew how to lie well.

'Is there anybody you want to contact? Any phone calls you want to make?'

'I told you. They were going to contact me at the hotel. Just leave the boy alone,' I added.

'You mean your travelling companion?'

'Yes.'

There was no answer. Then, 'You do know why you are being held by customs?'

'Some of it,' I replied tersely.

I fielded more questions for what seemed a long time. The interrogation came to an end when an officer I hadn't seen before came into the room. He pulled up a chair and looked at me thoughtfully. Then he leaned forward.

'*Chap chak . . . Frankie . . . Leng chye.* OK, Hui, what do those words mean, then?'

I was appalled. He had just proclaimed, in a reasonable Chinese accent, the special code words that I had given my men.

'Where did you get those words?' I demanded. I was breathing jerkily; the tension was getting to me. 'I tell you, I'm not answering one more question until I know who told you those words.'

He grinned. 'Your friends. Very helpful friends you've got.'

'Which ones?' I shouted. 'Give me their names. Tell me who told you! I'm not going on with this interview until you tell me exactly who they were.'

The man banged the table with his fist. '*We* say when the talking stops, Hui. Understand? And until we have the information we want, we don't leave this room, is that clear?'

'I need to use the toilet,' I said.

In the corridor on the way to the toilet I passed the cubicle rooms next to mine. They had pinned up the names of Roger and Paul on the doors. So they were being investigated too: I wondered how their interviews were going.

Back in the interview room I delivered an ultimatum.

'I'm going to keep quiet until you tell me the names of the people who gave you that information,' I said flatly. 'It's important to me, I need to know. You can't make me answer your questions.'

Not in England, I thought. *You aren't allowed to beat me up here.* I hoped I was right.

'And another thing,' I added. 'I'm hungry and tired. Please, can I have some food and take a break. Then I'll give my statement.'

The officers looked at each other.

'Fair enough,' said Gauld.

So I had half an hour to wonder how far the two lads in Amsterdam had co-operated with the police, and what sort of a story I was going to give the authorities. During the break a senior officer came into the rest room and asked me for some names.

'Your two associates have been arrested in Amsterdam,' he told me.

I received the news in silence, but inside I was furious. So they were the ones who had told.

'We need to know about James Chong,' added the officer.

'I won't tell you,' I muttered.

'Well, we know he was booked in at the Imperial Hotel in Singapore. We even know his room number, D312. We actually know quite a lot about your trip, Mr Hui.'

Now I was really frightened for James. If he was in Singapore going through what I was going through, he was a dead man. Drug-smuggling was a capital offence in Singapore, as it was in Malaysia. I was worried that my interrogation in London might have repercussions on his situation in Singapore, if he was being held there. So I kept my mouth firmly shut.

Two more officers from customs HQ arrived. They were very pleasant and asked questions that were straightforward. They seemed reasonable people, just doing their job, and I saw a glimmer of hope that I might be able to do business with them. I might be able to make sure that I was the only one who ended up facing charges. I decided to co-operate.

'I'll tell you what you want to know. I'll plead guilty to importing illegal drugs and be done with it,' I said.

'Good lad,' said the officer.

The officers who had interviewed Roger and Paul came in and asked me more questions. As they cross-examined me, I was astonished to find that they knew every detail of my previous trip. They knew how it was organised, where I'd gone, who I'd spoken to – everything. My heart sank. This was the end; it was hopeless. I was so angry that I wanted to kill Paul and Roger. They must have told everything they knew.

It was all supposed to be very different. I'd impressed on them before we left home what to do if things went wrong. If we were arrested they were to claim that they knew nothing about it, that they were just carrying the bags for me and didn't know what was in them. I was to do the talking, and they were to keep their mouths shut. It seemed the best way of dealing with possible problems. I would take responsibility for everything, and there was a good chance the others would get off without being charged. It was better one man in prison than a whole gang. And I reckoned that if they did get off, at least they would look after my interests while I was in prison. But it seemed that Paul and Roger had totally let me down.

The two HQ officers were frank with me. They told me what information they already had, and also that three of my associates had been arrested in Amsterdam and were now being interviewed by the police there. But one thing they didn't disclose was what had happened to James. Had he left Singapore in time, before information arrived from the British police, and been arrested in Europe? If so, James had escaped with his life. There was no death sentence for drug-smuggling in Europe.

So I had quite a lot to think about before the two HQ officers began their formal interview. I faced the most difficult decisions of my life. Should I tell them the whole truth? They seemed to have most of the important facts already, and what they had told me so far would guarantee a heavy sentence.

I thought back over what I knew. Three of us had been arrested at Heathrow, three more in Amsterdam. Who knew what others might be implicated? I had no idea what Paul and Roger were saying to the customs officers. The whole situation in fact was far outside my experience. In my worst nightmares about being arrested I had not imagined anything like this. The questioning, humiliation and arrest were all things that could have been predicted, but there was no way I could ever have foreseen the betrayal.

The interview went on until midnight. I co-operated fully as far as my own involvement was concerned, and refused to make any comments about anybody else's part in the smuggling.

Eventually I was taken to Heathrow police station for the night. They told me that the investigation would continue the next day. In the cold police cell I could not sleep, despite the fact that I was drained and exhausted after the events of the day and the long hours of questioning. Frightening thoughts were racing round my head. How long would my sentence be? Was James in custody or on his way to Britain or in gaol in Singapore, facing the death sentence? How much more did the authorities know? How much did they know about me?

I was taken back to Heathrow at 10.30 the next morning. On my way to the investigation room I saw James's name on one of the other doors. The relief was almost painful, and my joy at his escape from Singapore was not entirely unselfish. Had James's name appeared on the execution roll in a few months' time, then I would have had some awkward explaining to do to his friends and family.

During all this time I had not seen Roger since we were separated in the customs hall, or Paul since he had approached me in the public terminal. It was another two days before we were allowed to meet again briefly. The interviews were over; we were to be remanded in custody. Roger was under twenty-one years old, so he was sent to a youth custody centre. The rest of us were sent to

Wormwood Scrubs to be detained pending a hearing and to undergo further investigation. Paul was allocated to the same cell as James, and I was put in with Felix, a Swiss national, also arrested for smuggling drugs, with whom I made friends.

As we left for prison I said goodbye to Roger and tried to cheer him up. I reminded him we would meet at Uxbridge Magistrates Court. But he looked dejected and very young as they led him away.

11

PRISON

'So what happened at the airport? Did they give you a hard time?'

It was the daily exercise hour at Wormwood Scrubs. I had headed straight for James. I wanted to tell him how glad I was that he'd made it out of Singapore. And I wanted to find out who had betrayed us, who had ignored our carefully laid plans and talked all of us into prison. I made sure we were well away from Paul. I wanted to compare their stories. My questions to James were casual, but I was watching his expression closely as he replied.

'They really threw me,' he said. 'They knew everything about me.' He looked at me awkwardly. 'I thought you must have told them everything already. How else could they know? So I filled in the bits they hadn't got.'

I watched Paul walking several yards away, looking young and vulnerable in the crowd of hard, bleak-faced men, and my pulse suddenly raced.

'Paul,' I said tightly. 'It was Paul.' *The bastard*, I screamed inside. *He stitched us all up.* I grabbed James's arm. 'Don't you *see*? He told them the code words, they were interviewing me while they were interviewing him . . . Then later' – of course, *now* I was able to put the pieces of the jigsaw together – 'later on, they came in and told me they knew everything.'

'But not till after they'd talked to Paul,' said James.

I looked at Paul with loathing, but the warders were watching us, so I tried to keep my voice low.

'I'm going to kill him.'

'What with?' said James. 'That's not going to help.'

'I don't care if it helps or not,' I muttered. At that moment I hated Paul more than I had ever hated anybody in my life. 'Anyway, I'm going over there to tell him what I think of him.'

James seized my sleeve. 'That's stupid,' he said. 'You'll get into a furious temper and then you'll go crazy and then you'll start fighting. Everyone will laugh at you and you'll get into trouble with the warders. You don't want to end up in solitary when you've only just arrived.'

I bit hard on my anger and glared at Paul, who was watching us uneasily.

'I'll talk to Roger, get the details from him when we go to court,' I promised. 'Then I'll kill Paul.'

A day or two before we were to appear at Uxbridge Magistrates Court I was in my cell, sprawled on my bunk in vest and pants, moodily smoking and staring at the ceiling. Felix was reading a magazine. Neither of us had much to say. Suddenly there was a rap on the door.

'Visitors for Hui.'

'Where? Who?' I said sourly. 'There can't be; I don't know anyone in England. You've got it wrong.'

I had no friends in the country, and the few people I knew would hardly have bothered to come and see me to cheer me up. They would certainly not have wanted to attract police attention by revealing that they knew me.

'Come on, it's not a mistake, you're to come along to the interview room. Move it!'

I threw on a shirt, trying to work out who the visitors could be. I knew that my case had attracted wide public interest. The newspapers in Malaysia and Singapore had reported the arrests and written the story up extensively, because we had been carrying the biggest quantity of drugs seized from Malaysians for a long time. My case had an added public interest. Not long ago the Malaysian Deputy Prime Minister had presented a Bill to Parliament to bring

the full weight of the law to bear on Malaysian nationals
arrested on drugs charges abroad. The Bill proposed that
any Malaysian convicted of drug offences while in a foreign country would, when released and deported back to
Malaysia, face further prosecution under the Dangerous
Drugs Act – whether or not they had already served a
sentence abroad.

So who were my mystery visitors? More customs officers
wanting answers to yet more questions? Some solicitor
wanting me to sign papers about the court appearance?
Or staff from the Malaysian Embassy arranging for a trial
under my own country's drug offence law, perhaps leading
to my execution?

I was led by the officer through a rabbit-warren of
corridors and iron-barred gates into a part of the prison that
seemed deserted. We weren't going to the visiting room; the
familiar hubbub of conversation was nowhere to be heard.
Instead the officer opened a door and motioned me inside.
Four men and a Chinese woman looked up as I entered.

One face I recognised; it was a customs investigator from
Headquarters who had interviewed me at the airport. He
greeted me civilly, and formally introduced the others to
me. The woman explained that she was also from the Far
East, a law student working with my solicitor. The three
men were from Holland Park police station. They were
polite and businesslike.

'We're here to ask you some questions,' they explained,
'about three of your colleagues who have been arrested in
Amsterdam. You have been informed of their arrest.'

I was determined not to co-operate. 'They have nothing
to do with me,' I retorted. 'They're not colleagues. I don't
know them.'

The officers were unruffled.

'When did you contact these men? With whom did you
negotiate? How did you intend to pay them?'

'I told you. I don't know these people. There's nothing
I can tell you about them. Haven't I told you already?'

They would not be thwarted.

'Firstly, Mr Hui, we are in possession of the facts about your trip to Europe.' The investigating officer ticked off the points on his fingers. 'We know who you employed; where you were going; the names of all your contacts.' He reeled off a list of names, addresses, places. 'Do you want me to go on?'

I stared at him in horror. He had the whole operation at his fingertips.

'Furthermore, if the Dutch police are unsuccessful in obtaining a guilty verdict against your confederates, they will be deported back to Malaysia and handed over to the authorities.'

He paused, letting the full implications of his words sink in. Almost certain death for the three men, and serious problems for me when I was eventually deported to face the courts and the families of the men I had persuaded to die for me. As I thought about this, the officer took an envelope from his briefcase and began to lay out a series of photographic prints on the table. Stunned, I saw each of my men, clearly photographed in locations in Amsterdam that I knew well. Simon, walking along the Prins Hendrikkade, unaware of the cameraman probably concealed in one of the numerous alleyways; Choy drinking Dutch beer in a scruffy bar, puffing on one of the spindly, ragged Dutch cigars that he chain-smoked; Kasem, his arm round a beautiful Asiatic girl, beaming almost directly at the camera as if aware he was being photographed. Worse was to come. A fat folder was produced, stuffed with documents and photographs. Incredulously I saw that they were all about me and my smuggling activities.

'How long have you been collecting this?' I demanded.

'When you first came to Amsterdam. They had you under surveillance from the start. They were going to pick you up in Amsterdam but you had moved on when we came for you. But they've been tailing you for quite a while. We've had regular reports on your movements. Up till now, we just haven't had enough evidence to charge you.' Again he paused significantly.

The officers gave me a thorough summary of my activities: my routes across Europe, my accommodation, my contacts. They had a list of my European girlfriends, and the places we had been together. There were facts in that file that I had forgotten, and even some information that came as a shock to me. I had had no idea that I had been tailed by the Dutch police so thoroughly and for so long. My image of myself as a mysterious, glamorous underworld figure was suddenly severely dented.

'All right. Now, let's fill in the gaps.'

The questioning began again. The woman from the solicitor's office sat quietly to one side, taking notes. They wanted me to admit my connection with the three in Holland.

'Your statement would be important in securing a conviction,' they said. 'This would go in your favour when sentencing.'

'These people have nothing to do with me,' I growled. 'I'm not going to talk.' I folded my arms defiantly.

Then they told me that they had interviewed Paul earlier that morning, and now had enough evidence without mine anyway.

'Well, that's fine by me,' I said. 'It makes no difference. You can charge me if you like but I'm not going to tell you a thing.'

And nobody's going to be able to call me a supergrass, I added silently, rejecting one of the few underworld titles I did not crave.

I was taken back to my cell fuming at the thought that Paul had given away even more information. But I was glad I had been able to avoid having to explain to my friends that I had helped the police to convict them. At least in the future I would not have to face vengeful friends and relatives. I could hold my head high. I began to hope that the sentence would be a light one, that the Malaysian authorities would be lenient when I got home, that the good times might still come back.

The hearing at the Magistrates Court was straightforward. We were remanded for trial at Reading Crown Court, and sent to Reading Prison to await the trial. It was six weeks after the arrest. This time Roger was allocated a cell on the youth landing, and Paul, James and I were put in a single cell on one of the main landings. Light came from a window high on the wall opposite the door, and a grille of iron bars covered the window-glass in the door. A table, a small cupboard and a chair were the only items of furniture besides the bunks, a single on one side of the cell and an upper and lower bunk facing it. I took the bunk on its own. Nobody questioned my right to have it. There was a sullen acceptance that I was still the leader of our gang, even in prison.

I could just about bring myself to speak to Paul, but the atmosphere was full of hostility. I lost my temper easily. The smallest thing set me off; clothes left untidy, one of the others whistling, a radio turned up too loud. As Paul inadvertently revealed more and more of the things he had told the customs investigators, my frayed temper easily snapped and I flew into vicious tantrums. But I tried to keep calm. My solicitor had told me that I would receive the official statement from the prosecution, which would contain transcripts of the statements made by Roger, Paul and James. Then I would be able to do some cross-examination of my own; I would ask them exactly what they meant by betraying me.

As prisoners on remand we had no work duties and plenty of time to get on each others' nerves. The humiliating environment made it worse. At night, locked in our cell, we had to use plastic pots to urinate in, and each morning there was a frustrating and faintly odorous pilgrimage to empty them in the lavatory. Tempers were fragile, and there were often arguments and sometimes fights, leaving the lavatory in a filthy state for the landing cleaners to deal with.

We began to use prison language, picked up from the other prisoners. 'Recess' for the lavatory, and 'slopping out' for the dreary morning ritual were straightforward. 'Lead on', the usual command to get moving, and 'banged up' for 'locked away' were also simple equivalents; and prisoners referred to each other as 'cons', originally a half-humorous abbreviation of 'convict' and now just the normal word for a fellow-prisoner.

But most prisoner's slang was violent and destructive, and it suited our mood to use it. We were soon calling every prison officer a 'screw' knowing that it was a coded sexual insult. The most vicious language of all was reserved for cons hated by their fellow-prisoners: 'grass' and 'supergrass' were familiar terms for informers, but here they were deadly insults; and the most despised of offenders, child rapists, were 'nonces', the term delivered either in tones dripping with hatred or in a totally dismissive way that reduced the person to valueless nothingness.

On remand we received a small weekly allowance, which was enough to buy some tobacco, though never enough to last through the week. We were allowed visitors, but none came to see us apart from officials and legal representatives. Nor did we expect any. We knew nobody in Reading. The only contact with the outside world was through letters. Roger received one from his sister. She told him that our arrest was a major news story in Malaysia. She enclosed a news cutting reporting the case. He allowed me to read the letter; it was a loving, touching reassurance: 'We'll stand by you, whatever happens.'

The night I read her letter I lay in bed thinking about a thousand things. I thought of myself, the situation I was now in. I had no friends. Those I had thought of as friends had betrayed me under questioning; as for the scores of hangers-on who had enjoyed being seen with me when I was powerful, they were probably now attached to a new star, and had forgotten me. I had no family to support me. I dared not write to my mother or Tracey about what had happened. I reckoned I knew what their response would be: 'Serve him right.' In some quarters there would be celebrations, a general thankfulness that justice had been done and that I had been punished for my wicked deeds.

I wrestled with my misery in the darkness. If I had to be arrested, why at this particular point in my life? I was almost out of my difficulties. A few more trips would have set me on my feet. I would have had money and influence, I would have been the head of a big smuggling organisation. I'd put in so much hard work – and now it had all come to nothing. Just when I was nearly at the point where I could have gone to Tracey and shown her that I had solved my problems and could care for my family properly again.

Every time I have a daughter, I thought angrily, *my life goes to pieces*. My first marriage ended when my daughter Eunis was born; now my daughter Regina was six months old, and I was in deep trouble again. The more my thoughts revolved around my children, my family and my future, the angrier I became. I blamed everybody except myself for my troubles. Listening to the breathing and occasional movements of my two cell-mates, asleep in their bunks, I cursed them. Because of their stupidity we were all in trouble. My brother and sisters wouldn't want to hear from me after the disgrace I had brought on the family. I thought of my father, standing tall and big and severe, and wondered if the judge would be like him.

I'm the loneliest man in the world, I thought, *and I can't tell anybody about my problems*. It would be a sign of weakness, and I had to be strong. So I had to put on a cheerful, brave face all the time, as if everything was going to be all right. I was creating the image for myself of a hard man.

That was certainly my reputation at Reading.

The remand wing has three landings, one for young offenders and two for adults. The prisoners were 40 per cent Pakistanis, 30 per cent Africans and the remainder other foreigners and some local lads. There were a few

from my part of the world – a Chinese from Singapore
and two Singapore nationals – all being held on drugs
charges. Because we shared the same language we got on
quite well at first; but later we disagreed on some things
and began to drift apart. Before long we were no longer a
group within the prison population. We had all found our
own friends.

I found making relationships difficult anyway. My attitude was boastful and unyielding. I was quick to talk
about my own exploits but had little time for other
people's. As a result I got into heated arguments and
fights, but was always pulled back by other cons. Soon
I was known as a trouble-maker, someone best to avoid.
Being around Chan Hop Hui meant being identified with
trouble.

Two months after arriving at Reading I finally received
the prosecution statements from our solicitor, Mr Meredith.
It was a thick spiral-bound book of typescript containing
transcripts of the statements that had been made by customs officers, myself, Roger, Paul and James at the time
of our arrest.

I started reading after evening lock-up. Paul and James
were reading their copies too. There was silence. But after
a few pages I couldn't control my rising temper any longer.
I hurled the book at the window, missing Paul by inches.
Furious, I demanded an explanation.

'You've told them everything,' I stormed. 'More than
that, you told them all about James – his hotel, room
number, flight number, the lot – *while he was still in
Singapore!* You bastard, you might have got him hanged.
And you didn't care at all.'

I was appalled at the extent of his confessions. He even
told them what he knew about my previous trip, who I
had helping me as couriers, and the names of people he
knew were involved in other ways. It was a total, cynical
sell-out. He'd put us all in deep trouble in the hope of
getting a light sentence.

James stepped in quickly and stopped my harangue. He knew I was likely to go berserk. Anything might then happen in our small cell.

'Wait until our solicitor's had a chance to talk to us about it,' he suggested. 'Maybe there's something he can do.'

I reluctantly accepted, but from that time on my relationship with Paul was one of icy silence and contempt.

12

THE TRIAL

A few weeks later Mr Meredith came to see us again.

'I've brought your indictments,' he said. 'They set out the charges that will be formally made against you at the trial.'

I looked at the document, a bleak official form with the charges scrawled against our names. I was charged with two offences: I was charged jointly with Roger for unlawfully importing over 10 kilograms of heroin, classified as a class A drug; and on my own count with knowingly importing an unknown volume of dangerous drugs on my previous visit to Britain in April.

When I read this I was appalled, and then very angry. I could see what the police strategy was. Instead of charging Roger and me separately, the two suitcases were to be taken together in a single charge. The combined street value of the drugs was well over a million pounds. I found myself recalling a British law lord I once read about in a newspaper who established the principle that if anybody was found guilty of a drugs offence in the British courts, and the drugs seized were worth over a million, the minimum sentence should be between twelve and fourteen years. *They've got me*, I realised. *If they take the two bags together, they won't need that second count. They won't need to know how much I brought in last time. With Roger and me they've got all they want. They're going to put me away for twelve years minimum.*

'Is this true what I'm reading?' I demanded.

Mr Meredith smiled comfortably. 'Yes, but don't worry. It's going to be fine.'

'Fine?' I retorted. 'You must be out of your mind! Twelve to fourteen years in prison, and you tell me not to worry?'

'Who said anything about twelve to fourteen years?' asked Mr Meredith in some surprise.

I told him, in no uncertain terms.

'A lot of things can happen,' he smiled. 'Don't worry. We'll see what happens at the trial.'

I slammed the papers down on the table.

'It's me who's going to do the sentence,' I shouted. 'After this case is over you collect your money and go home to your nice house and forget it, you have a nice sleep; and I go to prison.' I calculated rapidly. 'Twelve to fourteen years, that's at least ten after remission.' I let my eyes wander round the drab interview room, the guard standing impassively at the door staring at the opposite wall, the flaking paint and shiny lino floor. 'And you tell me not to worry.' I buried my face in my hands.

I started to ask a torrent of questions. Why couldn't we be charged separately when we were arrested separately? We were each carrying our own suitcases, so why wasn't it being treated as two separate crimes? In any case, were the authorities allowed to do this?

Mr Meredith listened patiently as I harangued him. Eventually I ran out of questions and fell silent. He collected his papers together into a neat pile, placed them in his briefcase, and snapped the catches firmly shut.

'I said, don't worry,' he repeated. 'I know it's difficult, but you've got to have trust in me. I'll do my best. But you have to do some things for me.'

I looked up angrily. 'What?' I demanded.

'First of all,' he said firmly, 'calm down. You're not helping yourself by getting so angry. Then, when you're in a thinking frame of mind, I want you to write down your family background. Tell me all about how you were brought up, where you went to school, your hobbies and whatever else you can think of. Then write down how you became involved in drug-smuggling.'

I snorted. 'You want me to write out a full confession, is that what you want? Go to hell.'

Mr Meredith sighed, a frustrated, tired sigh. 'Don't be stupid. What you write will only be seen by me and my staff.'

'You're lying,' I snarled. 'You're in with the police. You want me to do ten years.'

'Do you want to help yourself?' demanded Mr Meredith. 'Because if you do, you can only do it this way. I need enough from you to put together some sort of convincing argument that you were led astray. Evil companions. Drink. Bright lights, too much cash, plausible friends. You know the kind of thing. If I were in your shoes, I'd start writing now.'

He picked up his briefcase and moved towards the door.

'Oh,' he said, 'by the way; I'll come and see you next week. Have something ready for me, there's a sensible chap.'

'All right, Hui,' said the guard, with every appearance of satisfaction. 'Back to your cell. Come on.'

Lying on my bunk later that day, going over and over the events in my mind, I saw that I was in bad trouble. Most of the cons in the prison who were caught carrying the sort of quantities I handled were doing between five and seven years. I sank into a deep depression and refused to speak to anybody, even to Paul and James in my cell.

I sat on my bunk with my head on my knees or sat staring bleakly at the door, wrestling with my anger and bitterness. What would happen now to my plans to be reunited with my family? A sudden memory of Tracey's beautiful face and the happy smiles of my children swam before my eyes. *I'll be nearly fifty before they let me out of here*, I wept. I thought about Tracey and my children for hours and hours, going over the good times, the bad times, the arguments with her mother; until eventually my mind was empty, the pictures mercifully faded into a dull-grey blankness.

Word spread that Chan Hop Hui was in a bad way, and some of the more kind-hearted cons tried to cheer me up. But I didn't want to be cheered up. I started to harangue them too, telling them at great length how badly I had been treated and how treacherous my companions had been. I warned them about Paul and James.

'They are evil people,' I said, 'they can't be trusted; see what happened when I trusted them.'

I wanted to make sure they would be friendless and despised for as long as they were in prison. The other cons listened, made some excuse, and went away. I was left on my own with my anger.

In any case I felt superior to the cons. I was a big-time operator; I'd brought over a million pounds worth of drugs into Britain; in the past I'd survived customs checks, police scares, suspicion, and the jealousy of rival smugglers. I was much bigger than they were. That was what hurt most. I believed in my capacity to think fast, to improvise on my feet: I was an accomplished liar and proud of it. If we were arrested, I'd promised them, we would be all right. I would tell a good story and get us all out of trouble. But I never stood a chance. Before I could tell my wonderful story my so-called friends had told them all they needed to know and more. I felt utterly helpless, like a sheep in its pen waiting to be slaughtered.

'Look on the bright side, mate,' said one prisoner cheerfully. 'You're a hell of a sight better off being caught in Britain than if you'd been picked up in Malaysia or Singapore. If you'd been arrested there you'd be swinging at the end of a rope by now.'

'I wish I were,' I grunted.

My visitor shrugged and went away. But I meant it. In the Far East, at least the question of who had grassed on who would have been a minor matter. The result would have been the same for all of us, we would all have hanged. But to have passed through the two most dangerous check-points in the world – Singapore and Malaysia – and then to be within a hair's-breadth of freedom at Heathrow, hurt. And it hurt most because of Paul and James. I'd promised them bonuses, I'd undertaken to protect them, I'd trusted them. And then they showed themselves in their true colours as soon as trouble started.

For several days after Mr Meredith's visit I did nothing but lay awake all night staring at the ceiling, my body tense and shivering in an agony of mind; and by day I slept with my head wrapped in my bedding to shut out the light and the ceaseless, infuriating chatter of James and Paul. There was no one I could turn to; I could trust nobody; and the people who might have been willing to listen to me and help me couldn't stand my depression.

Things became a little easier when Felix, my cell-mate at Wormwood Scrubs, was sent to Reading. At least I could talk to him. He was outside my immediate circle and brought a welcome objectivity to the situation, and so I began to regain some peace of mind.

Mr Meredith was Felix's lawyer as well as mine, and had told him also to prepare a document. So we worked on them together, and when Mr Meredith next came to the prison I had a statement ready for him. It was a cunning mixture of truth and lies. I was proud of it. It began with a brief account of my early life and my two marriages, and painted a poignant picture of a man driven to desperation by the need to support his family and an unfortunate drinking problem. I described 'Beng' as my Thai contact who saw my poverty and took advantage of it: 'He told me that his friends had connections in Europe, and asked whether I had the guts to accept an invitation to go to Europe. Instantly I knew what he meant. I knew that they were drug-smugglers. But beggars can't be choosers . . . '

This heart-rending account was of course very far from

the truth when in fact I had leapt at the chance to go to Europe knowing exactly what was involved and confident of enormous profits. For the benefit of Mr Meredith, however, I presented myself as driven to crime by my overwhelming desire to be a good husband and father. The fine clothes I had bought after my first trip, I explained, were a necessary investment. I had to make a favourable impression so that I could obtain the stock to start up in business: 'In order to reunite my broken family, I needed to start a decent business, one my wife could manage, to gain her confidence as I do love her and our children. I needed only some money to start all over again . . . '

Such was my arrogant contempt for the whole legal process that I even included a cynical joke: 'I knew that English law and penalties for this offence are very lenient. Beng explained to me about the Opium Wars in the eighteenth century and how the English government taught the Chinese to smoke opium . . . '

Mr Meredith read it impassively. 'This is fine, it will help me prepare your case.' He read it again, 'We won't be using the stuff about the government, of course.'

'Why?' I demanded.

'It's not going to go down very well with the judge. It will go against you.'

'So? What difference does it make? I got nothing to lose. I'm going to get twelve, fourteen years. That's the law, isn't it? So I can say what I like, I still get a heavy sentence.'

Mr Meredith smiled gently. 'You really must try to lose this fixed idea that you are certain to get a heavy sentence.'

The old familiar beating in my eardrums and the tightness round my forehead returned. My voice rose in anger.

'You are a *stupid* fool,' I stormed. 'You know nothing about it. You say have trust in you and how can I have trust in you? The judge will send me down for a long time.'

A kind of madness got into me. I swore at him in English and Chinese, using words I had only ever heard in seedy night clubs and gambling dens. I heaped abuse on his parents, and speculated whether they were married or not.

I shouted at the top of my voice, 'If you don't do what I say I will get rid of you. You are no good as a barrister. I will give you the sack!'

Mr Meredith threw back his head and laughed and laughed. Then he managed to calm me down.

'I'll do my utmost to secure a sentence that's as light as possible,' he assured me. 'Trust me.'

He gathered his papers together. Reading my statement again he smiled and put it with the other papers into his briefcase.

'I'll be in touch shortly,' he promised. As he was leaving he turned back. 'The Crown Court's got a heavy case load on at present,' he said. 'But I'll see whether we can get priority. As you're all pleading guilty it won't be a long hearing – so the trial could be quite soon.'

The guard opened the door for him, and he left.

The next few weeks were among the worst in my life. I hardly slept. When I did I was plagued by bad dreams – nightmares in which I was at home with Tracey and my children, having fun and enjoying life, when suddenly huge paper monsters from Chinese festivals appeared and carried them away; or grim-faced Triad officials cross-examined me endlessly about my statements, so that I woke with the word 'traitor' hissing in my ears. Sometimes I was a child again, standing in front of my father, knowing he was about to beat me and wishing he would stop lecturing me and get on with it.

Deep bitterness was putting down roots in my heart. There was nothing about the prison that I did not hate; and the people in my cell I hated most of all.

There was nothing to hope for. I was scared. The half-remembered newspaper article on drugs convinced me that the least I could hope for would be ten years. Anything less would be a miracle.

Miracle, I thought sourly. *As if God cared.*

'Hey, Hui – what do you know? Today's our ninety-ninth day in prison!'

James had been keeping count, circling the days on a battered calendar over his bed, left by a previous inmate. It featured a suntanned lady with a wonderful figure, and somebody had scrawled obscene messages across her limbs.

I smiled unpleasantly. 'You needn't be so happy,' I sneered. 'There'll be another ninety-nine to come. And another ninety-nine after that. And—'

'All right,' said James sourly, 'I only mentioned it.'

In the mid-afternoon a screw came to the cell. 'You're all to go to the canteen to collect your pay. You're going to court tomorrow for your trial.'

We greeted the news with ridicule. Mr Meredith hadn't warned us and we had had no official notification.

'It's a mistake,' I insisted.

'What's that got to do with you?' The screw was briskly efficient. 'Just go to the canteen like you're told. If it *is* a mistake it can be sorted out there. Get *on*.'

Five of us arrived in the canteen: myself, Paul, James, Roger and a Singaporean Chinese con, Ken. He had already been in court for two days, and the jury were to retire to consider the evidence the next day.

Five Chinese, I reflected resentfully, *I wonder what the judge will make of that.*

Afterwards Paul, James and I ignored each other for a long time. I tried not to think what sort of sentence I would get, and sprawled on my bunk with a pile of books and magazines. But it was impossible to concentrate. All I could think of was the utter impossibility that I would be leniently treated. After a while I sat up. To my astonishment I saw Paul kneeling on his bed, his hands clasped in fervent prayer. A hot rush of anger flooded to my head. I wanted to go over and kick and punch him. What right had Paul to pray, after what he had done to us? How could God protect an evil man?

I just hope he gets the same sentence as I do, I muttered, *then I can kill him slowly*.

The night passed. None of us slept. Only occasional words broke the silence. The same old worries kept coming into my mind. I turned on the radio; it annoyed the others but it crowded out some of the insistent fears that were tugging at my brain. Eventually I fell into a restless, tense sleep, from which I was woken by a screw banging on the door of the cell, shouting us awake. We were told to wash and go to the reception area.

An hour later we were driven to Reading Crown Court.

We five Chinese were locked in the same court-room cell. It was a dirty, small room, with scribbled obscenities and other graffiti all over the walls. The others chattered nervously. I remained aloof and said nothing.

A screw arrived and unlocked the door. 'Hui – come with me,' he said, and I followed him to another room, cleaner and brighter, in which Mr Meredith and some other people were waiting for me. He introduced his colleagues – one was the Chinese woman law student who had come with the party to Wormwood Scrubs – and then explained to me what would happen in court.

'Remember,' he emphasised, 'behave yourself – and don't start getting angry, whatever the prosecution witnesses say when they give their evidence. Even if you think it's a load of lies.' He produced my written statement. 'Now, this is fine for my purposes, and it's been a help in preparing the case. But I hope you won't be telling the judge some of the things you've put here.'

I laughed uproariously, partly from nervousness. Mr Meredith looked irritated.

'It's quite foolish to annoy the judge,' he urged.

'So what difference does it make?' I demanded. 'Twelve, fourteen years, what difference does it make anyway?

Whatever happens, I go to prison for a long long time. So you tell the judge about the Opium Wars. It will make me feel better, at least!'

The Chinese law student was watching me intently.

'Don't be silly,' remonstrated Mr Meredith. 'Just pray that the best will happen.'

'The best?' I queried. 'How many years do you think I'll get?'

He was silent for a moment, thinking. 'It will be somewhere round about ten years. Or perhaps less.'

I stopped fooling around. Ten years: 3,650 days. *That's a long time*, I thought. *I've completed exactly one hundred days, and I'm falling to pieces. What am I supposed to do now?*

Mr Meredith watched me thoughtfully. He probably knew what I was thinking. He tried to reassure me.

'Don't worry – trust me. I'll be trying to make sure you get a light sentence.'

I looked past him at the Chinese law student. She was red-eyed, and tears were glinting on her lashes. I couldn't handle the situation any more.

'Take me back to the cell,' I said to the guard.

In the cell I sat in stony silence. None of the others dared to say anything to me. They probably knew that things were not going well.

Several hours passed. A screw came and called Ken's name, and took him to the court room. I hoped fervently that he would be found not guilty and be set free to go to his home and family. I knew if I saw a friend from my own region given a heavy sentence, it would be difficult to find comforting words to say.

Suddenly a loud, anguished cry came from further down the passage. It was a woman's voice, sobbing uncontrollably.

I rushed to the cell door and shouted to a passing screw, 'What happened? What's going on? Did somebody get hurt?'

'She just got eight years from the other court,' said the screw. He smiled unconcernedly.

I wanted to know the details, and pestered him to tell me more.

'How much was she carrying?' I shouted.

'Two kilograms,' he called back, and disappeared down the corridor.

My legs buckled under me. I reached out blindly for the barred window of the cell door. Eight years! For two kilograms. And we had been carrying over 10 kilograms!

I forced a cocky grin, 'Well, good luck everybody,' I said. 'It's all fated, anyway. What will be will be.'

I had no idea why I said that. It seemed important that I, as organiser of the trip, should give some sort of spiritual comfort. But giving spiritual comfort to Paul made me feel sick. There was movement outside in the corridor. The door was unlocked and Ken came in, his face wreathed in smiles. Before he had a chance to sit down we besieged him with eager questions.

'What did the judge say?'

'What was the verdict?'

'How many years have you got?'

He beamed and sat down. 'The hearing's just finished. The jury are out to consider their verdict. But it went really well! I reckon my chances are really good!'

There was no more time to go into it, for our names were called, and we filed out. It was our turn now.

We were ushered through a side door into the court, where only a few people were present; some I took to be members of the public; there were some policemen in uniform; and Mr Meredith and several others in wigs and gowns were sitting studying thick files of papers. I was amazed how slack the security seemed. We were herded into the dock with only one screw sitting behind us. At the main door stood a uniformed policeman.

Roger was sitting next to me. I leaned over and whispered, 'I'm going to try for a breakout.'

He looked at me incredulously. 'Don't be a fool. You wouldn't get out to the street. And it would blow our chances to pieces. They'd never give us light sentences. Don't think about it, Hui.'

I didn't argue but made up my mind that if I got a heavy sentence I would give it a go. What could I lose? They could only knock a few months off remission.

I looked away from the door and saw Mr Meredith looking at me. I had an odd feeling that he knew exactly what I was thinking. I buried my head in my hands, pretending I was worried about the trial but in reality peering through my fingers at the main door, waiting for it to open a crack so I could try to see which way the corridor went.

'Be upstanding in court!'

We got to our feet as the judge entered, and the hearing began. First the prosecution barrister put his case; and then Mr Meredith got up and made his speech. But my English was not good enough to follow what they were saying. After a while I gave up trying and amused myself looking at the heavy gilt coat of arms in the panel over the judge's head. I wondered whether Mr Meredith was telling the judge about the Opium Wars. By my side Roger was gripping his chair, his knuckles white against the brown skin of his hands. Periodically my attention wandered back to the door, hoping to see it open a crack so that I could plan a little more of my escape route; I already knew in precise detail how I would get from the dock to the door.

There was a sharp pain in my side. Roger was digging his elbow into my ribs. Everybody was looking at me.

'The judge wants you to stand up,' hissed Roger.

I got to my feet, lazily, with studied insolence.

The judge looked at me; our eyes met. It was like confrontations I had had in night-clubs at home, when the enemy had possessed a weapon and I had not. I felt helpless, and was unable to hold his gaze.

He was saying something about evil deeds, that they should not go unpunished; that the crown had a duty to impose serious penalties on those who abused the law and who distributed dangerous drugs. He talked about my family; suddenly I heard him describing my father. It was the story I had prepared for Mr Meredith. Then he stopped speaking and looked at the papers on his desk for what seemed a very long time.

He's going to pass sentence, I realised, and heard my heart-beat accelerating. And then, to my surprise, I heard myself whispering inaudibly, 'God, help me – ten years would do . . .'

13

SENTENCED

The judge was speaking again. I had no trouble understanding what he was saying. He was sentencing me on the two counts of my indictment; the first count of smuggling 10 kilograms of class A drugs, and the second of smuggling an unknown quantity on my previous visits.

He pronounced sentence. On the first count, eight years. On the second, five years.

I turned to Roger. His face was wreathed in smiles. I turned to Mr Meredith and his colleagues. They were smiling too. *It's got to be good news*, I decided. I did the sums in my head, calculating fiercely. *Eight and five – and if it's concurrent it's only eight years.* And then there was remission . . . I bobbed an astonished 'Thank you' to the judge and sat down.

Paul, also indicted on two counts, was next. He was given seven years and six years. As the judge pronounced the sentence Paul shuddered and a strangled cry broke from his lips, 'Oh God!'

I wanted to leap to my feet and punch him in the face. He had expected a lighter sentence. I had no sympathy for him, and no desire to forgive him. I was hoping he would have got a heavier sentence than me so that I could tell him he deserved it.

James and Roger were more fortunate. They got five years and four and a half years. I was very pleased indeed, and made a great show of smiling at them and waving to them across the dock, studiously avoiding looking at Paul.

When the judge retired and we were taken back to the cell, Roger, James and I hugged each other with relief. Paul sat in a corner, ignored by us, making small talk with Ken who was waiting for the jury's verdict.

Mr Meredith appeared, full of good humour. We all shook his hand and thanked him for the good results he had obtained.

'I'll send you a Christmas card every year, you wait!' I cried delightedly.

While we were celebrating several customs officers came in. They spoke quietly to Mr Meredith and then came over to me. They asked me to follow them to an adjoining cell. I looked at Mr Meredith.

'Yes, go with them,' he said.

The cell contained a bare wooden table and chairs. The officers sat down on one side of the table and motioned me to the other chair.

'Congratulations,' said one pleasantly. 'That was an excellent result.'

'Thank you.' I waited cautiously to see what was the point of this interview.

'You realise that you will be eligible for parole when you have completed only part of your sentence.'

'Yes.' I was still waiting.

'We would like to help you with your application to the Parole Board when that time comes.' The officer consulted his notes. 'We would be in a position to do so if you were now to give us information about your three friends in Amsterdam.'

All my joy evaporated. I was bitterly angry, and rounded on the men sitting opposite me.

'What?' I demanded. 'You tried to fix it so I'd get a heavy sentence, you had Roger and me jointly charged so the street value would top a million, you knew that could get me twelve years minimum, you really set me up!' I banged the table. 'Now you want me to be a supergrass. Get lost, clear out, you hear?'

I turned on my heel. The policeman at the door moved to escort me back to the other cell. As I reached the door I turned and shouted back to the officers.

'We're all square now. I beat you once, this time you beat me. Let's see who will win next time round!'

Ken had gone back to court to hear his verdict. I told the others what the customs officer had said to me. In my rage, my anger turned on Paul.

'I suppose you're pleased now, you've done what you set out to do. You really repaid everything, didn't you? All the kindness, all the money and stuff you had off me, all the way I looked after you, you sure repaid me.'

Paul sat without replying. His face betrayed shame and confusion, and a kind of wounded pride. I continued to pour scorn and abuse on him, and he was still sitting mute and sullen when Ken returned.

Even while he was standing outside, one glance at his expression through the grille of the door was enough to tell us that it was bad news. When the screws brought him in, he told us what had happened.

'They voted me guilty. Majority verdict. Then the judge passed sentence. I got eight years. For two kilos.'

I groaned and turned away. I had no words to comfort him. I felt a sudden need to distract myself, to distance myself from the situation. I took a felt-tip pen from my pocket, and in flamboyant letters wrote the date of our sentencing on the wall, signing it with a flourish 'The Malayan Commandos'.

A heavy hand seized me by the scruff of the neck, so hard that I howled with pain.

'What d'you think you're doing, Hui?'

I pointed at the other walls, covered with obscenities and crude drawings.

'What are these, then?' I retorted. 'If I've done something wrong, you can report me to the governor, go on, you can do it, I don't care.'

I stuck my fists deep in my pockets, struggling against

an urge to hit the screw – even in that situation I realised that I was already in enough trouble. The argument became heated, and another screw came to find out what all the shouting was about. He didn't listen to my explanations but took the first screw away, banged the cell door shut, and locked it.

I finished my writing defiantly, and then sat down. Thoughts of revenge were filling my head. I knew that any attempt now to kill Paul would be thwarted by authority; but I nursed plans for a quiet revenge some time in the future, when we would be less under official scrutiny. After all, I had eight years to wait.

Back in Reading, no longer on remand, our brown clothes were taken away and we were issued with standard blue prison uniforms.

'You're convicted,' we were told. 'You lose your remand privileges. You'll be in the convicted wing now.'

Life was very different there. One major change was that I had to work, instead of spending long hours lounging with Paul and James in the cell. I was allocated a job in the prison kitchen where two friends of mine were also working.

The other remand cons reacted to our sentences in different ways. Some were pleased, but others had bet heavily on our getting double figures and were furious that they had lost their money. Before long rumours were circulating that I had obtained my light sentence by giving information to Interpol about my partners in Holland. That hurt, and I wrote to Mr Meredith asking him to send me the prosecution tapes. It was a matter of pride. I was desperately anxious to prove I hadn't grassed. My reputation as a successful smuggler was shattered, I'd been caught and punished. Suddenly my reputation for loyalty seemed very precious.

Working in the kitchen was demanding, but at least the canteen officers were kind to me. One of the perks of the job was that prisoners were allowed to cook their own food the way they liked. Rice and chicken were a large part of the con's diet, and I was allowed to cook my favourite fried rice and chicken soup for myself. I had a good relationship with the kitchen screw for the whole time I was at Reading, which was from mid-August, when I was sentenced, to 19 September when I was transferred to Bristol Prison for allocation to a long-term prison to complete my sentence.

A week or so after my trial I wrote to Tracey, telling her that I had been arrested and what my sentence was. It was a bitter letter.

'I suppose your family will be thrilled,' I wrote viciously, 'knowing I finally got myself into real trouble and locked away for a few years. At least they can have some peace in their lives now . . . '

At Bristol I was in a cell on my own for the first time. 'Banged up' for twenty-three hours, with an hour for showering, change of clothing and 'evening association', I was thoroughly miserable. With nothing to do I slept most of the day. Winter set in and I felt the cold acutely. My cell was damp and smelly. My prison wages were £1.50 a week, which was just enough to buy half an ounce of tobacco and stamps for letters. I had to forget luxuries like tea, coffee and sugar.

Tracey replied to my letter. I wrote again. She replied. But reading and re-reading her letters I could tell that she was determined to leave me. Looking back on our life together I could see why. My arrest must have been the final straw in a long catalogue of unreasonable behaviour, drunkenness and violence. But I loved her and my children deeply, and the thought that I would lose them drove me to distraction.

I had no idea what to do. There was nobody I could turn to in the prison, and nobody in all Malaysia who would be able or willing to help. The only outlet for my anger and frustration was to plot threats and violence. Rejection meant losing face; the prospect drove me to imagine vast schemes of revenge. When I got back to Malaysia there was going to be blood spilt, I promised, and the risk of the death penalty was no deterrent. So I whiled away the long hours, filled with hatred, plotting how to make money after my release and take my revenge.

A Sri Lankan con whose name was Sanjit seemed more thoughtful and peaceful than most of us. I alternated between despising him as a weakling and envying his tranquillity. One day he approached me when we were alone in a corridor.

'Are you doing anything special tomorrow?' he asked diffidently.

I laughed shortly. 'I'm going to a drinks bar until midnight and then going on to a night-club. Why? Want to come?'

He smiled. 'There's a meeting on this landing at six o'clock. It's for Muslims. I'm going. You come too.'

'You're a Muslim?' I glared at him.

Sanjit nodded.

'Well – I'm not,' I retorted. 'Tough. Forget it.'

'Anyone can come,' he persisted. 'You don't have to be a Muslim. It's a good way to find out about Islam.'

I squared my shoulders and spoke with measured deliberation.

'I hate your Allah. I don't believe in God. People who ask God to help them are fools. Why,' I waved my hand dismissively, 'there are dozens of cons in this nick that probably wanted God to help them. They're still inside.'

Sanjit was still watching me, as if he half-expected me to suddenly change my mind and agree to come. I pushed my face close up to his.

'There is no God,' I said defiantly. 'Take it from somebody who knows.'

As I stalked away I could feel Sanjit's placid eyes boring into my back. For all I knew he was still standing there as I rounded the corner, the last echoes of my atheism dying in the noisy air.

       ❖   ❖   ❖

Fluttering paper streamers, gaudily coloured, were swooping down from all directions. My children were cowering in fear, crying and calling for me. But I was fighting the dragons. They were coming at me again, trying to reach the children. I had no weapons to defend them. I was gesticulating with my bare hands, making the Triad signs, shouting the passwords that we used to identify ourselves in the underworld. Soon it was all over. The dragons seized my children and carried them off. As they soared into the blue sky I heard the voice of my mother-in-law, *'What sort of a father are you? Those children were your responsibility. Now what will happen to them?'* I turned on her and hit her, again and again, with my bare hands. As each blow landed, it sounded like a hammer stroke. She was still sneering, *'What sort of a father are you? What sort of a father are you? Now your children are gone.'* I hit her harder. Eventually she was silent, and only the sound of my hammer blows filled the world.

I sat up in my bunk shivering. The nightmare faded. The dragons were only a dream. My children were safe. The hammer blows, however, were real. It was the screw banging on the door. I had overslept.

I wondered what had caused the nightmare. *It's the filthy food they give you*, I told myself. I eased my body into a more comfortable position. After five months at Bristol I had still not seen rice served, and my weight had dropped from ten stone to eight and a half stone. My bones ached if I sat too long in one place. I reached for my blanket and folded it into a cushion, then sat back grimacing. The food at Bristol was enough to give anyone nightmares.

In fact I rarely slept at night, and then all my problems weighed on me in a crushing load, enhanced by the winter cold and the loneliness. The prison screws were unfriendly and my fellow-cons were hostile, especially those dishing up food, who missed no opportunity to provoke me and try to make me angry. They were chosen by the screws and thus regarded themselves as favourites in a position of power, which they exercised by handing out the smallest possible helpings to cons they disliked. The only way to get bigger helpings was to buy tobacco for them.

The situation starkly underlined all that I had lost; I too had had that kind of control over people, able to bestow or withhold favours. Now it was being done to me I writhed under the injustice. My threats were reported back to the screws and only made matters worse for me.

One day in the middle of exercise hour a con on my landing called a hunger strike for better food. Word spread quickly and there was solid support for a few days, but then people began to drop out and only the Asian cons were left. In the end we had to call it off. I was angrier than ever – my powerlessness seemed to have been sharply demonstrated.

Cons on the allocation landing were waiting to hear which of the long-term prisons they were going to. In the exercise hour the main topic was the British prison system. The most desirable institution seemed to be Long Lartin, which sounded like a holiday camp; and the worst, from the descriptions I heard, was Dartmoor, set deep on the Devon moors.

We Chinese were treated as outcasts because we were foreigners and, except Roger, spoke little English, and many of the cons despised us because we had been convicted of a drug offence. The screws on our landing told us that in their opinion we would be sent to Dartmoor. I didn't care what the others thought of the prospect. For myself, I reckoned it couldn't be worse than where I was. I was desperate to get out of Bristol Prison as soon as possible.

14

DARTMOOR

I poked morosely at a bowl of rice. A boiled egg lay on my plate, white and unappetising. The Asians had petitioned the governor for rice and curry to be added to the prison diet, and the rice was the first product of the new deal. The egg was a concession because I didn't want roast turkey. It was Christmas day 1985.

I spent Christmas and the New Year banged up in my cell. I had ample time to brood on other Christmases and on what my family was doing without me; and about what I was going to do to those who had put me in this situation. By the middle of January I devised a plan out of sheer desperation. I would swallow something poisonous – not enough to kill me – so that I would be too sick to be treated in prison and would have to be temporarily transferred to an outside hospital. I had no illusions that I would be able to escape, and my opinion of the British people was now so poor that I was sure that nobody would help me if I did manage to get out. But a stay in hospital would get me out of the prison for a while, and I would be seeing new faces and new surroundings instead of the walls of my cell and the same blank, negative faces of my fellow-cons. I began to look at soap and cleaning products with a new interest, trying to work out what the effects of swallowing them might be.

Before I was able to take the plunge, however, I was notified that my long-term allocation had come through. I was to go to Dartmoor with Ken. Paul and James were to stay at Bristol in the long-term wing. Roger, being under twenty-one, was allocated to Berkshire Youth Custody Centre. The cons heard my news with varying reactions. The few I got on with reasonably said they were sorry and hoped things wouldn't be too bad. My enemies, of whom there were many, expressed satisfaction. Goodbyes were brief and distant.

On 20 February a prison coach took me and a large number of other cons on the long journey to Devon. Much of the later part of the route was along country lanes. I scanned the trim hedges and the neat fields, looking for possible escape opportunities should the coach be forced to stop for any reason. As dusk fell we drove through small West Country villages, their streets lined with cottages. Behind the curtained windows lamps were being lit, and occasionally I caught glimpses of families preparing meals in warm, firelit rooms.

I wonder what Tracey and my children are doing now, I thought, and gripped the seat in front of me with tightly-clenched fists. I concentrated on the landscape to distract me. In the failing daylight I saw vast expanses of moorland dotted with rocky outcrops. A few sheep picked at patchy grass, and there was snow on the higher ground. *It wouldn't work*, I decided. *Even if I got away it would just be a matter of time before they came and got me. Nobody could find their way across this country*. Abandoning hope of escape was more than abandoning an academic exercise, a fantasy to pass the time on a long journey. Deep down I was remembering what the cons had said about Dartmoor. If it was all true, how was I going to complete my sentence? How would I survive in the worst prison in England?

On arrival we were put through strict reception formalities. A screw gave us a lengthy list of things we were or were not allowed to do. There was to be room inspection every day; bed sheets and blankets had to be stowed in their proper order; certain clothing had to be worn for certain activities. Any mistakes, however minor, would result in disciplinary action. The only bright spot in this new strict regime was that I would not be banged up all day in my cell. There were opportunities to mix with other prisoners in recreation sessions.

At weekends the local Salvation Army citadel organised informal hymn-singing hours, to which Christians from outside came. I sometimes went along for something to do, and even joined in some of the noisier hymns. I didn't try to understand the short sermons the Army officers gave; and I sneered at the bright smiles on the faces of the Christians. *It's easy to smile like that if you're only here for an hour*, I mouthed, sprawled in a chair at the back of the chapel. The words of the hymns meant nothing to me either. But a sing-along, even at the price of the irritating cheerfulness and religious fervour, was a way of passing an hour. I made sure the other cons knew I was not being taken in by any of it: a con who was thought to be getting religious would be ridiculed, and sucking up to the chaplain was reckoned to be a crude way of trying to get early parole. I stayed well away from him.

We were allocated work duties. Ken and I were given jobs in the kitchen. Mine was to work on cooking vegetarian food. I enjoyed the job. We were the only Chinese among the twenty-four people working in the kitchen – in fact the Catering Officer told me we were the only Chinese who had ever been cons in Dartmoor. Both of us worked hard and got on well with the screws in the kitchen. Our relationship with the kitchen cons however was not a good one. The same hostility that we had found in Bristol was also directed at us in Dartmoor. We were disliked because we were Chinese, and like most Asians we were not very tall – height is important in prison.

For some of the jobs we were dependent on work the other cons were supposed to do in the vegetable department, store-room and washing-up, but they refused to do it. As new cons still feeling our way we avoided arguments and did these jobs ourselves – but rumours

began to circulate that we were grassing on the others to
get them sacked from their comfortable kitchen jobs. They
had a very nice system going, and resented our allocation
to their department. Stealing and fiddling the store-room
records were common practice – anything stealable could
be used as barter for tobacco or drugs. Resentment flared
up when a few cooked chickens went missing and were
found under my work-table. The staff suspected me because
Ken and I had reputations as great eaters. But nothing was
ever proved.

'You ripped me off!'

I rapped out the terse accusation, my eyes fixed on the
man on the other side of my work-table. He was taller
than me, dangerous-looking, with intense dark eyes, a
fellow-worker in the kitchen.

He glared at me menacingly. 'So – who says?'

'I say,' I retorted. 'You owe me for gambling. You lost.
Now you pay up. Simple. Do it.'

It was pay day, the day I settled my gambling accounts.
I gambled every day during lunch breaks and evening
association times. Sometimes I won, sometimes I lost. Pay
day usually meant trouble and arguments over debts and
winnings. Fights were common. I was in one now. The big
man stepped closer.

'You're lying, Chink,' he said, and bent over the table
until his face was close to mine. 'I never owed you nothing.
I won you fair and square.'

'Back off,' I warned.

'You don't fright me, Chinky. I've fought real men, see?
You don't frighten me nothing.'

My eyes dropped from his, and he sneered. It was his
mistake. I quickly scanned the table top. The knife that
I knew was there was within easy reach; a long, well-
sharpened weapon like the triangular stilettos I carried in
Malaysia. It was in my hand in seconds.

'You ripped me off,' I repeated slowly.

The knife was poised, ready to slash and strike. I held his eyes with mine. This time it was he who looked away. There was an audible groan from the circle of his friends who were watching.

'I can't pay.' The admission came almost in a whisper.

I jabbed the weapon an inch from his throat.

'You pay me soon, understand? If I see you buy smokes, anything, before you pay me, I'll cut you. With this.'

He walked abruptly away and the crowd dispersed, talking among themselves and looking back at me with a variety of expressions. Ken congratulated me. I stared after the man.

'I want that money,' I said in a low voice.

It carried. He looked back at me, nodded, and hurried away. Inside I was laughing, but without humour. In Malaysia I had called out gangs of thugs to beat up people who owed me thousands of pounds in gambling debts. Now I was in a prison in England risking a knife fight for a few pence, with only Ken to back me up.

The screws heard about the incident, and it did little to enhance my reputation with the staff. The man himself asked to be moved to other work a few weeks later, so I had the satisfaction of knowing that at least I had scared him.

Ken, however, was not with me for long. He was transferred to Long Lartin for an education course. When he was gone I was the only Chinese prisoner in Dartmoor and was bullied by the other cons. Without Ken to stand by me I felt lonely and threatened, and had to develop a lower profile in the kitchen.

Two letters in my first months at Dartmoor added to my depression. The first, received early in March, informed me that my three colleagues in Amsterdam were found guilty and had been sentenced to ten, six and four years. In July I was sent my expired ticket by the Immigration Department. Legally I was not allowed to own a valid plane ticket, and the government would issue me with a ticket home when

my sentence was completed. I turned the slip of paper over
and over in my hands. Somehow, seeing it and knowing it
was useless emphasised that I really was stuck in a foreign
country far from family, friends and possessions, and likely
to spend some years there. The summer came and went. I
was preoccupied with my thoughts.

In October a young screw arrived from another prison
for two weeks relief duty. He drew up a new work roster
which took me away from my comfortable job in the
kitchen to other departments. I was outraged to find that
again other cons were supposed to be doing the work I
was now assigned to do, and were laughing at me while
they took things easy. The new screw seemed to single me
out for special persecution. Perhaps it was because I was
Chinese, perhaps because of my conviction or because I
stood up to him. Whatever the reason, not a day went by
without some new frustration. In the end I refused to do
what he told me.

'You're here on relief, and this isn't my work,' I protested. 'These others should be doing it. They aren't doing
anything. Why don't you have a go at them?'

He reported me to the Governor. He claimed I threatened
him. He was lying, though I certainly felt violent towards
him. The Governor ruled that I would lose a few days
remission of sentence; and I added the screws to the long
list of those against whom I planned vengeance.

Several weeks later I was again in trouble. It arose over a
fight about another gambling debt. This time I was lucky:
the Security Officer who broke up the fight arrested the
other man and he was fined a week's wages. When he came
back to work he tried to humiliate me at every opportunity.
I realised what he was doing and decided not to tempt fate
a second time by getting into another argument, and kept
my distance. But he stalked me like a hunter. One Sunday
when we were having breakfast he appeared at my table. I
ignored him. He banged the table.

'You used all the milk.'

I looked at him in surprise. It seemed a petty thing to be creating trouble about, but then all his accusations were petty ones. I looked round the room. All the milk containers were empty.

'Don't be stupid,' I said. 'Look. Everybody's milk is finished. You say I went round all the tables drinking up all the milk?'

He snatched my bowl and shook it in my face. 'You had it all,' he shouted. His mouth twisted in a grimace, 'I don't forget things like that, you understand?'

I looked right back at him. Not losing face was important to me. He turned on his heel and stormed off. Later that morning he reappeared at my work-table and stood for a few minutes staring at me without saying anything, a black scowl covering his face like a mask.

This has gone far enough, I told myself. *I've got to do something about it.* I slipped a sharp knife into my pocket and made some excuse to go to the washroom. I was sure he would follow me; he had dogged my footsteps for days now, and was especially keen on cornering me in isolated places and threatening me. When he came in, I would kill him. I stayed there as long as I could without arousing the screws' suspicion. He didn't come. I emerged warily, but he wasn't waiting for me outside. I went back to my work, looking for him as I went. I was so angry I was prepared to knife him openly. I asked a few quiet questions, and was told he had been moved to work in another wing. But when he got back it was nearly time to deliver the midday meals to the wings and matters had to be left for a while.

That same afternoon I had a visitor. I had no idea who it could be as I had no friends in Britain, and visits from lawyers, police and immigration officers had long since ceased. In the visiting room I was surprised to see a man I had known quite well in Reading Prison. I knew he was released but I had no reason to think I would ever see him again. There were well-known ways of getting round the rule that ex-cons were not allowed to visit. But why had he bothered? He had two Chinese companions with him. They gave no indication why they had come.

'Hui's been quite a villain,' grinned my friend. 'You wouldn't believe what he's been up to.'

He gave them a brief summary of my activities, and they listened calmly. Sometimes they asked me questions, apparently casual ones, though afterwards I realised they had extracted quite a lot of information from me.

'So you've a good many friends in Malaysia who are – let's say – not entirely hand-in-hand with the police?'

As the stranger spoke his eyes were boring into mine. His arms were extended on the table in front of him. The fingers of his left hand were twisted into a familiar gesture. With a jolt I realised what had been bothering me ever since I came in: they had been giving numerous Triad hand-signs.

A screw was standing by the door, watching us without really paying much attention. At least, I hoped he wasn't. For a moment I had the ludicrous feeling that he would realise that the secret signs of Oriental thieves, smugglers and assassins were being displayed under his nose in a prison in rural English Dartmoor.

I leaned forward and lowered my voice. 'Look, what do you want with me? Why have you come?'

The two strangers exchanged glances.

'We're, uh, associated with, uh, business activities in Los Angeles. We've built up a good distribution network all up the West Coast.' Their hands were moving fluently, interpreting and expanding the veiled allusions of their stilted speech. 'We reckon the time's ripe to restructure our operation. We want to deal direct with our Far East counterparts. Buy in direct, cut out the middle man, go for the big deals.'

My friend from Reading cut in, 'These boys are big, Hui, they're the best.'

I looked at him sourly. I wasn't sure I wanted this kind of attention nor how far the screw was listening.

'You can help,' he added. 'Your contacts are pretty good. These guys can set things up for you so when you get out, you just walk into the big money. This is the big one; this is the big break, Hui.'

And what are you getting out of all this, I wondered. The strangers were looking at me expectantly. I made up my mind.

'I can't give you an answer now,' I said, 'I need to think about it.' I pushed my chair back and stood up. 'Leave it with me.'

We shook hands. It was an odd experience to feel once more the unique grip and pressure of the House of Fragrant Blossoms. It was as if for a brief moment I had tasted the wealth and power I had enjoyed in Malaysia.

'There's something you can do for me,' I said. 'I need some jobs looking after in Malaysia. And I want to make contact with some friends in Amsterdam.'

After they had gone I had a long think. I'd opened a door – carefully, and in such a way that I could shut it if necessary – to possible deals with the Triads. But I wanted to find out more about my visitors. I was not going to open up to them fully until I'd tested their power and found out whether they really were in close contact with the Chinese underworld. If they proved satisfactory I knew exactly how I was going to use them. They would be useful in my quest for revenge. I could easily fix a deal for them. I could even send them to the Far East to meet some of my old contacts with a view to setting up long-term projects. And once over there, owing me favours, they could easily bring about some of the devious and evil revenges I had dreamed up for Tracey's mother and the gang who had humiliated me. It was a delightful prospect, and I felt more relaxed than I had in months.

That night in my cell I returned to the matter of my more immediate tormentor. I had spent the day with the knife in my pocket looking for a chance to kill him. Now I wove complicated plans to wreak a greater revenge than murdering him; I would attack his family. I decided to make every effort to overcome the enmity between us. I would seek for ways to befriend him, promise to arrange for drugs to be brought into prison for him – whatever he wanted; and all the time I would try to discover his home address. Then I'd make use of my visitors. I would promise to do what they wanted only if in return they would arrange for his family to be attacked. Wherever they lived, I was sure my visitors would find them somehow. I realised too that I could make arrangements for my enemy himself to die in prison, if the right contacts could be found.

The next day I began to put my plan into action. First I made an official application for my 'accumulated visits' to be spent at Reading Prison. This was a system whereby cons like myself, serving time in prisons where they knew nobody locally, could be transferred to a prison nearer their friends for a week or a fortnight, so that they could have visits. I'd accumulated a fortnight's worth of visiting orders, and at Reading I could continue the conversations with the mysterious visitors.

This is a master plan, I told myself, and set in motion the first stage: befriending my enemy. Though it wouldn't be easy, I told myself it was the only way to achieve my plan without being suspected. During the physical exercise periods I played on his side in the games and took every chance to dispel the tension. It didn't work out as I'd hoped. He assumed I was scared of him and bullied me all the more over trivial matters. Some workmates told me they thought I was being treated badly.

'You shouldn't be so soft on him, things are getting out of hand,' they said.

Privately I agreed with them, but pretended to be extremely humble.

'I'm just trying it for a few days to see if he will change his attitude,' I explained meekly.

A couple of days later he came up to me when I was playing cards during the lunch break in the kitchen.

'You lost me a week's wages,' he said. 'When the screws broke us up it was me that got hauled up before the Governor. It should have been you. And you know it.'

A circle of his friends gathered round and watched the scene with great interest.

'If you don't pay I'm going to smash your head in.'

I was willing to pay him something to further my revenge, but with about ten people standing round listening to his threats my pride would not allow me to do it. If I gave in in front of them the whole prison would have heard about it in an hour.

I got to my feet. 'I'm not going to pay.'

He dropped into a crouch and moved towards me, looking for a chance to get the first blow in. There were no knives within reach. I had just my bare hands. An exultant thrill coursed through me. This was what I was good at, what I knew how to do. *Maybe I can kill him now, with my hands.* I was smaller than he was, but I had something he didn't have: desperation.

His friends rushed in and pulled him away, swearing and struggling.

'I'll get you, Chink bastard!' he growled.

They calmed him down a little. I took the opportunity to slip a knife into my pocket. For the rest of the afternoon whenever I looked in his direction I could see his flushed, angry face watching me.

That night I lay awake in my cell. It wasn't just a punch-up any more. An accusing voice in my head was testing my resolve. *Are you really ready for blood? Have you got what it takes to kill him?* Deep in my heart I acknowledged that I was, and I had. *I'm going to kill him myself,* I vowed. *Not by the Triads, not by doing deals with drugs barons.* How many years would be added to my sentence if I killed him? Five? Ten? At home it wouldn't have been a consideration. I would have killed him before this. As soon as the bullying started my people would have dealt with him. Here, I was in a foreign country and in big trouble already. I began to think about home and my family. If I had my sentence increased, when would I see my children again? What sort of a future would they have growing up without a father – and one who would provide for them?

Inside my head the accusing voice whined on. *What sort of future would they have, with a father like you anyway? How have you helped them, being locked away in this cell?*

'What am I going to do?'

The cry broke from my lips, it echoed round the tiny cell. I was afraid somebody may have heard. For several minutes I listened carefully, my heart pounding, in case other cons were jeering that the hard man Hui was cracking. But there was only the usual night-time noise, subdued activity, footsteps scraping as screws paced the iron landings.

How had I got into this situation, I wondered, not thinking of the story I had gone over so many times in my mind, but of the long road I'd walked from my childhood home on the school compound to an English prison on the windswept moors. How had it all gone so wrong? My eyes were smarting with tears. I wiped them away angrily, and wondered why I bothered; there was no one to see Chan Hop Hui weeping. But my pride forbade me to weep. Only small men wept.

For some reason I began thinking about the prison sing-alongs. In the middle of the night, weeping in my cell, I couldn't get the hymn tunes and the radiant faces of the Christians out of my mind. Why? I knew well enough that cons turned to religion when things got tough. But I always laughed at the Christians with their talk of a God who was actually alive and loving. And yet as I thought about the chapel services and remembered them talking about the God they said they loved, I was beginning to feel what I had not felt for a long time: peace.

A bizarre medley of bits of hymn tunes was playing in my head: 'The Old Rugged Cross', 'Onward Christian

Soldiers'; hymns that didn't belong to my world, Asia, or in any world I ever visited before – but I found myself humming the tunes and occasionally fitting in a few half-remembered words. I shook my head angrily. Sure, the feeling was very nice, but I would not go running to the Christian God. How could he help me? On the other hand I wanted to know more about the strange feeling of peace. Maybe there was more to it than a string of sentimental tunes. Maybe there was something there that could really help me.

The thought crossed my mind that the chaplain might be somebody I could talk to about my confused feelings. But in a maximum security prison like Dartmoor, seeing the chaplain was a complicated procedure. You had to submit a formal application and he usually came to see you in your workplace. Maybe I would have forgotten the strange emotions I was experiencing by the time he came to see me. Perhaps I would look a fool. *And perhaps you would look weak*, I reminded myself. In prison, if you have troubles you don't share them. It shows a lack of strength and other cons look down on you. The kitchen workers often made applications to see the chaplain. I'd seen him arrive and seen him leave, and then I'd been among the first to ridicule and humiliate them. No, seeing the chaplain was not the way to do it.

I was stiff and sore, hunched on my bed. When I looked at my watch it was 3 a.m. At 6.30 the screw would come to unlock us for work. I pulled the blanket over my head and tried to go to sleep. It was impossible. Confusion and a dread that I would never see my children again wrestled with pride and a determination not to lose face. Chinese men hold on to their children tenaciously. Losing them is a mark of humiliation. I lay on my back, glared at the ceiling, and screamed my helplessness.

'God – help me, please help me!'

I had no idea who the God was to whom I was calling. Not the God of the chapel hymns, and certainly not one of the many gods of Asia, the army of deities among whose images and temples I had grown up. Nor even those to whom I had sacrificed and prayed on my initiation into the Triad. In fact I was uncertain that there was any god to hear my cry. But I wanted there to be.

That morning the Principal Officer told me my application for an accumulated visit to Reading had been accepted. I was to go the next week. It was wonderful news, and had come sooner than expected. I went back to work and told my Kitchen Officer.

Nearby I could see my enemy eavesdropping. He walked away, and avoided me for the rest of the day. His change of attitude puzzled me; until then he had missed no opportunity to harass me and make my life a misery. But of course word had gone round that I had had visitors, and that had attracted some attention. The cons were used to my boasting of gangster activities in Malaysia and I had told some of them about my Triad membership. I had also bragged about other men in Reading on drugs charges who were influential in the circles in which I moved. My forthcoming visit to Reading was seen as an ominous step. I ignored my tormentor. Outwardly I was calm. But inwardly I knew I was going to kill him. My two visitors would certainly play their part – when I had devised exactly how I could make use of them.

In the evening association hour I was sitting with a Londoner, John. I got on well with him, we shared an interest in sport and had no problem finding things to talk about. John was a Christian, though we never talked about religion. A Salvation Army officer I knew by sight from the sing-alongs came over to us. He greeted John, who invited him to sit with us. I assumed there was some personal matter he wanted to talk about, so I got up to leave.

'No, stay with us,' said John.

'I just came by for a chat,' explained the officer.

I sat down again. He put me at my ease, talking pleasantly and asking a few polite questions, such as where

did I come from and what did I think of English football.

'I've seen you at the sing-alongs,' I ventured.

The officer smiled. 'I've seen you there,' he said.

'Why do you wear that uniform?' I asked.

He explained, 'I'm in an army, Hui – God's army. We
work in all sorts of ways.'

He told me a little about what the Salvation Army did,
and it suddenly occurred to me that here was a chance to ask
questions without the disadvantages of seeing the chaplain.
John wouldn't see it as an admission of weakness, and there
was no need to make a formal application to see this man;
he was here, sitting at our table.

'Tell me about Christianity,' I said abruptly.

The transformation was remarkable. His face lit up, and
he broke into an enthusiastic description of the major points
of the Christian religion. He told me about Jesus Christ,
what he could do in a person's life, about the crucifixion and
the resurrection. He really tried to make me understand.
He drew on his own experience, not using long theological
words, and answered my questions patiently. I could see
how much it meant to him. He was talking not about a
religious system, but a person, Jesus. I listened to what he
was saying, but for me it was like one of the stories of great
men that my father had told me, of mighty heroes who did
wonderful things and whose example was hard to follow.
Inside I felt no response. When he went on to talk about
salvation, the kingdom of God and eternal life I switched
off completely. I was not interested in heaven and hell. As
far as I was concerned I was in hell already. What did it
matter to me where I went when I died? It was where I was
while I was living that was my problem. I was still young,
I had a lot to look forward to when I was released, and I
wasn't going to die for a long time yet.

John was quietly watching my face. I was sure he knew
what was going through my mind. When he saw me looking
at him he smiled.

'Hui, it doesn't make sense now, I know. But some day you'll understand, you really will.'

I smiled back. Christianity was a Western religion and my interest was mere curiosity. Yet why was I feeling so peaceful chatting about a belief in which I had no real interest?

'I'd better go and fill my hot-water bottle.' I got to my feet. 'I expect I'll see you later.'

I had no intention of coming back.

I sat in my cell writing a few letters until lights out. The talk about God still bothered me. After a while I pushed my writing pad away and tried to think the matter through. True, lately I had felt good when Christianity was mentioned. But I knew from my father's teachings that to concentrate on good and perfect masters was a way of growing in spiritual purity. Perhaps that was what Christians got from their Jesus, and what I was getting in a small way by finding out a little about him. But what did it add up to? Could I live my life on good feelings? What should I do when things got too tough to bear – find somebody to tell me about God?

As far as I could see it was a load of comforting rubbish. If God really loved me, Chan Hop Hui, why did I have to go through all this suffering? Why had he not protected me at the airport? Had I succeeded on that trip and made the money I ought to have made – then he would have made me happy. But if, as the Christians said, God could do anything, how could it show me that he loved me when he had let me go to prison to be despised, attacked and watched every hour of every day?

Gradually I began to rationalise. The good feelings were just emotional desperation. If God was the answer to my problems, he'd been very clever at hiding the fact so far. I was wasting my time and energy trying to find out more. He was a good God to the Western people, but he wasn't going to help me. Strangely, this left me feeling more at peace.

During the days before I left for Reading everything seemed to go well. My tormentor left me alone. I amused myself boasting that I would be meeting powerful people in Reading, people with a real influence in the outside world. That was the kind of help you needed to survive in prison, not good feelings and endless talk about a God who couldn't do anything.

15

SAVED

One night in Reading gaol I woke up and found myself talking to God.

'I don't know much about you, God. I don't even know what your proper name is. Sometimes they call you Jesus. So I don't know what to call you. But they say you can help people and do miracles.'

I shook my head in perplexity. *I must be going mad, I'm talking to God*. I ploughed on.

'Now, look at me; if you're really here, listen to me. I'm in desperate trouble. I'll probably kill a man when I get back to Dartmoor. That will put an end to his tormenting me. But it will mean I'll be punished, lose remission, be in prison a whole lot longer. I won't see my family for even more years. I don't know what to do. Why don't you help *me*? I need one of your miracles.'

The cell was empty. Nothing happened. No blinding light, no apparitions, not even the chill atmosphere of a brooding, anonymous supernatural presence that I had felt the night I was initiated into the Triad.

'Told you so,' I muttered, and curled up to sleep again. I wasn't surprised. I didn't believe in God. How could he have spoken to me?

I felt oddly disappointed.

I sent out a visiting order, and the two men came to Reading. I lounged back on my chair and stared at them arrogantly.

'OK, I'll help you. But if you want to do business with me, first you have to do something for me.'

They nodded cautiously. *They're hooked*, I thought exultantly. I looked round the visiting room. The screws were not listening. I leaned forward.

'There's a guy at Dartmoor I want taken out. I want him killed. Soon.'

They looked at each other, an unreadable look.

'Who?' they asked.

I told them who my enemy was.

'If you can get somebody inside to do it, then I'll know you've got the contacts, you're the kind of people I can work with. Then we make business in Penang together. But first you kill him.' I winked conspiratorially, 'It's a test, see? So I know you can be trusted.'

They didn't react. They merely absorbed what I'd said.

'And the Penang operation?'

I got to my feet with a lordly gesture. Suddenly I was feeling very powerful. The others rose reluctantly.

'Next week. We talk next week. I'll send you visiting orders. Be here.'

As I walked back to my cell it seemed as if the weight I'd been carrying since my arrest had lifted slightly.

Reading, with its change of routine and less strict discipline, was like a holiday; and I was free from the hostility of the Dartmoor cons. But it was only for a fortnight, and the satisfaction of being the kind of person that important drug dealers wanted to talk to paled as I realised I would soon be back on the Moor. I contemplated my murder plans. Maybe this time I'd planned it well; I might even escape being found out. But how did I know it would be the last time? Sooner or later my violent temper was going to lead to another killing. Next time I might not be cool enough to cover my tracks. I might never get out of prison.

Matters were not improved by the coldness of Tracey and the lack of information about my children. They were growing older. I wondered what they looked like now, what their interests were. For all I knew they might be budding sports enthusiasts. I could have helped them so much. If I had made that last trip successfully, I could have bought them anything they wanted. I realised they hardly knew me. I wondered what Tracey had told them about me and about my arrest. I wept hopelessly.

When in that mood I sometimes considered asking to see the chaplain. In Dartmoor it was a problem; here, few people knew me. I could ask him to tell me more about Christianity, and ask some difficult questions. But my pride got in the way again: I couldn't bring myself to ask for a meeting to talk about God.

My pride, however, took a severe blow next visiting day when my contacts didn't turn up. All my complacent delight in the deal I was planning evaporated. Had something gone wrong? Or were they just not interested? I was left confused and fearful. Robbed of my chance of rebuilding my Asian empire from a British prison cell, and confronted with the problem of going back to Dartmoor to face my enemy and my own violence, I almost went to see the chaplain there and then; but again what was left of my pride stopped me. Soon my fortnight's leave was over and I had to return to Dartmoor.

It was a bitter, windy day when the prison coach left Reading. I was travelling with other cons for Exeter Prison and would be taken on to Dartmoor the next morning. But the weather worsened as we travelled west, and black skies and flurries of snow on the hills were alarming omens for the night to come. We arrived at Exeter late, in driving snow. After reception procedures we were ordered to our cells. Mine turned out to be filthy, with no heating and hardly any light or fresh air. I piled my clothes on top of the blanket and fell asleep, tired out from the long journey. In the morning a screw came to my door. Heavy snow had piled up in the Dartmoor area and all traffic in or out was at a standstill. I would have to stay at Exeter and wait for the next escort to Dartmoor, in a week's time. I would be banged up in my cell the whole time except for an hour's exercise each day.

As we filed into the exercise yard, a tiny, clock-shaped area, I was furious. I only had a shirt, pullover and denim jacket to protect me against the freezing cold. I stamped my feet to keep them warm, grumbling all the time at the screws, at the cons, even at God.

'I'm worse off now than I ever was!' I told God. 'I was stupid to think you might help me. I should never have listened to what those fools in chapel said.'

I increased my pace, shuffling impatiently. Into my mind came a memory of Dartmoor chapel and an enthusiastic Christian urging his beliefs on the rest of us.

'Give it a try, give it a try,' he'd said, 'Jesus will answer if you call.'

Not to me he won't, I reflected, and almost swore out loud.

My thoughts were interrupted by a man walking alongside me.

'Where are you from?'

'Malaysia,' I said reluctantly, and tried to move away. I mistrusted cons who were over-friendly to newcomers. It meant they were scroungers.

'My name's George,' he said. I remained silent. 'Do you know Thailand?'

'I used to live there,' I said, wondering what he was up to. Probably, like many cons, he was fascinated by anything to do with the Golden Triangle or drugs. 'Come and see me there in 1989 after my release,' I said with a humourless smile. 'I'll help you make a small fortune. I know my way round the drug scene.'

I hoped he would be satisfied and leave me alone.

George's smile was open and broad. 'I'd have come like a shot not long ago,' he admitted. 'Not any more, though. I can't. I've become a Christian.'

I was scandalised. I looked round instinctively to see if anybody had heard. Didn't he realise what people would

say? Didn't he know that cons despised churchgoers, that
he'd be marked as a grass, a nonce, a parole-seeker –
a nutter? I'd been fascinated by the Christian God for
months, on and off, but nothing would have persuaded
me to mention it to another con.

'What are you in for?' I asked, embarrassed at what I'd
said about drugs.

For half an hour he told me about himself; how he was
sentenced for grievous bodily harm and became bitter and
depressed in prison; how God had come into his life; and
then how he had experienced God as somebody who could
actually change his life. As he spoke the same kind of
joy came into his face as I'd seen on the face of the
Salvation Army officer in Dartmoor. It was a look of
simple gratitude.

I listened with real interest. I'd heard such stories before,
but not from a fellow-con. I admired what George had
experienced, even envied it; but I found it hard to believe
that it was something that could happen to me.

'Lead on!'

The cries of the screws signalled the end of exercise
hour.

In my cell I picked at my evening meal. My appetite
had disappeared. I was thinking about George. Perhaps
there was something in it for me after all, I thought.
Then I pulled myself together, put my tray on the table
and stretched out on my bunk, staring at the darkening
sky through the tiny barred window. But troublesome
thoughts persisted: George's story, my own predicament
at Dartmoor, my wife and family thousands of miles
away. I needed something to distract me. As a prisoner
in transit, all my possessions were held in Reception. I
opened my locker hoping to find a magazine or newspaper
left behind by a previous inmate, but it was empty. I had
better luck with the two drawers, which yielded a Bible
and a dishevelled story book. At last, something to while
away the boring hours. I put the Bible to one side. It had

lost half its pages and I knew where they had gone. In prison there is nothing as good for rolling cigarettes as Bible paper.

The story book had no cover or title page; most of its pages were loose and the corners dog-eared. I smoothed them flat and put the pages into the right order. They seemed to be all there, but without the cover I had no clue what the book was about. The first chapter was called 'Bangkok'. I was immediately interested. A book about Thailand – a wave of almost painful nostalgia swept over me. I flicked through the text and saw references to Australia and Hong Kong. *A travel book*, I concluded. *Just the thing to take my mind away from this freezing hole.* But later chapter titles included 'Arrest', 'Betrayed' and 'Lard Yao'. I knew the last name. Lard Yao was a famous women's prison in Bangkok. I'd once had a flat not far away. *A book about Far East prisons; I wonder how they compare with British ones.* I settled on my bed and began to read.

At school I had learnt English but my reading ability was only average. Since then my choice had been magazines, especially pornographic ones with lots of pictures. But with time on my hands I managed fairly well. As the story unfolded I began to have a strange feeling of recognition. The woman telling the story had been duped by two Hong Kong Chinese and used as a courier to smuggle drugs. Aspects of the story seemed extremely familiar. I even began to think I recognised the men involved. Finally, two or three chapters on, I recognised the woman.

It's Rita Nightingale, I realised. *It has to be her.*

Memories of her arrest in 1977 flooded back. Yes, here it was in black and white; she stayed at the Asia Hotel, almost next door to me, and was arrested at the airport. Because of her I'd had to lie low in the southern province for a year. Because of the international publicity that her arrest provoked, the Thai government clamped down so heavily on security and customs checks that my business was ruined.

Rita Nightingale, the stupid English nurse who caused so many of my problems. How many nights I'd drunk myself into unconsciousness – because of Rita Nightingale!

Well, let's see what she has to say for herself, I decided grimly, and read on. By the time I had read half-way my hatred of her had turned to sympathy. The book told the story of her imprisonment in Bangkok, and I identified completely with her feelings of anger and frustration as a foreigner in a hostile prison. She even started to wonder about God, in the way I had done.

I began to think of friends of mine still in prison in Malaysia and Thailand, some of them convicted on drugs charges and facing the death penalty. Suddenly I was really scared, not only for them but for myself as well. If I went ahead with my plan I could be in as deep trouble as they were. With that realisation came the awareness that my shirt was sticking to my back in a cold sweat.

There was a noise at the door; a screw was opening up for tea. I went to the recess and poured cold water over my head, then collected my drink and went back to the cell, to be banged up until the morning. I lay on the bed and tried to forget God, George and Rita Nightingale but they would not go away. I picked up the book again. Soon I was absorbed. I really wanted to know whether God had done anything for Rita Nightingale. She said prison visitors had talked to her about somebody called the Lord Jesus. They told her he was God; that he could carry her burdens, forgive her for all the wrong things she had done and give her joy and peace. Rita had become a follower of Jesus, and her life had completely changed.

Her story matched mine in so many ways, and her needs were so similar. Yet she was describing how she had found peace of mind and the ability to forgive the people who had betrayed her. I tried to imagine myself forgiving Paul for what he had done to me. *That's what I want*, I echoed, and a small hope began to rise in me; if I could find the same God, discover this Lord Jesus, he might help me the way he had helped Rita. But who was Rita's God? Was it the same Jesus the visiting Christians had offered, urging 'Give it a try, give it a try!'? And if so, what would the other cons say? How exactly did one make contact with Rita's God and ask for his help? Would he want to have anything to do with me anyway?

I finished Rita's book with tears pouring down my face. I knew I had just read the story of someone who had suffered in exactly the same situation as I was in, and had found an answer – an answer that might be available to me. *Look at me, what have I achieved?* I asked myself. *Nothing but trouble.* Perhaps I could go to Rita's Jesus secretly, so that nobody would know. But how?

As I sat deep in thought I noticed the tattered Bible lying where I'd tossed it earlier. For the first time in my life I wanted to read the Christian holy book. I opened it expecting to find deep moral teaching and a code of pure and ethical behaviour. After a few pages I shut it in disbelief. Abraham . . . Isaac . . . Jacob . . . Judah . . . mothers, fathers, long lists of names . . . it was like reading a telephone directory. I wept with frustration and threw the book against the wall of the cell, where it fell in a pile of ragged pages. *This stuff isn't for me*, I raged. *This is a list of people God decided to speak to. I need somebody who knows how I feel, what I'm going through. I don't need a telephone directory.*

As I buried my face in my pillow in bitter disappointment, waves of sleep hit me. I was mentally and physically exhausted. *Maybe I'll talk to George about it tomorrow*, I muttered.

I sought out George during exercise hour.

He smiled a welcome, 'How are you getting on?'

'All right. I read a book yesterday.'

'Which one?'

'I don't know – it didn't have a cover. It was about Rita Nightingale.'

George's face lit up. 'I know it. What did you think of it?'

I paused before replying, choosing words carefully.

'It impressed me. It impressed me a lot. She felt like I do. The same situation, same kind of arrest, everything.'

I hadn't the courage to tell him I wanted to know more about God. But George raised the topic himself.

'Rita really experienced God's love in that prison, didn't she? I love reading her story. It shows how great God is.'

He began to talk about God, in the way you might talk about a very powerful friend who had done many kindnesses for you. Shortly before exercise hour finished I plucked up my courage.

'How exactly do you become a Christian? What do you have to do? What did *you* have to do?' The screws were looking at their watches. 'Do you think you could write out the things you have to do? I'm interested to know.'

George's eyes sparkled. 'It would be a pleasure,' he said.

I collected my meal and went back to my cell. I had a lot to think about, and my head was bursting; but there was a different feeling in my heart. George was like Rita; he too had become a Christian in prison. Hearing him talk I recognised that he knew Rita's God. While he was speaking something strange had happened. I began to feel, in a weird way, that Rita's God was actually in the exercise yard with us.

I'd been looking for a God. I wanted somebody to help me, to get me out of the suffering and misery of prison. It was obscure to me who it was I was looking for, but there had been many clues that somebody was there to be found. What if the God I sought, the answer to my problems, was the same Lord Jesus that Rita, George, the Salvation Army officer and the Christians in the sing-alongs were talking about? They all said the same thing – that God had come to them, that they hadn't found God by themselves. *Was that why there was a snow storm*, I wondered, trying to fit in the next piece of the jigsaw. *Maybe he's going to come to me here.* I thought meeting God was something you had to do in a big church, or in the prison chapel. The Chinese gods would never enter filthy cells or dreary prisons. But maybe he *was* coming here – here; not Reading, not Dartmoor, but right in this cell.

I knelt by my bed, tears streaming down my cheeks. Suddenly I knew what all those good feelings meant. God hadn't forgotten me. My fears and doubts lifted like a weight from my shoulders. I found myself repeating, over and over again, 'Thank you, God! Thank you, God! I know who you are! You're Jesus, aren't you! You're the Lord Jesus! And if that's who you really are, God, then please – help me to find out more about you!'

I don't know how long I knelt there. Eventually I climbed on to the bed. A new feeling was filling my heart, not just the warm, good feeling I had had before, nor even the absence of fear. It was a feeling of pure, undiluted joy.

There was a quiet knock on the door.

'Hui! It's me, George.'

The bell for recess must have rung. He pushed a piece of paper under the door. He had written out some instructions and a brief prayer of repentance and commitment. As I read about repentance a profound feeling of remorse swept over me. So approaching God was not a matter of following a set formula, of offering a suitable sacrifice in the way that my neighbours gave food in the temples at home. If I were to come face to face with God I would have to bring with me all the evil things I had done, all the grief I had caused, the violence and aggression that had been in my life since my early teenage years. I couldn't hide them away out of sight. I thought of the lives that had been ruined by the drugs I had bought and sold. For all I knew, people had died because of me, families wrecked, young people's futures ruined. For the sake of money I had spread sickness and misery and death. *And now you propose to talk to God*, the familiar accusing voice inside my head said flatly.

But George had said God did not turn away people who were truly sorry for the wrong things they had done, however terrible they were. I re-read his piece of paper; yes, it was written there quite clearly.

The lights on the landing were turned off. My cell was in darkness. The noises of the prison had died down and a dead silence had settled. I knelt down and smoothed George's piece of paper out in front of me. I read his instructions once more and then closed my eyes.

'God, please forgive me for my sins.'

I said the words out loud. It seemed an enormous thing to ask. I said it again.

'God, please forgive me my sins.' I paused. Then, 'I want the Lord Jesus to come into my life.'

It was as if a searchlight had been suddenly switched on. My heart and body were rocked by a surge of sublime joy. It was unlike anything I had ever experienced before. There was a meaning to it; it wasn't just emotion, though I was weeping and smiling a wide, beaming smile at the same time. This was the joy of salvation that George had told me about. This was the joy of knowing that God had accepted you for what you were, that there was no need any more to struggle to find him, that he had found and rescued you because he wanted to. And with the joy came peace, a final laying to rest of the torturing anguish and heartache. My doubts and fears were destroyed. A hurricane was sweeping away all the paper dragons. Sitting in that tiny cell, I was free. No more terrors, no more despair, no more bad dreams. For the first time since I was sent to prison I slept like a baby.

Next morning at slop-out I met George on the landing, as we joined the queue to empty our urinal buckets.

'I did what you said.'

That was all I managed to say before George over-whelmed me.

'Praise the Lord!' he shouted, his face glowing.

He grabbed my hand, shook it enthusiastically, and then threw his arms round me and hugged me. I was acutely embarrassed, and looked round furtively to see if anyone was watching. George had no such inhibitions.

'Now we're brothers in Christ! I'll give you all the help I can.'

During exercise hour later we talked again, and in my cell afterwards I read the battered Bible like a hungry man suddenly finding a fresh loaf. I understood little of it, though George had suggested which parts I should start with.

'Ask for a Chinese Bible when you get back to Dartmoor,' he had advised.

In the meantime I found plenty to fascinate and excite me in the Gospels.

I re-read Rita's book, which George told me was called *Freed for Life*.[1] The more I read, the more aware I was of my past wrongdoing and the more I was ashamed of it. My life had been one of pride, violence, drunkenness, women, discothèques and a constant struggle for wealth and power. There had been no love, only hatred and exploitation. This growing awareness brought me to my knees several times as I asked Jesus to forgive me. I prayed George's prayer again as I went to bed that night. As I drifted off into a warm, joyous sleep I had an extraordinary sense that Jesus was actually in the room with me. I wouldn't have recognised him if I had seen his face; but I just knew that he was there.

Next morning it was just the same; no fears, simply peace and hope. Even the cell looked different. But I knew that it was I who had changed.

A few days later George came to find me. He was very excited.

'I've just been told that I've been allocated to Dartmoor to finish my sentence. We'll be going down together with the same escort!'

---

[1] Marshall Pickering, 1982.

It was something else to thank the Lord Jesus for. I was going to have a friend of my own in prison who could help me find out more about Jesus.

Together we looked back at how he had answered my cries for help, in his own time and place. He had done it all. In Dartmoor and Reading I had kept him at arm's length by my busy work routine, my wild behaviour and my gambling. But he had brought me to Exeter in a blizzard, because that was where he had decided to speak to me.

16

BACK TO DARTMOOR

For the rest of the week I was in Exeter Prison I read Rita's story over and over again, and asked George dozens of questions. I remained very unsure exactly how the Lord Jesus and the Christian God could be the same person, but what George was able to tell me thrilled me. Words heard at the sing-alongs began to make sense. In particular the phrase 'born again' fascinated me. Previously I'd dismissed it as puzzling and slightly repellent, one of those phrases that meant everything to the people who used it and nothing to anybody else. But now it made sense. I was beginning my life all over again.

In my cell I was at peace with myself. I slept soundly. The nightmares were gone completely. I had my worries and doubts about the future, but the seething hatred and bitterness had vanished. My desire for revenge was gone too; the whole reason for my visit to Reading was a remote and unreal shadow from a past that seemed far away. Sometimes the feeling of peace in the cell was so strong I thought I could reach out and touch it. Above all, I wasn't alone any more. Jesus was in the cell with me. I knew it in the same way a blind man knows not what someone's face is like but when that person is in the room. Because he was there I talked to him. I told him all my problems, 'but you know all about them anyway, don't you, Jesus? Please help me sort my life out, please help me like you've helped all these others . . . ' The future wasn't filled with fear any more. It was shining with hope.

'You see, Hui,' explained George, 'You're a Christian now. God has a plan for your life, just like he has for everybody. And he'll show you what that plan is in his own good time.'

My life so far had been dominated by my own desires and a determination to get my own way regardless of who I hurt. The idea of handing over control to anybody had never occurred to me. Now I had to face up to the fact that Somebody intended to demand exactly that.

The idea felt good.

One long discussion with George was about Dartmoor. It is a top security prison and a prisoner's every movement is watched by the screws. You can't go where you like. Where you go, a screw accompanies you. When you mix with other cons in evening association or exercise you don't talk about religion, unless to mock it or ridicule religious people. Otherwise you are labelled a deviant and the cons put pressure on you in a hundred different ways.

How, I asked George, was I going to live as a Christian there? And where would I find help to learn about the Bible and the Lord Jesus?

George was worried about that himself, and we agreed to pray to Jesus about it and try to leave it to him to sort out.

We arrived in Dartmoor together on 6 March. I told nobody what had happened in Exeter. For several weeks the only person who knew was George, and during exercise periods or in any chance meeting he encouraged me to read the Bible and pray. But as the weeks passed the catering staff noticed that my attitudes had changed. I didn't argue all the time or try to get into fights. My old tormentor had unaccountably changed also; now he left me alone. Sometimes I noticed him watching me with a worried, quizzical expression. After finishing my daily duties I didn't hang about any more causing trouble. I hid myself away in a corner to read.

My books were borrowed from a small Christian collection donated to the prison library, including *Born Again*, the story of Chuck Colson; and *Chasing the Dragon*, by an English girl, Jackie Pullinger.

Colson had been close to Richard Nixon and was heavily implicated in the Watergate scandal; he'd become a Christian. He too had been a prisoner, living with men whose sentences he authorised when he was in power. I was fascinated by the paradox. I devoured the story of how one of the most powerful men in the world had turned his back on his own ambition and had founded Prison Fellowship for Christian prisoners and prison visitors. Jackie Pullinger's story was also extraordinarily interesting. She lived in Hong Kong's Walled City, talking to drug addicts and criminals about Jesus. Hardened Triad members had been transformed and addicts released from their addictions. It was a world I knew; but I had never come across what she was describing.

The more I read books like these, the more I wanted to know about God. I read all the Christian books I could find, and went back to parts of the Bible that had previously perplexed and confused me. I picked my way through genealogies, baffling lists of laws and regulations, and strange prophecies, searching for clues to help me understand God more.

I was still reluctant to apply to see the chaplain; I didn't want him to come to the kitchens.

In the end the first person I told about what had happened in Exeter was my wife Tracey. I wrote to her a fortnight after coming back to Dartmoor. For the first time in my life I managed to summon up the courage to confess that I had done wrong and to ask another person for forgiveness. Weeks later her reply came. It was a cautious, brief note. She said she was pleased to read my letter and that I should continue to seek God. She said nothing about the future, nor had I expected her to. I was left with a mixture of hope and frustration, wanting things to move much faster.

One night I poured out my problems to Jesus. I knew that if I stayed in Dartmoor until my release I would make no progress.

'I'll never manage as a Christian here,' I said. 'The other cons are trying to make me go their way, and the prison system won't help me to go straight either.' I remembered the hostility and fights since I arrived in Dartmoor, and longed to be somewhere else. 'Please take me away from here, Jesus – please take me somewhere with some Christian cons, or at least Christians nearby who will visit me and help me to understand the Bible.' I paused for breath.

The prison was virtually silent, and the cell was in darkness.

'Apply to go to Long Lartin Prison.'

The voice was small, but quite distinct.

I looked at the door, expecting to see someone standing there, but there was nobody. The voice had been close at hand, but I was alone. I repeated the words wonderingly. *Go to Long Lartin*. I knew little about the place except what I had heard in Bristol. Why had the name come to me like that? With an exultant thrill, I realised that Jesus had spoken to me.

Next morning I went to see the Assistant Governor.

'I want to be considered for transfer to Long Lartin,' I said.

He raised his eyebrows. 'Any particular reason?'

I plunged in, knowing that if I stopped to think about it I would never manage to tell him.

'I want to start again,' I explained. 'I'm a Christian now. I've made so many problems for myself here I want to go somewhere else and start afresh. Sir.'

He didn't reply for a moment or two, but remained deep in thought.

'I realise your position, Hui,' he said gently. 'You're the only Chinese here and I'm not unaware of what that means. You've had a rough time.' He opened a drawer and took out a printed form. 'Fill in this form,' he said. 'I'm prepared to support your application.'

I was so excited I almost grasped his hand.

'I should warn you, however, that the decision isn't mine,' he added. 'The final ruling will come from the Home Office.'

I went away and prayed fervently that the Home Office would say yes.

Six weeks later I was called to the Assistant Governor's office. He was smiling broadly.

'Look,' he said, and showed me a letter on Home Office notepaper. It was written in very complicated English and I found it hard to understand. I looked at him enquiringly.

'You've got it, Hui, you've got your transfer.'

I was overwhelmed. The Assistant Governor smiled.

'I'm very pleased. You've got a mate at Long Lartin, haven't you?'

I thought of Ken the Singaporean.

'Two Chinese together,' said the Assistant Governor. 'You'll be able to back each other up. Jolly good. I'll fix up your transfer date as soon as possible.'

I told my workmates my news.

'I got my transfer! Thank God, thank God!'

They were incredulous.

'How come you got a transfer? You're a foreigner, you don't get visits, you don't have any relatives to be near – you're not even on any training courses. How the hell did you manage it?'

'God did it for me,' I said.

Three months ago I would have boasted about the strings I'd pulled. Now without thinking I gave all the credit to God. There was something else too. It was the first time I had indicated to them my belief in God.

When I saw George he congratulated me generously; I would be leaving him behind but we were going to keep in touch.

* * *

In almost twenty-five months since I came to Dartmoor I
had never attended a Sunday morning chapel service, but I
was now desperate to do so. My desire to go was stronger
than the fear of my workmates' ridicule. I was also still distressed by Tracey's lukewarm response to my letter. *I must
put myself right*, I vowed. One Sunday morning therefore
I plucked up the courage to tell my Kitchen Officer that I
wanted official permission to go to Sunday service.

'Are you feeling all right?' he demanded.

'I feel fine, sir. I just want to go to chapel.'

He laughed outright.

'Come on, Hui, what are you up to? Have you gone mad,
or what? How long have you been here – two years? You
never went before.'

His words were a barrage and I couldn't get a reply in.

'You're supposed to come here to work, that's what you
get paid for. I don't pay for you to play around in church.
If you want to do that, that's your affair – but you'll have
to find another job.'

The old anger began simmering, but I turned on my heel
and sat down at my workplace without a word. Some of
my workmates had overheard the exchange and told others.
Soon the teasing started.

'Hui going to church? Ha, ha!'

'Hey, everyone, Hui's got religion,' shouted a Welshman
in a mock-pious voice. 'He's got God running errands for
him! Hey, Hui, your chances of parole look pretty good
now, don't they!'

Before, I would have leapt at him and tried to smash him
to the ground. But now I stayed seated while the laughter
echoed round me. I wanted to fight them and my fists curled
automatically; but something stopped me.

After a few minutes a Catering Officer, Mr Hamilton,
came over to me. I had a lot of respect for him, and he
was always gentle and considerate with me.

'Get along, son, or you'll miss the duty officer. He's
escorting the churchgoers from this wing. Off you go.'

So I attended my first-ever Sunday morning service.

The date set for my transfer to Long Lartin was 1 May 1986, but a nation-wide prison officers' strike delayed it. We spent most of the strike locked in our cells, and there was much anger against the screws.

Probably because I was disappointed at having my transfer put back, and also because I was outspoken in my criticism of the staff action, my relationship with several screws deteriorated sharply. I was in particular trouble with one of the kitchen screws who took to ordering me to do the dirty jobs, which was not part of my work as a diet cook. Whenever I had a few moments to sit down he found me something else to do. I protested but it was useless; I was told that I had to obey my orders. Matters came to a head when I was preparing to fry eggs for 600 inmates.

'Hui! Take the swill buckets out.'

'I can't; I'm out of time for this job.'

He insisted. I lost my temper.

'I've had enough!' I stormed. I gathered my things together. 'I'm not going to work here any more.'

He said nothing. He escorted me back to the wing in silence. Next morning I was summoned to appear before the Governor. I was charged with refusing to take orders and refusing to work. I argued that I had resigned from my post, which as a prisoner was my right; that far from refusing to work I had actually been escorted to the wing by the screw, which meant that he must have accepted my resignation. But when I accused the screw of lying about me and about other cons, I lost my case. The verdict was three days loss of remission, overnight detention in the cell block, and a fine of two days wages.

The cell block was cold and dirty. There was nothing to read and no writing materials. Smoking was not allowed. The screw in charge was abusive. There were lines in the corridor floor, beyond which cons were not allowed to step, and every move was watched closely. We couldn't even empty our urinal buckets without a screw following close behind. The screw on guard took every opportunity to humiliate me. At lunchtime he jeered as he unlocked my cell door, and made noises as if calling a caged animal to eat. I had never been treated like it in my whole life. When I refused to eat anything the door was slammed shut, and I heard the screws laughing outside.

That night I was cold, hungry and bitter. In my anger I turned upon God, 'Why has this happened to me? Where are you now? I haven't done anything wrong – why have I been punished?'

My new-found faith was cracking. Against my will pictures of revenge began to form in my mind. I turned the problem over and over, until in the early hours of the morning when I was almost asleep I heard the small voice again, 'You will be all right, son. Have faith in me.'

I went to the door-grille, the voice still clear in my ears, but there was nobody there. *It's the voice of God*, I said to myself in awe. I knelt down and thanked him for coming to me in that dirty cell, and the sense of quiet, strong peace returned.

When I got back to my wing, having lost my kitchen job I was banged up for most of the time except for exercise periods and meals. But my new transfer date was set for the following Friday. Soon I was packing my few belongings and saying my goodbyes.

A con I knew quite well told me he needed to make contact with one of the cons in Long Lartin.

'What do you want me to say to him?' I asked.

'It's a money problem. Look, I'll tell you about it.'

'Don't,' I said. 'It would take too long. Write to him. I'll get the letter to him.'

Strictly speaking it was against the regulations, but I was feeling in a generous mood. This was my big break. From now on it was going to be wonderful.

17

LONG LARTIN

As the prison van rumbled on its way to Long Lartin Prison, I pondered the few facts I knew about the place. It was a top security prison. I'd heard a lot about its modern facilities, and about the sort of con that ended up there – serious crime offenders such as major bank robbers, murderers, IRA men and drug barons. A small shiver of excitement went through me as I thought how I'd sought out such people in Malaysia and Thailand. Now, I began to daydream, I would be living with them every day . . .

I shook myself awake. Those thoughts belonged to the past. I was finished with all that, living a new life and given a new start in a new prison. When the van came to a stop in the reception area some time later I was still feeling rather subdued.

The main prison building was modern. There was a large playing field. The screw at reception was actually friendly. It was unlike any of the other prisons in which I had been. Soon I was sitting in a quite pleasant reception room, waiting for the reception screw to take me to my allocated wing. The door opened and I got to my feet expectantly. But it was a different screw, the one who had taken my baggage for security checking. He had some paper in his hand, and was very angry.

'What's this?'

He slammed it down on the table. My heart sank. It was the letter I'd agreed to deliver.

'Transfer to cell block tomorrow,' he snapped.

The reception screw arrived and took me to D wing. I followed him, barely taking in the new sights and sounds of a different and pleasanter prison. My mind was racing. *It was all going to be so different*, I thought angrily. *So much for my new start. I'm in trouble already and tomorrow I'll be in the cells.* I didn't expect to sleep that night, but I did; partly from tiredness after the journey and partly because even though I was emotionally tense and angry, deep inside I had a feeling that even in this kind of crisis things would be different now that I knew God.

Next day I was summoned to the Governor's office. He had the letter in front of him on his desk.

'You knew it was against prison regulations to carry mail without permission?'

I nodded. His face was neutral, giving nothing away.

'Then why did you do it?'

I decided to tell the truth. I took a deep breath.

'He had money problems. He wanted me to talk to his friend about it, but I didn't understand what it was all about. I told him to write a letter.'

The Governor looked at me thoughtfully.

'You're charged with a breach of prison regulations. From what you're saying I take it you're pleading guilty to that charge.'

'Yes,' I said, and stared bleakly ahead, waiting to hear my punishment.

'Your private cash spending will be stopped for six weeks.'

I could hardly believe it – it was an unusually light punishment.

'Thank you, sir,' I stammered. *Thank you, Jesus*, I echoed silently.

'I don't want to have this kind of behaviour from you again,' the Governor said firmly. 'I'm giving you an official caution. I will not tolerate deliberate breaches of prison regulations.'

Later I met Ken during free association time.

'How did you get on with the Governor?'

I beamed. 'Fine. He let me off. Well, six weeks loss of private spending.'

His eyebrows lifted. 'Is that all?'

'Oh – and a caution. Not to do it again.'

Ken thumped me on the back. 'Come on, I'll show you round.'

He was a valuable guide for me as a new inmate. In prison you are lucky if somebody explains the system to you; normally you have to find out for yourself and there are many ways you can get into trouble out of ignorance. But Ken was there to welcome me and explain anything I didn't understand. *Another thing God did for me*, I marvelled.

I had arrived at Long Lartin on 23 May 1986 and before the month was out I had made many friends in D wing. On 11 June I was given a job in the prison kitchen.

It was not difficult to see how Long Lartin had acquired its reputation among British cons. Even apart from the modern buildings and ample sports facilities, the cons were different. It was a 'dispersal' prison – most of the inmates were lifers, with sentences from ten to twenty years. It was a different atmosphere from other prisons. The cons had a different mentality, a sense of pride.

'Nobody gives you any trouble – unless you go looking for it,' Ken instructed me.

I'd already noticed that cons were allowed to wear their own clothes. Wages were paid in cash, not into a prison bank account as in my previous prisons, and the canteen opened four times a week. You could even order your own food and cook it in the wing, and when the other cons found out I was a good cook I was soon earning a little extra money cooking their meals for them. It paid for tobacco, toiletries and other small luxuries. Long Lartin inmates were not usually inclined to interfere in other people's business, and I avoided known trouble-makers. So there was none of the pressure of resentment on me that there had been at Dartmoor. Also, I enjoyed the sports facilities. I played football, basketball, badminton and other games.

After a while I summoned enough courage to ask my Kitchen Officer for permission to attend the chapel service. To my delight he not only encouraged me to go but also offered to make arrangements for somebody to work my shift if I was due to work on Sunday morning. There were several services for different denominations. I went to the Church of England one, and enjoyed singing hymns and praying, though I didn't understand some parts of the service. I was disappointed by the attendance – only a handful out of about 600 cons – but I recognised the Gymnasium Officer there. During my time at Long Lartin we rarely talked together as Christians, but the way he lived his life was an inspiration to me. He was a consistent, likeable Christian.

My attendance at chapel raised no comment from my fellow-cons, and I did not talk about it. Indeed I told nobody I was a Christian. I wanted to, but the right situation didn't appear.

In the evenings I read my Bible. There were also a few Christian books in the prison library. But though I enjoyed the freedom to get to know the Bible better, I was still worried that my new-found joy and peace might disappear. Something seemed to be missing. I knew that attending services and trying to be good was not enough. Many Chinese and Malaysian religions demanded only that. There had to be more, though I didn't know what it might be. God had taken over my life and knew what was going to happen next, and so I prayed to him before I went to bed. *Please send me someone to minister to me*, I asked night after night. *Send me somebody I can have fellowship with*. The words 'minister' and 'fellowship' were ones I'd learned from the Christian books I'd been reading.

'Excuse me.'

The speaker was a fat con with a wide, genuine smile that lit up his bearded face. When I entered the prison library he was the only other person in the room. He came across and stood next to me. I was looking at the religious books, hoping to find a new one.

'Yes?' I responded, my gaze still on the books.

His voice was quiet, but confident and friendly.

'Are you by any chance a born-again Christian?'

The words were so out of place in that environment that I would have laughed out loud, if I had not been so thrilled to hear them spoken.

'Yes, I am,' I said. 'How come you know that?'

'I've been watching you since you were transferred here,' he said calmly. 'I've seen your quietness. You're a peaceful, cheerful sort of bloke. And of course I've seen you going to chapel.' He stuck out his hand. 'Name's Bob,' he said. 'I'm a lifer. Been a born-again Christian for a long time.'

We clasped hands.

'Come over here,' he said in the same low, soft voice. 'I'll show you something you'll want to see. Have you got a Chinese Bible?'

He led me to the end section of the shelves.

'Here – I don't know whether it's Chinese or some other language.'

There, sitting tidily on the shelf, was a Bible in Chinese characters. I picked it up delicately, as one might handle a jade vase. For two and a half years I had not seen a Chinese book. I gently turned the pages. The Gospels, parts of Acts, other passages I knew in English were suddenly presented to me in the language of my childhood. With a surge of excitement I realised that I could now study the Bible in both languages. I stammered my thanks, and we arranged to meet as soon as possible to pray together and talk about the Bible.

Now that I had a Chinese Bible my understanding quickly increased. Bob helped me to understand many of the parts I found difficult, and as we prayed together I began to make real progress. I knew what Jesus Christ had come to earth to do. Not to introduce new rituals; the services in the chapel, though important, were not the key to Christianity. He didn't come to found a system of ethics, like the ancient Middle Way of the Buddha. Now I belonged to him I knew that much of my behaviour would have to change, but that was not the heart of the Gospel. He didn't come to found a religion, although millions looked to him as the historical founder of their faith. He really did live, Bob assured me.

'You can go to Israel today and walk in the same hills he did, see the same mountains,' he said.

What he came to do, I now realised, was simply to change people's hearts and lives. I had seen it in myself; I knew God had accepted me and was changing my life. And I knew he had saved me from the punishment I deserved. The prison sentence was nothing in comparison to the horror of dying without knowing God. Jesus died to save human beings. And to save me. This made him far more powerful than any of the gods I had been told about as a child.

'You see,' Bob explained, 'he hates sin. He hates all the things you and I did. The things that put us in here, the things we did that never got found out. He hates it all. He just can't stand to have anything to do with it.'

I shivered, remembering the violence, the selfishness, all my greed, the way I'd treated my family. I thought of Tracey and my children back in Malaysia, and I covered my face with my hands.

'Then he hates me, Bob. I'm full of it. You don't know.'

Bob reached out one of his large hands and grasped mine comfortingly.

'But that's exactly it, don't you see? He hates the sin, but he loves you. That's why he came and found you in Exeter. That's why he wants to help you get rid of all the crap in your life, all the stuff that's tried to bury you, keep you from ever knowing God. Did you ever think about him in Malaysia?'

I shook my head.

'Well then, he must love you if he followed you all the way here.'

One thing became very special to me. I devoured all the Bible verses about how Jesus treated the people he met who were depressed and troubled. His words seemed so kind and understanding: 'Have faith in God, don't be troubled! There's no reason to worry.' When I read such words in the Bible I remembered the clear voice I'd heard twice, and its calm reassurance: 'You'll be all right, son. Have faith in me.' In the Bible I found a Jesus who hated fear, who showed people that they must live by faith, who was able to give confidence, faith and peace to anybody who came to him wanting help. I knew this from my own experience, but seeing it spelt out in black and white lifted my heart.

I became convinced that the Bible contained the foundation for everything I needed to know. At home people worked hard for their religion, I had watched them blindly obeying rules and regulations, following endless rituals, paying out large sums of money; but they were like sheep, just following orders. From talking to Bob, reading the Bible and Christian books, I glimpsed that Christianity was a relationship with a real person, Jesus Christ, through whom I could know God. And one of the keys to that relationship was a mysterious thing called the Holy Spirit, described in the Bible sometimes as an invisible person, sometimes as an unseen force like the wind, but always – confusingly – as God.

After several weeks, in which we became close friends and spent many hours together, Bob was transferred to The Verne, a prison in Dorset. Despite my disappointment, I reminded myself that God had answered my prayers by sending Bob to me. Who could tell what he had in store for the future? So we parted brothers, and I continued to read my Bible and praise God for the help he had given me so far and the wonderful situation he had put me in in Long Lartin.

The months passed. I worked hard on the sports field and was picked for football matches against teams from outside. I enjoyed my work in the kitchen too. I learned a lot about living as a Christian simply by watching the everyday behaviour and conversation of the Gymnasium Officer. He was kind to me, though the relationship between screw and con never allowed the same friendship and fellowship I'd had with Bob.

But life was great. I basked in the sunshine of God's goodness, thanked him every day for what he had done for me, studied my Bible, worked hard, and waited expectantly for him to send somebody to replace Bob.

Looking back I suppose it was another of God's blessings that I was given those months of happiness and spiritual growth. For very soon everything was to fall to pieces.

18

CAST DOWN

'Hui!'

I stood rooted to the spot. Ken was backed against the wall, watching warily as the English con crouched ready to rush him, holding a wooden chair at arm's length poised as a weapon. His eyes remained fixed on the other's face, while he shouted out to me. I was standing in the circle of spectators.

'Come on – help me! Take the chair off him . . . '

The other cons broke into a ragged cheer.

'Go on, Hui, give him a hand!'

'Stay where you are, keep out of it!'

I could feel the old anger rising inside me. Deep in my pockets I clenched my fists. My fingernails bit into my palms. In my chest a tiny pulse was fluttering. *Go on*, I thought to myself, *what are you waiting for? He's your friend, isn't he?* Before I was a Christian I would have been the first to join in a fight. It was partly my natural pugnacity and partly a desire to protect my honour and that of my people. But since God came to me in Exeter Prison, though often tempted to fight, I had always been able to resist by praying as the situation arose and leaving as soon as possible. But this was different. This was Ken, my closest friend apart from Bob, and with Bob gone the only person really close to me in prison. Jesus, help me, I prayed.

'Come *on*,' cried Ken.

Suddenly it all seemed easy. I stepped backwards through

the onlookers and walked quickly away. The jeers of the cons followed me to my landing.

Ken had shown no interest when I broached the subject of Christianity. He was a Buddhist with a strong commitment to his culture and the ancient traditions of his family, and had no use for any other religion. We had remained good friends, however, until the fight. When we met again he was bruised and swollen from the beating he had taken, and was bitterly angry with me.

'I thought you were my friend,' he accused me. 'I thought you were a Chinese brother. That you knew what loyalty means.'

His anger was echoed by his friends. Some of the Asian cons who disliked me took the opportunity to pass remarks behind my back. Some said I had been on the Englishman's side all the time and that I had walked away to make sure Ken lost the fight. It seemed that the pleasure of coming to Long Lartin was already spoilt. My relationship with Ken deteriorated hopelessly, and I missed his friendship. The other Asians lost interest in taunting me, but there was still an undercurrent of resentment. I put up with it and got on with my life, but I felt as if a shadow had fallen across my path.

So it was with something of a sense of inevitability that I received the really bad news after only a few months at Long Lartin. The Prison Authority had reviewed my record and reclassified me from a category B to a category C prisoner. I was no longer a dangerous con who must be kept in a high security prison. I was eligible for transfer to a semi-open prison.

In one way it was welcome: a lower category was an acknowledgment of good conduct. But I was not sure I wanted to leave. I had a good job in the kitchen with good wages, and that meant I was eating well. I had a lot of freedom too; Long Lartin was a place where the screws weren't watching you all the time. In fact my relationship with the screws was good. The kitchen and gymnasium screws especially were kind to me, but all of them were friendly and usually gave me whatever help I needed. Compared with the Scrubs and Dartmoor it was paradise. No, I didn't want to leave.

The Assistant Governor told me I was being silly.

'You should go to a category C prison,' he said. 'It will be a stepping-stone to being considered for early deportation.'

Early deportation was the equivalent of parole in the case of non-British prisoners not resident in the United Kingdom.

'I'm not worried about early deportation, sir,' I said. 'I want to finish my sentence here.'

I knew my crime as well as anybody: two counts in a drug case had brought a sentence that was already lenient. Compared to others it was a good result. I wasn't counting on being allowed out early. On the other hand I had survived two and a half rough years in various prisons and now with God's help I had found somewhere I could learn and grow. I tried to explain some of this to him, and he said he understood.

'You are allowed to petition the Home Office about this,' he said. 'I'll give the petition my support.'

Full of gratitude, I left his office rejoicing at God's provision yet again. The Assistant Governor would see that my petition was accepted. Hadn't Jesus brought Bob along at the very time I needed him? And hadn't I prayed every night for the past few weeks that he would send somebody else? I was sure he would. And now it seemed as if I was going to be able to stay in Long Lartin, the first place I had been really happy since my arrest. Two weeks later my petition went to the Home Office. The result came in due course. My request was rejected. I was to be transferred to a category C prison.

Prisoners are offered a choice of transfer in order to make it as easy as possible for relatives to visit. The options were Channings Wood in Devon or The Verne in Portland. I had no relatives to consider, so the choice of The Verne was an easy one. That was where Bob was and I was longing to see him again; and Roger, Paul and James were there also, transferred from the Youth Custody Centre and Bristol Prison. Roger was due for release next May. If I applied for The Verne I could be with him for the final months of his sentence. I wrote to Roger, and he told me about The Verne and its systems. It sounded quite attractive. He also mentioned that there were half a dozen Chinese from Cardiff who had recently arrived charged with assault.

When I heard that, I wondered whether my decision was the right one. I realised that too many Chinese at The Verne might turn out to be a problem. I love my fellow-countrymen and we have a tradition of helping each other, in family life and society in general as well as in the Triad oaths. That was why Ken had been so angry with me for not helping in the fight. But what would Roger and the others say when they knew I was a Christian? How would they react to the changes in me? I was not the person they used to know any more.

I prayed at every opportunity, asking God whether I should cancel my application. But every time I prayed I felt a quiet sense of peace. After a few days I was convinced that God wanted me at The Verne. When the official transfer notification arrived I accepted it with genuine thankfulness. For a time the shadow of Ken's bitterness lifted and I felt secure and protected in God's care.

Winter came and great drifts of snow swirled around the prison. The football field was unplayable, and we trudged from building to building on slushy walkways. Some of the cons cursed the weather but I welcomed it. It reminded me of the wonderful experience I'd had in Exeter. One December day I was looking out of a window at the swirling snow. Birds were being tossed like black rags in the bleak white sky. Cons were shovelling snow from the walkways, their breath curling like smoke in the icy air. Indoors it wasn't too cold. But the view from the window reminded me of Christmas scenes from English books I'd seen as a child.

Christmas, I thought suddenly. *This is going to be my first Christmas as a Christian!*

Christmas in Malaysia and Thailand had no religious significance. It was a Christian festival and I'd despised it as I despised all religion. It was an excuse for a good time, lots of drink, maybe a new woman. Remembering the old days I was horrified, and promised myself it was going to be different this year. When I found out that there was to be a carol concert in the chapel a week before Christmas, I began to count the days. Long Lartin seemed the best place in the world, and I thought myself the happiest person in England.

It was while I was rejoicing in God's love and care for me that Tracey's letter arrived.

'I'm pleased to see you've had a change of heart,' she wrote, 'but there isn't any real chance of a reconciliation. Too much has happened between us. I've met a good man, an accountant, who lives in Kuala Lumpur. We are together now.'

I read on mechanically. My hands were shaking. A mental picture swam before my eyes. Tracey and her man, living with my children in one of the trim bungalows in the wealthy suburbs of Kuala Lumpur where accountants lived:

> It's good you've come to your senses wanting to help bring up the children, but I doubt very much that you can just come back from prison and take them. The only thing I can suggest is that if you are willing to set up a trust fund for the children, then I will allow them to stay with my mother. You could have access to them at weekends if they wanted it.

The remorseless sentences went on:

If you want to fulfil your responsibilities and keep
contact with the children you will have to pay maintenance to me. Also, I have the opportunity to start a
business with a friend. It's my opportunity to start my
life again after you broke up our home. You should
pay compensation for what you've done. I need
capital for the business. It should come from you.

There were figures in the letter, neat totals of Malaysian
dollars, carefully set out: her accountant boyfriend had
shown her how, I knew. I barely took in the amounts,
which seemed astronomical. The letter ended tersely:

In any case, I don't believe you should have custody.
I would contest it. My new boyfriend has more right
to them than you have. They like him, and he isn't
in prison. But if you face up to your responsibilities
and pay what I have said, you can have access
at weekends.

A great roar escaped from my lips as I flung the letter
to the floor.
'*Bitch!*'
I didn't care who was listening, still less that a few cons
on the landing were watching with interest through my
open cell door.
'The *bitch*, the stupid bitch!'
I will not write down the words I shouted after that.
All the filthy and vicious language I had used every day at
home came back as if I'd never stopped using it. It was like
a spiritual earthquake. The foundations of my life for the
past months disappeared, and everything collapsed into the
hole that was left. The peace that had accompanied me since
I left Exeter was replaced by a black rage that thundered
in my ears and filled the whole world. I reached down and
picked up the letter again, then ripped it into tiny pieces.
She's worse than I ever was, I thought bitterly. *I would*

never have taken anything from her. This is extortion.

For a while a kind of madness possessed me. We Chinese never allow our wives to have custody of our children when we divorce. After my first marriage ended, drink and gambling had made me forget what had been drilled into me since childhood. Now in prison, with almost everything taken away, my rights and duties as a father seemed very important to me. It was not merely a matter of male pride. My children carried the family name, and if I let Tracey do as she wished my relatives would never forgive me. Neither, for that matter, would my ancestors.

I banged the cell door shut and sat with my head in my hands, moaning and shaking myself backwards and forwards. After a while the worst of my passion subsided, and I was just sobbing quietly. Eventually I began to pray. I was furiously angry but I did not shout at God. I asked him questions instead, endless angry questions, 'Why did you allow this to happen? Why haven't you done something to change Tracey's heart? Why did you allow her to meet this man? You are the most powerful being in the universe; why didn't you do something to stop all this happening? You could have done it – so what have I done wrong that you don't? Where *are* you, God?'

Tiredness overcame me at last and I lay down, still arguing with God, but before long I drifted off to sleep, sprawled on my bed in my clothes.

I woke feeling stiff and uncomfortable. It was past midnight. My cheeks were damp; I had been crying in my sleep. My mind was blank. I could hardly remember anything of my raging. The situation revolved endlessly in my brain. Revenge was out of the question, I decided, though my reasons were strictly practical ones: a family tragedy would certainly follow, there would be bloodletting on both sides and innocent people would get hurt. But I was full of hatred towards my wife and her boyfriend.

'If I can't have my children,' I said, 'then nobody will.'

What was I to do? Losing a leg or a hand you could bear, but losing the children was unthinkable. I knew I had a responsibility to pay maintenance to my family; but how did she expect me to pay those sums? I would have to go back to drug-smuggling to raise the money. *She's using my love for the children as a way of taking revenge on me*, I moaned. *She's trying to destroy my faith in God. Otherwise why would she tell me about her new boyfriend and all her plans for the future?*

I believed that God knew all about my problems – but where was he now? Why was I so distressed? It was almost a year since I had felt this low.

I had some money in Thailand, but not nearly enough to meet Tracey's demands. I could end by losing everything: children, Tracey, even enough to live on when I went home. I could operate the drugs racket from inside prison; I had the contacts. But how long could I do it before being caught? Was Tracey trying to set a trap for me, by tempting me into breaking the law and probably getting a life sentence? As I pondered this eventuality I became very frightened. If it was a trap, then surely it wasn't Tracey who was attacking me: it was the devil using her to destroy me.

I knelt down and prayed fervently and at length. I opened my Bible and read whole chapters, looking for God to give me a special message. But nothing happened. No illuminating thoughts came into my mind. I saw no visions. The small clear voice that had spoken to me in the past was silent.

In the morning I reported for work as usual and sought out the Kitchen Officer.

'A serious problem has come up. I need a day to rest and think about it.'

He looked at me curiously. I must have looked terrible; I'd hardly slept and the hours of crying and tension must have shown on my face.

'What's happened, Hui?'

I told him the truth. He was sympathetic.

'All right, Hui. Take the day off.' He clapped me on the shoulder, 'Get some sleep.'

Back in my cell I drew down the curtain and was asleep as soon as I lay down. I slept until the early evening. When I woke up a trickle of cons came to the cell, worried by my absence after the storms of the previous day. To most of their questions I just answered 'family problems'.

Ken heard about my distress and came to cheer me up, and I was glad to see him, though our conversation wasn't as relaxed as it used to be, and it became clear that he still hated me for letting him down. After he left, another con came to the cell, a man from the north of England called Bill with whom I was friendly. He was a tall, gangly man with a deceptively tough air.

'You look like you could do with a real sleep, mate,' he said. 'Look, have this.'

He dug into his shirt pocket and produced a tobacco tin. Inside was a twist of silver paper. He unfolded it with deliberate care and smoothed it flat. I knew what the waxy brown substance inside was. Bill winked at me, and proceeded to take cigarette paper and tobacco, crumbling and sprinkling the marijuana along its length. He rolled it expertly, licked the paper and surveyed the result of his work critically: a plump cigarette, its contents showing ragged at each end.

'A nice, fat joint,' he said approvingly, placing it on the table. 'A reefer. Marree-jew-anna. That'll relax you. Now, take it easy. And if you think they will help you get your sleep back, I can get you more. OK?'

When he was gone I lay face down and wept. All these good people wanting to help. Even Ken had come to me in my hour of need, when I had run away from him when he needed help. What was wrong with a joint? It wasn't like taking heroin or cocaine. It was just a relaxant. Something to make me feel better.

I rolled on to my back and looked at the joint lying on the table. It was so tempting; just to pick it up and light it. *I need to sleep*, I told myself, *I won't be able to, I've been asleep all day, but I'm still exhausted. And I've got to work tomorrow.* Surely Jesus would understand. Maybe Bill was even his messenger, bringing with him God's gift of sleep. At last I talked myself into believing it, and picked the joint up. I cradled it in my hands for a moment, and then reached for my lighter. As I did so, my Bible fell off the table and landed open on the floor. I leaned over to pick it up. Words caught my eye:

> If you love me, you will obey what I command. And I will ask the Father, and he will give you another Counsellor to be with you for ever . . . the Counsellor, the Holy Spirit, whom the Father will send in my name, will teach you all things and will remind you of everything I have said to you.

It was as if a voice was speaking the words, quietly in my ear: 'Peace I leave with you; my peace I give you. I don't give to you as the world gives. Do not let your hearts be troubled and don't be afraid.'[1]

I read the whole chapter enthralled. That mysterious Holy Spirit again! I realised that the voice that had spoken to me before was now speaking to me in a different way, through the pages of the Bible; but I knew it was a direct message to me at that particular moment. Jesus promised his followers that the Holy Spirit would be a teacher and a counsellor who wouldn't go away. *I'm a follower of Jesus too*, I realised. *It's for me too!*

The joint remained unlit and forgotten as I sat deep in thought. George had been my teacher and counsellor in Exeter and Dartmoor, until I was transferred; at Long Lartin I'd found another teacher and counsellor in Bob, but he had been removed though we would meet again in The Verne. I had been building my hopes for growing as

---

[1] John 14:15–16, 26–27.

a Christian on finding human beings to help me; but now Jesus was showing me that the Holy Spirit would be my teacher. This discovery so elated me that I immediately began to talk to God, thanking him for the promise he had given me. There was still much about this Holy Spirit I couldn't understand – why the Bible spoke of it as a 'he' though it was invisible, for instance – but I wanted to find out. I alternated between praying and reading the Bible until tiredness swept over me and I fell asleep.

Was it a dream that followed, or a vision? All I know is that for what seemed hours that night my mind dredged up hundreds of memories of my childhood and life in Malaysia. My life was presented to me like a film running at lightning speed, until finally I was remembering the years I spent with Tracey, and all the tensions and bitterness that had developed between us. But I was remembering in a curious way. I was seeing myself being thoughtless, spendthrift, unkind, cruel, harsh with my children; I was hearing my voice saying vicious things. I watched myself consumed with anger, hitting Tracey and pouring out strings of foul-mouthed abuse. And as it all unrolled in front of me I felt real shame for all that I had done.

I woke exhausted, perplexed as to why it had happened. I worked in the kitchen and got through the day somehow, but the next night exactly the same thing happened. It was as if something was being meticulously worked out, step by step; as if, while I slept, my life was being put on some sort of trial. I tried to fight it, to switch my mind off; but it was impossible. The remorseless trial went on, and as I watched I was judge and guilty party all in one. It was the same for the next six nights.

During that long week the accumulated resentments and bitterness broke down. I realised that Tracey had been right. I was a failure as a father and as a husband. Neither she nor the children had had the love or the things that wives and children ought to have. I had had money to squander and spent it all on myself. As I understood just how badly I had behaved I was covered in shame. On the last night I finally realised what was happening. It was the Holy Spirit showing me the things I had done wrong in my life and making me see them as if for the first time. Through that week-long scrutiny the Holy Spirit showed me that I needed to go to Jesus and repent of the evil things I had done to my family.

I wrote to Tracey, weeping. I asked for her forgiveness. I wrote knowing that I would never be able to win her back; but I had regained the deep sense of peace inside me. As I recognised it once more, I knew it had never gone away.

The carol service in the prison chapel was wonderful. Only about thirty cons attended, but some Christians living nearby came, and members of the prison staff with their families, so that in all we had a congregation of around 200 people. I will never forget it. When we sang about the peace of God it was as if I could have reached out and touched it, like an enormous embracing blanket wrapping me from head to foot. In my heart I was sad about Tracey, but the radiant faces of the Christian visitors were like a message to me personally from God, telling me that peace and love were not just words.

Just before Christmas I had another new experience: my first Christmas card as a Christian. It was from George's wife Mary; she sent it from them both and as he had promised to keep in touch I was delighted. When I wrote to thank her I asked her what it was like being the wife of a man who was in prison. I was trying hard to see things from Tracey's point of view.

In January my faith was severely tested again in a series of setbacks. Two things kept me going and prevented my bruised faith from slipping away. One was that Mary was writing to me regularly, encouraging and guiding me as I struggled on. The other was that the activity of the Holy Spirit in my life was an ever-present fascination to me. It was as if no part of my life, past or present, was safe from his searching gaze. When I was tempted to give up in despair, it seemed that passages of the Bible had been written specially for me. Words casually spoken in chapel helped me in unexpected ways. My old problem of anger was controlled on several more occasions as I was given the ability to walk away from explosive situations. And in the middle of it all the Holy Spirit went on showing me attitudes, actions and thoughts that needed to be changed.

Sometimes in conversation with somebody I would suddenly see very sharply how my words sounded to the other person, and as I changed my approach to soften an unintended harshness or criticism I would recognise that the Holy Spirit had intervened. In difficult decisions the Holy Spirit often showed me unmistakably the right step. More than once, having made a choice I was unsure about, I literally had no peace of mind until I had altered my decision, often in some embarrassment.

Before long I was depending on the Holy Spirit for guidance in every aspect of my life. When I prayed to Jesus about something, I waited for the Spirit to show me the answer. When I read the Bible, I was alert for the characteristic feeling of certainty that I was reading something God particularly wanted me to know.

How the Lord Jesus, God and the Holy Spirit all fitted together, and how they could all be one God, I couldn't fathom. Of the three I knew least about the Holy Spirit. But I could see exactly what it – he – was doing in my life.

19

THE VERNE

The Verne is a granite stronghold on the bleak hill overlooking Portland near Weymouth. The road zig-zags uphill from the tidy modern bungalows of the town, climbing through scrubby moorland to the massive prison gates.

I arrived at The Verne on 26 February 1987. Once again I found myself in a different environment. Most of the cons were Kenyan or Nigerian Africans on short-term drug sentences ranging from three to five years. There were also eleven Hong Kong Chinese. As I left the reception room Roger and James with some of the Chinese were there to greet me. They helped me carry my belongings in.

I was allocated a room in B1 wing, on the top landing. Prisoners were given keys to their rooms and told to double-lock their doors as a protection against petty thieving. I was to learn the wisdom of this a few days later when I forgot and left my door open all day. I returned in the evening to find three bars of soap had disappeared. Paul and James were in B1 with me, but Roger and the other Chinese were in a different wing. Bob also was in another wing and we could only meet in the free association period, which was a big disappointment to me.

Paul and I had parted on bad terms, and now we were in the same prison it seemed impossible to rebuild any sort of relationship. We were uneasy with each other and tried not to meet when we didn't have to. On the other hand I trusted James and Roger. The three of us and the other Chinese had good conversations together. The Hong Kong cons were in

their twenties, very relaxed and tolerant. We spent hours
fooling around, cracking jokes and teasing each other. We
reminisced a lot about the prisons we'd been in, swapping
lurid anecdotes and trying to cap each other's accounts of
the past two and a half years. But I couldn't bring myself
to tell them I was a Christian. Bob, quiet and understanding
as ever, didn't press me to do so, though I think he was
worried that I might find my young and inexperienced faith
struggling in this new environment.

The tall, lanky clergyman stuck out his hand.

'Name's Derek Cordell,' he said affably. 'Good to have
you with us this morning.'

It was my first meeting with the chaplain, a relaxed,
friendly man who put me at my ease immediately.

'Now, can we meet up some time soon for a chat?
Give us a chance to get to know each other. How about
tomorrow?'

The Revd Cordell's job included a lot of work on
prisoners' welfare, and I got to know him well. He took
a particular interest in me as a foreigner without family in
Britain. I enjoyed his Sunday services, which were attended
by around forty inmates, mostly Africans, though there
were also Europeans and South Americans. It was the
first time I had worshipped in such a mixed group, and
the hymn-singing was wonderful. I found the chaplain's
sermons difficult however and the theological words he
used went over my head. When I got to know him better I
told him so; and it says a lot about him that he accepted the
criticism without becoming angry. For his part he often had
the task of curbing the enthusiasm which sometimes made
me impatient of prison rules and regulations. Though I
never succeeded in tying his theological expertise to my own
demands, this kindly, smiling priest was a very important
part of my Christian life at The Verne.

At chapel services I saw a number of people from B1
including Mr Dunk, my Wing Officer, whom I knew only

from admission procedures and day-to-day prison regulations. Some cons looked as if they really were worshipping
God, and I felt sure Officer Dunk was too. But I was too
shy to ask him.

Bob and George had both explained that it was important
to tell people about my new faith as soon as possible, but
somehow the timing was never right.

Jesus, help me to tell somebody, I pleaded. *I can't
do it myself.*

It was the same in working hours. One of the work
options available in The Verne was full-time education,
and I was accepted for courses in English and mathematics.
Inmates from various wings turned up to the classes, and
I knew many of them from my time in Reading, Bristol,
Dartmoor and Exeter. Some of the Asian cons remembered
me from 1984 and 1985, when I was first imprisoned. On
occasions, turning suddenly, I caught them looking at me
with odd expressions. One day I challenged one of them,
a con I'd met in Reading.

'What are you staring at?'

'You've changed, Hui.' He was embarrassed. 'Your attitude's different. You're smiling too much. You're always
cheerful. And you've quietened down. What's happened?'

I almost told him then, but something held me back.
Later I tried to turn the conversation round to the same
topic, but there was no recapturing the opportunity.

My chance to speak about Jesus finally came when I was
walking along the landing and saw a face I recognised.

'Sanjit!'

Sanjit was the Sri Lankan at Bristol who had tried
unsuccessfully to persuade me to go to a Muslim meeting.
He beamed delightedly and grasped my hand.

'Hui! I've seen you around but haven't had a chance
to say hello.'

I shook his hand rather self-consciously, because of our
last meeting when I had told him there was no God.

'At Bristol you were a real trouble-maker, Hui,' exclaimed

Sanjit. 'You were full of hate, a most violent man. I remember you well!' He looked at me quizzically. 'Then when I was transferred to Dartmoor you had gone to Long Lartin, but they told me all about your activities in Dartmoor. And they told me about your trip to Reading too. A most violent man, a violent man indeed! But now, when I see you you've changed. You're not trying to break the system. You aren't fighting every day. You speak differently. What's happened?'

I smiled. 'I'm a Christian now, Sanjit. I'm saved, by the grace and mercy of God.'

'What are you talking about? Is that a joke? You're the last person I'd have thought would have any interest in God. Go on – tell me how it happened.'

It was the invitation I had been waiting for. I poured out the whole story of Exeter: how I found Rita's book in my cell; how George talked to me and showed me how to become a Christian; even something of the joys and depressions I experienced. I finished, and waited for his response. He seemed interested.

'So we belong to different religions now – even so, I'm glad you've found a faith, Hui. You're certainly a different person,' he said.

Among my possessions was a mah-jong set. It's a game much loved by my people. In most Chinese communities you can see people absorbed in the play of the small ivory tiles. We Chinese cons, already a close-knit group, formed the habit of playing at the weekends and on occasional weeknights, always meeting in wing B1. As the eldest of the group I was accorded some respect, and Roger and James were my close friends; but the coldness between myself and Paul remained. He kept to his own friends, mainly Pakistani cons he had known in his previous prisons, and they met in the evening in the room opposite mine.

'You know they have drugs in there?' remarked one of my mates, indicating the noisy laughter coming across the landing.

Stupid fools, I thought. Actually I had some sympathy for Paul; his father had died since he was sentenced and his mother was ill. I could imagine the pressure he was under. But my struggle over the marijuana joint in Long Lartin had left me convinced that drug-taking was not the way to deal with such problems.

James and I talked about Paul but neither of us was prepared to speak to him about the drugs. I tried to introduce the topic obliquely by saying, for example, that I had heard about a con who had become an addict during a prison sentence. But Paul's attitude was edgy, and he never said anything in reply. It was an odd situation for me to be in: a convicted drug-smuggler; associated with drug-traffickers; member of a Triad that was inextricably involved with the trade; and now trying to preach to Paul. Yet I had never taken drugs myself and had forbidden my workers to do so.

My life had certainly turned upside down since I encountered Jesus in a prison cell in Exeter. I was trying to live in a way that would make him pleased with me. I knew I was changing, and others could see it too; other cons, the Prison Authorities, even Tracey had grudgingly acknowledged that I'd changed. In The Verne I went to chapel on Sunday, and made it a habit to spend some time there every morning as well, praying and reading my Bible. The other cons joked about me, and sometimes there was a sharp edge to their comments. The Chinese accused me of becoming westernised.

'You're worshipping the Western God,' they jeered.

Bit by bit I explained that I really did worship the Western God now, and he was helping me to change; that there was an amazing thing called the Holy Spirit that was also part of God, and this Holy Spirit was going through my life showing me what was wrong and needed to be changed. I tried to tell them about Jesus' promise of 'another Comforter', but I hardly understood it myself. None of it made any sense to them anyway, and the fact that

I tended to speak my mind strongly on most matters only
added to their annoyance. They reacted badly, and often
the mah-jong tiles were abandoned as everyone turned on
me, ridiculing my Christian faith and humiliating me in
various ways.

I prayed about each incident, and discovered that Jesus
really was a friend who could help me through times of
criticism. It seemed as if I was wrapped in a cloud of love
and strength, like a butterfly wrapped in its cocoon and
growing all the time.

But by no means all of my problems were so easy to sort
out. Faced with the fact that drugs were circulating in the
prison, I was uneasy. My reaction to Paul's involvement
was mainly one of contempt; Paul was weak. But part of me
was concerned on a much more personal level. Though still
far from reconciled to Paul, I was genuinely concerned that
he should not become an addict. This prompted thoughts
that I didn't feel ready to deal with yet. The prospect of
Paul becoming hooked made me think of the hundreds and
thousands of people who had bought on the streets the
drugs I had sold. From my padded suitcases little packets
of destruction and death had circulated all over Europe and
Asia. Divided and re-divided, packed in smaller and smaller
quantities, my shipments of heroin and cocaine had wrecked
families, destroyed lives and certainly contributed to tragic
deaths. How could I live with that knowledge? What did
God think of it? What would I say if I ever met the parents
of addicted children? And how could I ever put anything
right again?

When such thoughts came I wrestled with them but could
not resolve them. In the end I always put them on one side,
to be dealt with later. Being a Christian in prison gave me
enough problems to handle already.

20

MORE SETBACKS

[The Prime Minister of Malaysia] said the government
made no apology for the country's tough *dadah*
[drugs] laws as it regarded the death penalty not only
as a deterrent but also as an appropriate punishment
for 'these criminals for they are worse than murderers
who deliberately spread misery and death in their
quest for easy wealth' . . . The aim was to inculcate
in Malaysian youth the total rejection of *dadah* as the
most evil of human vices.

Berita Malaysia, October 1986

Dadah, or drugs, was a word to send a chill of fear down
travellers' spines.

A few weeks after my arrival at The Verne a letter was
forwarded to me from Long Lartin. It was a copy of a
reply to a query sent by the Prison Probation Officer to
the Malaysian High Commission in London, and enclosed
a news cutting announcing further tightening of Malaysian
anti-drug trafficking legislation. The letter was brief and
to the point. 'This is to inform you that the advice
given to us is that action can be taken against Mr Hui
Chan Hop under the Dangerous Drugs (Special Preventive
Measures) Act 1985.'

I knew what the measures might be: arrest when I
returned to Malaysia; questioning about not only the
offence for which I had been imprisoned but also all

my past activities; a possible further period of imprisonment; perhaps even the death sentence. Rumours abounded in the prisons about the harsh penalties being imposed in Malaysia and other Far Eastern countries for drug-trafficking offences; and the grim warnings – placarded with grinning skull and crossbones – exhibited at airports and border posts: '*Dadah* is death'. I knew government control was stricter now than when I was trafficking, but even then the death penalty had often been imposed.

I put the letter away carefully and tried not to think about the future.

It was not the only news I had from Long Lartin. Ken was to be transferred to The Verne. When I heard that, I was extremely depressed. He hated me for my failure to go to his help in the fight. He was not going to be an ally when he got here and could well be an enemy. Relationships already frayed by my attempts to talk about my faith could well be put under more stress.

My worst fears were realised. Ken was allocated to my wing and quickly made friends with the Chinese cons. Soon there were whispered conversations and clumsy allusions to the fight in Long Lartin.

'Of course,' a con whispered loudly to his neighbour in the exercise yard, 'Hui ain't really Chinese at all – worships European gods now. Every morning. Reads their holy book. And he don't help Chinese people, not like a real brother would.'

He spoke with exaggerated clarity, wanting me to hear every word. There were other comments.

'He turned his back on his own.'

'He got no interest in us.'

'See Hui there? You can't depend on him. He got religion, that's the end of him. Don't trust him.'

'Traitor . . . Traitor . . . Traitor . . .'

The whispers, vicious and hurtful, followed me wherever I went. Within two or three days I was the most unpopular person there.

Six days after his arrival Ken was involved in his first
fight.

The dining-room was full of cons finishing their meal. I
concentrated on my pudding. The duty screws were standing in position, their gaze wandering round the room. James
and some Chinese cons were on my table, though we hadn't
talked much during the meal. I scraped the last fragments
of food from my plate methodically, carefully licking my
spoon, postponing the moment when I would have to get
up and endure a lonely free association period.

A scuffle on the far side of the table made me look up.
James was fighting with one of the English cons. I had no
idea what had started it. Almost immediately five of the
Chinese joined in and beat up the English con. Though
I was sitting very near I ignored the fight and went on
picking at my plate.

'Hui!'

One of the Chinese, Chang, called to me to join in, but
I pretended not to hear. All kinds of thoughts were going
through my mind. I knew if I joined in, and fought as well
as I knew I could, I would be popular again; the Chinese
would like me, I would regain the respect I had had as
the eldest of our group. No more lonely evenings; the
gentle click of the mah-jong tiles, the sweet smell of cheap
cigarettes, only the occasional tolerant joke about my faith,
just like it was before.

'*Hui!*'

Chang looked incredulous as I sat without moving. Some
of the English cons were moving purposefully towards the
fight to help their friend.

'Come *on*, don't just hang about. What are you *doing*?'

I knew that Ken was nearby. With a sick feeling I saw
him coming across. One of the Chinese lads waved at me,
and I realised he was giving a Triad sign, the gesture of
summoning help. I remembered the oath I'd sworn, and
the recriminations when I walked away from the fight at
Long Lartin.

Suddenly the screws were at the table. Swiftly and efficiently they separated the Chinese and English. The two sides drew apart sullenly, glaring at each other. One or two of the Chinese were glaring at me.

The screws decided that the situation was under control, but feelings were still running high. As they turned away a second fight broke out. This time it was between the English con whose argument with James had started the whole thing, and Ken. The Englishman had gathered his own mates and was looking for revenge. He had been beaten up by a gang of Chinese, and Ken was Chinese.

Looking round for help Ken saw me. His expression was half ironic, half bitter. Then the fight took off in earnest. Tables were upturned and chairs flung across the room. Cups and plates crashed to the floor. Before the screws could intervene the violence had become savage and several cons were badly hurt. Soon others joined in and the fight turned into a giant free-for-all.

A blinding jolt of pain exploded at the back of my skull. I'd been hit by a tea mug. Instantly my temper rose. I swivelled round, looking for the con who had thrown it. The centre of the fighting was a few paces away. I got to my feet, my fists clenching, the old red mist beginning to swirl across my vision.

But that was as far as it went. I couldn't beat up the con who threw the mug, even if I could find who it was. I couldn't move. I was paralysed. It was as if something had locked my arms and legs solid. As I stood there, unable to move a step, my anger evaporated. The fighting seemed to recede a fraction, as if I was watching it through a double-glazed window. I seemed to be detached, thinking rapidly and coolly. *It's happened again*, I told myself wonderingly, and walked away from the fight to my room upstairs.

'Are you a chicken, or what?' demanded Chang later as we passed each other in the corridor.

I didn't answer. I just smiled, thinking once again of that extraordinary power that had overridden my anger.

It was the Holy Spirit, I decided, and debated whether to tell Chang. The other Chinese cons saw us talking and came over.

'Maybe you're looking for parole,' suggested Chang.

The same insult had been tossed at me after the fight at Long Lartin. I remained silent.

Ken swore. 'Hui's all talk,' he said. 'All that boasting about his big activities in Malaysia. All the fights and gang warfare. Never happened, did it, Hui?'

He pushed his face close to mine. 'Cos you don't know how to fight, do you, Hui? You're just a lying bastard. You don't have no reputation. You're nothing.'

The others sniggered approvingly.

I shrugged my shoulders. 'I've had enough,' I said quietly, and went on to my own room.

The following week eight Chinese cons were transferred to other prisons. The Prison Authority was afraid that Triad activities would flare up in the prison as a result of the gang fight. Before they left the Chinese put the blame on me, claiming that I had advised the Authority to split up the Chinese group. It was an insulting remark, especially spoken by a Chinese about another Chinese. It underlined the fact that the cosy group of mah-jong players in my cell was over, that I was no longer accepted and trusted by them.

I didn't mind what they said about me. One wonderful, glorious fact now dominated my thinking entirely. God had demonstrated beyond a shadow of doubt that he was able to help me overcome my pride and my violent anger. I was coming to understand that Christianity was about a God I could talk to; about a book that said true things; and about power, real power, incomparably more meaningful than the power-games I used to play in Malaysia, Thailand and the English prisons. As I tried to fit these pieces together they seemed to add up to a God who was bigger than I had dreamed. *How much more is there to find out about him?* I wondered.

21

THE TURNING POINT

I was in prison and you came to visit me. (Matt. 25:36)

The Wing Officer of B1 was a stocky, pleasant man whose face was permanently wreathed in a broad grin. Melvin Dunk's attitude to the men was strict but fair. Watching him at work and in various situations during my first days at The Verne, he impressed me in the same way as the Gymnasium Officer at Long Lartin. However it was only after the fight that we had a real conversation. I was shy, and had sheltered in the loud and cheerful companionship of my Chinese friends. Now I had lost my friends, and despite the leap forward in my understanding of God I was feeling depressed and alone. One evening I wandered into Mr Dunk's office with a minor problem, and hung around after he'd dealt with it. He sat back in his chair and looked at me with interest.

'I've seen you in chapel, Hui. Tell me – are you a born-again believer?'

I nodded enthusiastically and with some relief. 'Yes, I am!'

His grin seemed to touch both ears.

'That's wonderful, brother! How did it happen?'

I told him the story, and he listened enthralled. I discovered that Melvin always heard news of what God had done for other people with as much pleasure as if it had happened to him. When I had finished he told me how he became a Christian.

' . . . and there are quite a few Christian brothers on this wing. You've seen them at chapel, I expect. Let's go and meet them properly. This is wonderful, Hui!'

His enthusiasm was infectious, and a great burden seemed to have disappeared from my shoulders. He led me through the wing to a door behind which a conversation could be heard. Pushing it open without knocking, he took my arm and led me inside. A small group of men looked up. They were sitting in a cramped circle, with open Bibles in front of them.

From my loneliness and humiliation I was brought into a circle of instant friendship. I was amazed that there was a group of Christians in B1 who met for Bible study and fellowship every evening. They welcomed me warmly. The leader's room was near mine, and we became friends. Up to ten of us met from seven to ten o'clock, reading the Bible, discussing what we had read, and praying together. Until then I had read the Bible on my own or at most with one other person. Now as part of a group I discovered that God speaks to people in all sorts of ways. I shared my experience of reading Chapter 14 of John's Gospel the night I was tempted to smoke the joint at Long Lartin; others told how God had used the Bible to speak to them too. What was fascinating was that in each case it was a different part of the Bible: some passage that had seemed to me unimportant, difficult or just plain boring had actually changed somebody else's life.

'It's the Holy Spirit,' explained Bob. 'We can't see him. But he stands by us while we read the Bible and shows us what God wants us to know from it.'

Discovering the group was a major step forward for me and would have sustained me for months. Coming immediately after the fight and the loss of my friends, finding people I could really think of as my brothers was as much a miracle for me as those I read about in the Bible. In the group I could ask about anything that puzzled me; for example, the whole question of baptism fascinated me. Brought up in Malaysia in a Chinese family, I had never heard of it happening to anybody I knew. But now I had read about it in the Bible, and being immersed in water seemed to be a very important and necessary step for Christians. But what happened when you were in prison, where there wasn't even a swimming pool?

I asked the chaplain about it, and he tried to explain.

'Not all churches baptise by immersion, Hui. In the Church of England what usually happens is that the person is sprinkled with water.'

'But in the Bible—'

'Well, surely what matters is what's *happening* when somebody's baptised. The Bible makes it clear that baptism's a picture. Sprinkling is a different kind of picture, but it's a picture of the same thing.' He was speaking carefully, making sure I understood. 'Different denominations have different practices. Some do it one way, others another.'

'I don't understand,' I said doubtfully.

'Why are you interested, anyway, Hui? Do you want to be baptised?'

'I'm not sure,' I replied. 'I'm thinking about it.'

A little later he stopped me on my way to work. 'D'you want a visitor, Hui?'

I thought he was joking.

'Who's coming?'

He explained, 'It's a Prison Visitor – she has permission to see prisoners, help with any problems, give what assistance can be given from outside.'

I frowned. 'Is she police?'

He smiled broadly. 'She's a Christian lady, Hui. I told her about you and she would like to meet you.'

That was how I met Grace Walker, who was to be my friend and counsellor. She was the first Christian outside the prison whom I came to know personally.

'I'll visit you regularly,' she promised.

Again I marvelled at the goodness of God, who had added this new friend from outside to the ones I had found inside. Yet there was still more to come. Six new Chinese cons arrived at The Verne. By their use of sign language several of them were Triad members. Not long ago I would have sought them out and made friends, partly because they were Chinese and partly because they were the sort of people I most admired. I had different priorities now and saw little of them. One day Derek Cordell called me to his office.

'You've got another visitor, Hui,' he told me.

'Is it Grace?' I was surprised, because it was not her day for visiting.

'It's not Grace, no,' he explained. 'What's happened is that a Chinese pastor and a Christian lady have come over from Cardiff to see one of the new boys – he was doing a Bible correspondence course with them in Cardiff Prison. But I've told them about you and they would like to meet you.' He waved in the general direction of the visiting block. 'Might be a good idea to have a chat with the pastor – I told him we'd been talking about baptism and other things.'

I was delighted, and made my way to the visiting room.

It was wonderful to be able to speak to a Chinese Christian. Pastor Wong had been spending a year in England and was shortly to return home. He introduced his companion, a white-haired lady with a kind face.

'Annette has been a Christian worker in Malaysia for many years,' he said. 'She knows your country and your people well.'

He spoke in Chinese, but when he introduced Annette she responded in Chinese too. With a shiver of astonishment I recognised exactly the same accent and character of voice that my mother had. I could hardly speak, because the amazement of hearing my mother's voice on a stranger's lips took away my words. Then Pastor Wong asked me to tell them how I had become a Christian. I told them everything from my earliest memories in Georgetown to the wild and reckless life I led in my twenties, my involvement with the Triad, the gang warfare, and the drug-smuggling.

The whole story poured out. They didn't say anything, apart from occasional promptings and questions.

I told them about my arrest and early days in prison, about Exeter, and all that God had done for me since. I talked for over an hour, and finally fell silent, exhausted, with much still untold.

Pastor Wong broke the silence.

'Hui, that's a wonderful story. Thank you for sharing it with us.' He reached for his briefcase. 'Let me tell you something about what we are involved with in prison work. Do you know about the organisation Chinese Overseas Christian Mission?'

'No,' I replied.

'It's usually called COCM for short. It organises correspondence courses on the Bible.'

I must have looked bewildered, because he hastened to explain further.

'They're lessons you can study here. You write down answers to questions about what you've learnt. Then you send the answers by post to a teacher who marks them and helps you with anything you haven't understood.'

It sounded incredible; I knew that some prisoners were studying by post for various things, but it had not crossed my mind that one might be able to study the Bible that way.

'I expect it costs a lot of money,' I said wistfully. I really would have liked have to taken such a course.

Pastor Wong smiled, 'It doesn't cost anything to join the course,' he said. 'Of course, you'd have to pay postage, buy envelopes and so on.'

'No trouble!' I beamed. 'I get paid for my work in the kitchen, I can buy stamps here. How long before I can start?'

The pastor took some papers from his case and laid them on the table.

'I've got the first lesson right here,' he said. 'I will leave it with you today. When you have completed the questions, send it to me and I will mark it and answer your queries.' He pushed the papers across to me. 'I am leaving Britain shortly, but Annette will mark the rest of your answers.'

I looked at the papers he'd given me.

'It's in Chinese!' I exclaimed.

'Yes,' replied Pastor Wong, 'and of course Annette has a very good knowledge of Chinese.'

We prayed together before they left. My heart was overflowing with gratitude to God for the opportunity to study the Bible in my own language. But even that gratitude was overtaken by my feelings as I listened to Annette praying in fluent Chinese, in my mother's language and my mother's accent. When we opened our eyes, mine were full of tears.

It was a turning point, the major turning point in my life as a Christian. I had made my acquaintance with God as the source of the good feelings that came inexplicably as I listened to his followers singing hymns about him. In Exeter I'd experienced Jesus as an almost tangible presence. I had seen the power of God changing my life, altering situations that I had thought unbearable, and seen him answer my prayers. I had experienced the Holy Spirit: but until now I had been relating to a God who was like a schoolmaster, a figure of authority wanting the best for me but to whom I must submit myself completely. And now I had seen a completely new aspect of God. To make it possible for me to study the Bible was a good gift; yet to send as his messenger a woman who spoke to me with my mother's voice was unbelievable.

He didn't have to do that, I told myself. *It was unnecessary. It was a gift, nothing more, nothing less. God sent me a present. He sent me my mother's voice.*

As I thought about it that night, lying wide awake as gratitude and incomprehension rolled around in my brain, light finally dawned. *No, he didn't have to do it,*

I acknowledged. *People who give presents don't need any reason except one.*

The night-time corridor noises seemed to fade away as one thought filled the prison universe.

This God I've discovered – he loves me! No strings – no conditions – no price tag on the wrapping paper. The God the Bible talks about loves me, Chan Hop Hui! He sent me a present because he loves me!

From understanding God as a superior version of the Chinese gods, a heavenly Mr Bhang who was on my side and had a supernatural agent called the Holy Spirit, my concept of him turned a somersault. He was my Father, he loved me, he wanted to give me presents for no other reason than pure affection. *He even allowed his own Son, the Lord Jesus, to die instead of me.*

The Christian group was having one obvious impact on me: my language was changing. For a while now I had tried hard to stop swearing, partly because it used to be important in my old life, and partly because I knew using God's name or violent sex words to relieve my feelings wouldn't please him. Most of the time I was able to keep my tongue in check, but sometimes anger, frustration or merely forgetfulness defeated me. I was helped in my struggle by watching how other Christians acted; in this and in other ways. Melvin Dunk set an example that I could try to follow. The prison terms 'screws' and 'cons' also lost their bitterness. Prison slang was a useful shorthand, almost a foreign language we all had in common, but it was violent language. Now, however, I could speak the word 'screw' without any destructive or violent connotation.

And there were new words I had never used in the sense that the Christians used them. To them – many in prison for serious crimes, from rough and violent backgrounds like my own – every Christian was a 'believer', a 'brother' or a 'sister'; they spoke of 'fellowship', 'ministering to each other' and 'blessing'. It was strange to hear at first, the sort of talk you might use to a member of your family. But that was exactly what it was. Now I could see what it meant to be in a group of people who all had the same Father in heaven, and with my new discoveries about God's love for me I was ready to see the word 'father' in a new light.

The group was linked to the Pentecostal Church. Local Pentecostals prayed for them and wrote letters of encouragement, and there were other links of various kinds. I found that in many ways the Pentecostals were different from the Church of England; through comparing Derek's Sunday service with the worship services led by a local Pentecostal pastor, I learnt that different churches had different ways of talking about Christianity.

Bob helped me to understand.

'Isn't it that you are either a Christian – or you're not?' I demanded. 'What does it mean, being an Anglican or a Methodist or a Pentecostal? Why not just one label?'

Bob explained about Christian denominations, and pointed out that they shared the same love of God and desire to be obedient to him and the Bible as we had.

'But the church is made up of human beings, Hui. Sometimes there are problems of pride, even unfaithfulness. The Bible says that in the last days people will turn right away from God even while they look as if they're following him.'

He drew a Bible from his pocket. A passing con looked at us with amusement. We ignored him.

'Read Matthew's Gospel,' said Bob. 'He talks about it in Chapter 24, how even God's people might be deceived.'

'So what can anybody do about it?'

The seriousness in Bob's voice was disturbing. He tapped his open Bible with his finger.

'You have to ground yourself in what God says in here,' he said. 'That's how God has promised to protect us. And when you look for a church to join, that's the kind of church you should look for. One that's really committed to this book.'

The little group of Christians on B1 was certainly committed to the Bible. We read it every night and shared our understanding. In my first few weeks as a member I learnt more than in the whole of my Christian life up till then.

I was also attracted to the group by the welcome and friendliness extended to me. I felt one of them. It marked the beginning of a separation: the evenings spent in my room playing mah-jong and swearing and boasting with my friends seemed a long way off. I knew I could not go back to them. When you are born again you are born into a new family. These were my friends now. I talked like them, I shared most of my free time with them. They were more than friends. They were my brothers.

22

THE CIRCLE WIDENS

Annette Harris's strong, neat handwriting covered the page in regular, legible lines. My childhood training in Chinese calligraphy made me take pleasure in good handwriting when I saw it, but the contents of the letter were much more interesting to me at that moment:

> Yes, it's true. God does love you. He sent his only son, Jesus, to die on the cross for you to take away your sins. So who is God? He's not a Western god, but the Creator of the universe. The one and only true God, who has made himself known to us, first through Creation, in which we can see his power and wisdom; then through the Bible, in which we can learn more about his character and deeds, then last of all through his son, Jesus Christ, who came in person to show us what God is really like.

I had begun the correspondence course and finished the first lesson within a few days. Annette wrote to acknowledge receiving it, and there was an exciting postscript: 'There is a young Christian engineer here from Penang called John Lee. He's going home to Penang at the end of July. Would you like him to take a letter to your family?'

My immediate reaction was to say yes; a letter taken by hand would be much better received than one by post. But as I thought about it dissatisfaction crept in. I'd heard nothing from Tracey; as far as I knew she had finished with me completely. I'd written pleading for forgiveness and offering help with the maintenance of the children from the money I had in Thailand; but she ignored my letters, probably because I refused her the money she was demanding to set up her business. The prospect of sending a letter by courier merely reopened some of my old resentment, and I struggled as I prayed, pouring out my troubles to God.

I was having several problems spiritually at the same time. The most serious was that, as I prayed to the Holy Spirit to continue showing me what was wrong in my life, I realised that I had never faced up to the question of forgiving Paul. I'd begged Tracey's forgiveness many times, yet I could not bring myself to think of a reconciliation with him. *But think what he did*, I often said to God as I prayed late at night. But there was no response, nothing to fuel my bitterness, just a quietness, a sense that God was waiting for me to make the next move.

I told Melvin Dunk what was happening. He was sympathetic.

'I'll tell you one thing, Hui,' he remarked. 'You could have predicted you'd be feeling like this, a fortnight ago.'

'What do you mean, predicted?'

Melvin smiled. 'Well, look at what the Lord's given you recently – Annette and Pastor Wong's visit, the correspondence course, the chance of John Lee taking letters to Penang, a deeper understanding of the things of God – you wouldn't expect the devil to sit quiet while all that was going on, would you!' He shook his head vigorously. 'No, you would not. He's trying to spoil it all for you. He's trying to tempt you to lose your trust in God. That's how he works.'

I knew Melvin was right, and said so.

He shrugged, 'Not me, Hui. Just my Senior Pastor the Holy Spirit!'

He was a man who did not forget he was a prison officer. I never saw him break a prison regulation; he gave Christian

cons no special privileges; and he would not have allowed
the officer–prisoner relationship to be compromised. But
Melvin had numerous ways of showing love and concern.
A look could speak volumes, and to sit across the table from
him could be a closer fellowship than kneeling side by side
with many another.

Under Melvin's guidance I began to make progress.
Though I found it hard to forgive Paul, at least I realised it
was something that God wanted me to do. And there were
further outside encouragements. I kept in touch by letter
with Mary, for example, and three weeks after Annette and
Pastor Wong had visited me Mary shared my story with the
congregation of her local church, St Austell Baptist Church
in Cornwall:

> After I'd finished [wrote Mary] only the Holy Spirit
> could break people down like I was witnessing . . .
> Afterwards so many people came up asking if they
> could write letters – so you might be receiving more
> letters. Also I told them about your wife and children
> and the whole church is making them a special prayer
> request for you. You see, my dear, even though you
> are locked away you can still work and minister to
> people outside. These are your fruits, Hui.

As Mary had predicted, there was an immediate and
thrilling response. Letters of encouragement, support and
promises of prayer arrived. People I had never met promised to pray for specific things: my future; my life in prison;
that I would be faithful in my Christian life; that the Holy
Spirit would teach me everything God wanted me to know
about himself; and some promised to pray regularly for my
family in Malaysia.

I was overwhelmed. The language of the letters was
deeply moving. These people did not know me, yet they
were addressing me with more affection than I'd experienced in a long time.

I showed the letters to Bob and Melvin, and we rejoiced. I made progress again in my studies, and my depression lifted. I wrote a belated letter to Annette to ask John Lee to visit my children at my mother-in-law's house.

One shadow did not lift. In the normal process of English law my eight-year sentence would be due to end after five years, with remission taken into account. The date of my release, once far in the future, was now something to be reckoned with. I would be compulsorily deported to Malaysia. Sometimes I thought of the new strict laws against drug-smuggling in my home country, and the words '*Dadah* is death' came back to me. There was every likelihood that when I went home I would be in very big trouble indeed.

'I don't intend to appeal against my deportation order,' I wrote to Annette. 'I trust my Lord Jesus and honestly believe that he is looking after my future. Man can keep me away behind the prison doors, but God will be there to unlock doors that men cannot open. Praise his wonderful name.'

They were confident words, and for most of the time I believed them. But I was still a very new Christian, and however hard I tried not to, I wondered what lay ahead.

23

BAPTISM

In August I was given a new job, that of gymnasium orderly. I revelled in my new duties, and was soon organising football matches and other sports. I continued the COCM correspondence lessons, and as I learnt the basics of Christianity and began to gain a picture of what the Bible taught on issues that had often perplexed me in the past, I felt I was growing as a Christian by leaps and bounds. And all the time I had the fellowship of my group, the careful and thorough teaching of Melvin Dunk, the visits of Grace Walker, and regular letters from Annette Harris, Mary and the members of St Austell Church.

There was more to tell Annette. The cons were by now very well aware that I was a Christian. I was known to be a member of the group; my cell was decorated with Bible texts and pictures; and I had a shelf of Christian books that I often lent out. I had many visits in the evening from my fellow-cons. Some were frankly curious about the goings-on of the drug-smuggler who had become religious, but some genuinely wanted to talk. Ranji was one of the latter. He came to my cell on some trivial pretext, but soon made it clear that he wanted to talk. Sitting on my chair he seemed tense, his refined, aquiline features furrowed as if deeply anxious. I began to pray silently as he made small talk. *Lord, what is he really trying to say? Help me to know how to answer him . . .*

In that first meeting he confided several personal problems and worries, and somehow I managed to find some words of advice that were helpful. Later on he took to dropping in during recreation periods, and began to ask questions about Christianity, though always in a detached, academic way. Recently his interest had become much keener. The leader of the fellowship group got hold of a Hindi Bible for Ranji to read, and he came to my cell every night to talk about it. By July he was openly wanting to know all about Christianity. When I showed him the letters I had received from Christians outside the prison he was visibly moved. But there was something blocking Ranji's way, a burden of depression and fear that showed itself every time he talked about his home and family and his plans for the future.

'Please pray for this poor friend of mine,' I wrote to Annette. 'I need your prayers to win him to the Lord Jesus. He understands a lot, but he won't let go of his burden.'

One result of my letter was that Ranji began the correspondence course. And he was not the only one.

The second new student was Alan Parkinson. Alan was an English con, recently arrived in A wing. He was some years younger than me. When we met conversation seemed to turn instinctively to Christianity. He asked me how I'd ended up at The Verne, and before long I was telling him my story. He listened with interest as I talked on. I could see it was having a strong effect on him. I was used to being interrupted when I told my story – 'Oh, that was just fooling yourself' or 'Come on, Hui, you got religion so you'd look good before the Parole Board' – but there were no interruptions from Alan. Afterwards he just nodded thoughtfully and went back to his cell.

The next day he came looking for me.

'I need help, Hui. My life's in a mess.' He took a deep breath. 'Fact is, Hui, I decided after we talked. I really made my mind up. Hui, I want to be a Christian. I've asked Jesus Christ to be my Saviour, like you told me yesterday. Help me, Hui.'

As I answered, it was as if a separate part of me was singing praises to God while the rest of me talked to Alan. I explained to him how to grow as a Christian, how to learn more and become stronger in faith. I talked with a confidence fed by Annette, Melvin and my correspondence lessons.

'It can be hard in here, Alan,' I said. 'But when I think of all the wonderful things God has done for me since I became a Christian . . . '

Before we parted Alan had decided to start the correspondence course, and so I was able to write to Annette and ask her to make the necessary arrangements.

It was not long before half a dozen of us were studying the Bible through COCM.

In the months since I mentioned the subject to Derek Cordell, my interest in baptism had become stronger. The correspondence lessons had pointed me to Bible passages that impressed me all the more as I studied them. I spent a long time discussing the question with Melvin, and decided that baptism was something God wanted me to do.

'It's an act of witness to other people,' Melvin pointed out, 'and it's an act of obedience.'

As I read the various Bible commands that Christians should be baptised I echoed the words of the Ethiopian eunuch in the New Testament, who asked the apostle Philip, 'Why shouldn't I be baptised?'

Once I had made up my mind, Melvin discussed the matter with Derek Cordell. My request involved a major upheaval in prison procedures, because I had come to the conclusion that my baptism must be by total immersion. First it was not the common practice of the Church of England, where, as Derek had explained, it is normally conducted by sprinkling; and he had never officiated at a baptism by immersion. Secondly he was also dismayed by the sheer practical difficulty of getting anything into the prison that would hold enough water. So a large

number of people had to be convinced about the proposal.
I was worried that the chaplain would say it was out of
the question. Perhaps there was some prison regulation
which would make it impossible. I spent the day worrying
about what Melvin would report when I met him in the
evening for prayer.

He was in a very good mood.

'Derek couldn't have been more helpful, Hui. He really
got behind the idea.'

Melvin's grin was even wider than usual, a huge pleasur-
able beam that radiated happiness.

'Of course, it's going to be difficult. But he's determined
to make it happen. You've got a friend there.'

In the weeks that followed Derek went to enormous
lengths to make my baptism possible. He knew avenues to
explore when it looked as if it was never going to happen. It
was through his persistence that a small tank was eventually
found that could hold enough water for me to be immersed,
and through his negotiations with the prison authorities that
the tank was successfully brought in and, suitably adorned,
installed in the chapel.

He was also flexible about the form of service. When he
realised that I was unhappy with aspects of the Church
of England baptism rite, he agreed to incorporate some
elements from the Pentecostal tradition. Through his help
the Governor gave me permission to invite my Christian
friends from outside the prison to attend the service in
the chapel at The Verne. The date was set for 27 September 1987.

There were only two things that made me sad.

The first was that George, through whom I had encountered Jesus in Exeter, was not allowed to be present. He
had completed his sentence and was home with Mary.
But prison regulations restrict access by ex-prisoners to
prison premises.

'Don't be sad and hurt because George is not allowed in
to see you,' wrote Mary. 'He will be sat outside the prison

in the car praying and praising God with us. He will be
with us in spirit.'

But George's absence still cast a shadow over my
happiness.

The second sadness was that Annette wouldn't be present.
It was a long way from Cardiff, she was finding it difficult
to travel as she became older, and she was not sure that the
Governor would allow her to attend. But she was thrilled
that I was to be baptised.

'I really wept for joy when I read your letter,' she wrote,
but added, 'humanly speaking, it will be impossible for
me to attend.'

Some weeks before the baptism Derek asked me to see
him in the chaplain's office to discuss some details of the
service. He was filling in a form.

'What's your Christian name, Hui?'

'I haven't got a Christian name,' I said. 'My father named
me Chan Hop, but I'm a different person now. Those aren't
Christian names.'

Derek tapped the form with his pen. 'We have to put
something here. But it's no great problem. You're free to
call yourself anything you like. So what Christian name
have you chosen?'

I had already thought about that. I answered immediately.
'George.'

What better name could I choose to symbolise my new
life and new birth than the name of the man who was
sent to me by God to help bring about that new birth?
Unfortunately, although George is a common English
name, it is difficult for Chinese people to pronounce. I
tried, but it came out as 'Shawsh'.

'Pardon?' Derek queried politely.

'Shawsh,' I said firmly.

Derek scribbled on a piece of paper.

'Well, it's a good biblical name,' he commented.

I didn't understand until I saw the programmes that
were printed for the baptism. My new name was given

as Joshua. I was appalled, because I didn't know anybody called Joshua. I decided not to raise the matter with Derek as the programmes were already printed, but I was grieved inside.

Then Annette wrote to me, having seen the programme. 'It is an excellent name, full of meaning,' she said, and showed me how to find the story of Joshua and the great promises God gave him when he took over the leadership of the people from Moses. As I read the chapters she suggested, I realised that I wanted to be called Joshua. It was a name that symbolised God's calling, his gifts and his promises; and, as Annette pointed out, its meaning is 'Jesus is the Saviour'.

And that was how I came to change my name at a 9.30 a.m. service in the chapel at The Verne. It was a joyful time attended by over a hundred people, many of whom had set out in the early morning to be there on time. A party came from St Austell Baptist Church, and so I met some of the well-wishers who had been writing to me since Mary told them about me. People came from Jersey, Cardiff and London as well – all friends who had heard about me from others who were writing.

Miraculously Annette was there, having solved all the problems that had seemed likely to stop her coming. And in the car park outside I knew that George was praying and praising God with us.

Derek and the Pentecostal pastor led the baptism together. It was a simple and very beautiful service. At the beginning I read a statement of testimony that I had prepared, in which I told how I had found faith in Jesus, how he had made himself known to me in Exeter, and his goodness to me ever since. It was an opportunity to witness to some to whom I had not talked about my faith: many of my fellow-cons were there, some out of friendship but others cynically, wanting to see what the funny religious Chinese was doing in a big tank of water. But as I looked round the chapel all I could see were smiles. As we sang 'Jesus is King, and I will extol him', I knew that Jesus was present in the chapel.

Afterwards many were weeping with joy. Annette and Grace Walker hugged me and my friends shook hands and embraced me. Grace Walker took my arm and led me to a lady who was in tears.

'This is Beryl,' she said. I cried and hugged her. She was one of my faithful correspondents from St Austell's.

The Assistant Governor tapped me on the shoulder. 'Where is your friend from Exeter Prison?'

'He isn't here,' I explained. 'He applied to come, but you weren't able to allow it. But it's all right, he's in his car outside, and he's with us in spirit.'

The Assistant Governor smiled. 'I'll see what can be arranged,' he promised, and went off with Melvin Dunk.

A few minutes later Melvin returned looking radiant. 'You can meet George in the visiting room afterwards,' he said. 'The Assistant Governor's given permission!'

So I came face to face again with George, whom I had last seen in Dartmoor.

While talking to him in the visiting room I noticed a couple at another table, with a baby. We both knew the man, Barry, a con from Dartmoor, who was serving a new sentence in The Verne for a crime committed after his release. Their faces were grey and miserable. The woman was crying. The baby was very young, only a month or two old, lying placidly in its mother's arms staring at the ceiling. I looked at them, and back at the radiant faces of George, Mary and my friends from St Austell.

A conviction formed deep inside me. *That's what I want to do with my life. I want to help people like that, Lord*, I vowed. *Please show me if there's any way I can help anybody in this place.*

When I looked back on that moment days later, it seemed a sort of commissioning. I felt that on the day of my baptism God had given me a sign that my life was going to be spent helping people in some way, whatever I did and wherever I might be, whether in the city, the countryside or a Malaysian prison.

Chan Hop Hui belonged to a past world of bright lights and dark alleyways; where people's lives were traded like small change as packets of drugs were sent out to do their work of addiction and death. I could not put right the destruction I had caused; five years in prison could scarcely begin to pay the debt. But Jesus had paid the debt for me. In the service of baptism I had acknowledged that on the cross he paid all debts, and every evil thing that I or anybody else had done could be wiped out in God's eyes because of what Jesus had done.

So it was possible to talk about new lives, new beginnings, new names. Chan Hop Hui was no more. Joshua Hui was a new person, a person born again, and the baptismal service was a picture of it. Chan Hop Hui had been Chan Hop Hui's man. Joshua Hui belonged to Jesus.

The evening after my baptism, after lights out, I sat close to the grille of my door to catch the light from the corridor, and wrote to Annette:

> I'm still hanging on cloud nine, rejoicing every moment at what the Lord has given to us. I could hardly find words to express my feelings. I've been repeating over and over again, 'Thank you Lord, thank you Lord.' It was the most wonderful day of my life, nothing can be compared to it. All day I couldn't stop singing the songs that were sung on Sunday.

Whatever the future might hold, it was going to be different.

24

NEW DIRECTIONS

The cold rain was sheeting down, forming puddles on the uneven stone flags of the walkways. In the early evening dusk the sky had looked deceptively clear a couple of minutes previously when I set out from B wing for the chapel. I was not wearing my coat, and was regretting it. As I ran a man in a raincoat came into view. I slowed down and recognised Barry, the con in the visitors' room after my baptism. We sheltered together in the doorway of one of the prison buildings.

'How long have you got left to do?' asked Barry, raising a perennial topic of conversation between cons.

'A couple of years,' I said, 'give or take.' My wet socks were squelching in my shoes and my pullover was beginning to steam gently. 'I lost remission – about a week – a fight, a year ago.'

He nodded bleakly. 'Bastards. They just knocked me back on my parole,' he growled. '*Bastards*. And my wife just had a baby. She can't manage without help. I got to get to her.'

I didn't know what to say. The shadows wrapped themselves round us, forming a wet shroud of darkness that hid his face and made his expression unreadable.

'I saw her in the visitors' room. After my baptism service. Saw your baby as well.'

He didn't answer. Suddenly he spoke forcefully.

'I'm going to break out,' he declared.

The rain glistened on the rough granite surface of the main gate arch.

'I'm going out, you'll see. I don't care where they pick me up. Just so long as I have a bit of time with her. And the kid.'

He spoke the brave words in a soft, toneless voice, and I knew it was not bravado. He really was going to try to escape. The rain showed no sign of stopping, but he moved off towards the football field. I followed him, running to catch up. I was soaked. I could feel the rain running in trickles down my back inside my shirt, but it didn't matter. As we trotted along I was praying silently and fervently.

'Breaking out won't help,' I said at last. 'They'll catch you in a day, and you'll end up with all your remission lost and then where will your wife be?'

He became calmer, and we were able to talk about his problem. I promised to see Derek and ask him if he could help.

Derek contacted Prison Christian Fellowship, the organisation for which Rita Nightingale worked, and they were able to visit his wife and help her in a number of ways.

The incident was one of several confirmations of my intuition on the day of my baptism, that I would have a ministry of helping people.

In the meantime, I needed the help of other Christians to grow spiritually myself. One of the things I found exciting about being a Christian was that God brought different people into my life at different times, knowing when I would need the particular gifts each person possessed.

He brought Bob into my life when I was first a Christian. Bob's firm but careful teaching had been just what I needed to build me up as a spiritual baby. Now Melvin Dunk became my guide and teacher. If I had any time to be bored he made sure it was filled; he gave me Christian books, tape-recorded talks and constant advice and guidance. My Bible knowledge was progressing too through the COCM

lessons; and Annette wrote at least once a week, full of
advice and encouragement.

In October the long-anticipated news from John Lee
arrived. He had visited my children in Malaysia, and had
spoken to my mother-in-law. She was unwilling to believe
that I had changed, and insisted that she would only accept
it if she saw it with her own eyes. But he reported that my
children Ryan and Regina were well, and described them
to me. Having missed several years of their childhood, this
was the first I knew of what they even looked like. Some of
the old resentment flickered into life. But I talked to Melvin
and my friends about it, and after much prayer I was able
to accept that this was a step forward, even if not such a
big one as I wanted.

My correspondence was increasing too. My baptismal
testimony had been printed for distribution at the service,
and Annette had asked if she could circulate it among
Christian friends. It was published in October in a local
magazine of the Prison Christian Fellowship, and the
following month in the main newsletter of the Prison
Christian Fellowship United Kingdom. As a result of the
publicity I received letters from all over the British Isles,
including one from Rita Nightingale. It brought 1987 to
a joyful end. Rita, whom I had hated for what she had
done to my successful drug business, and then despised
for her stupidity in getting caught, was the person whose
story had opened my eyes to the wickedness of the life I
had led and my desperate need for God. I was thrilled as
I read her warm, friendly letter.

So, surrounded by the love, prayers and support of
Christian friends, both inside and outside the prison, whose
cards and letters decorated the walls of my cell, I celebrated
Christmas as Joshua Hui.

In January I completed my COCM Bible course, and
Annette enrolled me for further studies organised by the
Emmaus Bible School in the north of England. David
Thompson, my new tutor, was a sympathetic teacher and

wise counsellor. I began a series of courses on 'What the Bible teaches', 'Searching the Scriptures', 'Men who met the Master', 'Servant of God', and others.

As I completed each course I was sent a certificate, and the growing collection on the wall of my cell was often a starting point for conversations with cons visiting me for the first time. Many of them revealed deep problems. In some cases the Holy Spirit prompted me to say things which seemed to help; and in others I arranged for the person to see Melvin or the chaplain or other helpers. My letters to Annette were full of requests, and she was often helpful not only in providing answers to other people's problems, but in dealing with my own.

Among the books Melvin gave me was *The Fourth Dimension* by Pastor Yonggi Cho, minister of the world's largest church in Korea. I read it over and over again. Yonggi Cho was writing about the Holy Spirit, and what he was saying was new and revolutionary to me. He talked about the 'fruit of the Spirit', something I recognised: the Holy Spirit had restrained my anger, given me patience to bear crushing frustration and despair, and transformed my personality. As I watched people in the group growing as Christians I could see the Holy Spirit was changing them too. But what was different and astonishing to me were the *gifts* of the Spirit. He wrote of people prophesying as the Bible prophets had done; about 'words of knowledge' by which people knew supernaturally what they could never otherwise have known. Diseases were being miraculously cured. And it seemed the common experience in his church in Korea that people prayed in languages they didn't know, with the 'gift of tongues'. He said this gave their prayer a new dimension of meaning and power, that it opened up whole new ways for God to work, and that it was mentioned in the Bible in the context of normal Christian life and worship.

I'd read something about these gifts in Jackie Pullinger's book, *Chasing the Dragon*, though assuming they were

just for the particular case of drug addiction. At the time
I read her book I was still thinking of the Christian God
as an alternative version of the Chinese gods, and so it had
seemed reasonable that he could produce extraordinary
magic as the situation demanded. But Yonggi Cho was
talking about something God wanted to give the whole
Church, gifts for everybody in every place.

I was enthralled by this discovery, but I soon found to
my dismay that not all Christians agreed with Yonggi Cho.
Some in the prison didn't want to discuss the 'gifts of the
Spirit'; others said they were gifts the Church had once
enjoyed, but were no longer relevant to our age.

'That doesn't explain what's happening in Korea,' I
said to Melvin.

'No, it doesn't, does it?' he replied. 'Hui, this is a very
important subject.'

Melvin was one of the few Christians who called me
Hui nowadays; it was his way of gently underlining the
officer–prisoner relationship. Characteristically, however,
his 'Hui' seemed to convey more affection and concern
than many people could express in my new Christian
name Joshua.

'You know, Hui, I've been praying with you and sharing
God's word with you for a while now. And what I've been
trying to do is to ground you in principles, in scriptural
principles. I've been trying to ground you in the Bible, and
I've been trying to push you on as well.'

I nodded.

Melvin continued, 'And now this is a very important
scriptural principle you've met with. You've discovered
that the Lord Jesus has deeper things for you to learn.
That's why I gave you Pastor Yonggi Cho's book. The
Holy Spirit does equip us with power, and the gift of
tongues is a sign of it.'

Melvin's office was very quiet, and I felt a great peacefulness as he explained to me, in his matter-of-fact voice,
that the gift of tongues was sometimes given by God to a

believer as a miraculous private experience, and sometimes it involved other Christians laying their hands on the believer and praying with them.

'I'm not going to pressure you, Hui. I believe that God's good timing is perfect. When you're ready to take this next step forward, ask me and I'll be glad to pray with you and lay hands on you.'

I knew that I very much wanted this gift, but something made me hesitate.

'Melvin, I believe everything you say and I know it is God's words you are speaking. But I don't want to receive this thing from anybody but God. I want to ask God to give it to me himself, without anybody laying their hands on me.'

If he was hurt, no trace of it showed in his face. I doubt if resentment even crossed his mind.

'That's fine, Hui. God has his timing, and everything will happen when he chooses.' He hesitated. 'But if I can help you in any way, then you won't waste any time, will you? You'll come straight to me?'

'You know I will,' I replied.

From that time I devoured every book I could find about the Holy Spirit; I spoke to anybody who had experiences to share; in my letters I asked people's opinion and advice. And in all my prayers the matter I brought to God again and again was speaking in tongues. I was like the woman in one of Jesus' stories who made the judge weary by her persistence. Like her, I was determined to obtain what I was seeking.

25

THINKING OF HOME

'Take it, Hui!'

I lunged sideways to catch the ball, but the pass was clumsy and my attempts to intercept it no better. My right hand brushed the ball as it hurtled past. There was a sharp tearing pain. I doubled over, gasping in agony. The basketball game came to a stop and everybody gathered round me. Reluctantly I straightened up and looked at my hand. My thumb was sticking out at a peculiar angle, already inflamed and throbbing.

The Gymnasium Officer examined the injury cursorily. 'You've dislocated it. Don't think of playing on. Off to the Medical Officer.'

A chorus of ironic cheers followed me as I left the gym, nursing my wounded hand. It seemed that ever since my baptism I'd been experiencing injuries at work, from minor cuts and bruises to more serious accidents. I'd never had so many accidents before. In my mind I was sure that the devil was trying to attack me by spoiling the recreation I most enjoyed, sport. On the way to the Medical Officer I decided to make a stand. *The devil doesn't have to win*, I vowed. *Lord, you can heal this thumb. Please help me.* Gingerly I held it in my good hand and began to manipulate it back into place, gritting my teeth in preparation for an agonising few seconds. There was no pain. The thumb slid neatly back into position, and apart from soreness it worked as well as ever. The next morning there was some swelling, and the prison doctor sent me to Weymouth Hospital for an X-ray.

224

No broken bones were revealed. The thumb had relocated perfectly. A few days later the swelling disappeared and I removed the bandages. It was Good Friday.

I wrote to tell Annette what had happened, and rejoiced with her over the healing I had received. I wrote knowing she would be particularly concerned to hear I had damaged my hand. For Annette and I had a project, and I needed my hand for it.

At the beginning of 1988 she had drawn to my attention that my story was being used in several ways, that people were finding it challenging and inspiring, and that it was a sign that God intended to use it to help others.

She said, 'You should think seriously about writing a book.'

It was a new idea, and I was attracted to it. But I knew that my English, though improving, was not good enough, and I asked Annette if she would help me by turning my writing into good English. She agreed to do so.

So for some time now I had been writing an account of my life, and she had been correcting my English and commenting on what I had written. We had not progressed far – I was still writing about my childhood – but we were both excited by the project, and people to whom Annette showed it were encouraging. I had been aiming to write a chapter a fortnight, and so a damaged thumb would have seriously interrupted the job.

The devil was attacking me in other ways that were not so easily dealt with. It was as if the prospect of a book about what God had done in my life incensed Satan and inspired him to new attacks. For instance, there had been a spate of relationship problems between the Christians. On one occasion a letter I wrote to a friend in St Austell was misunderstood, and though it was unintentional I was miserably aware that it was caused by my own careless writing. It took much prayer and the help of sensitive friends to sort the problem out. The fellowship group too went through a difficult time, and for a while I stopped going, confused and distressed by the sight of Christian brothers in conflict with one another. In that situation again my own mistakes didn't help matters, and several Christians in and out of The Verne had to spend time counselling those of us who were involved.

Besides friction with Christians, there were always problems with cons who ridiculed our activities and saw every open act of witness as an attempt to win favour with the Governor and gain early parole. Many of the problems in our group were made worse by the malicious interference of such outsiders.

At the time I was helped by a sermon Derek Cordell preached about Simon carrying Jesus' cross. He pointed out that if Christians relax and lay down their responsibilities they become part of the problem that oppresses them, and increase the weight of the cross. Melvin Dunk too was a constant source of comfort, though he never allowed me to relapse into self-pity.

'There are no back-line soldiers in the Lord's army,' he reminded me, and opened his Bible at Isaiah 30:20. 'Look, Hui. "Although the Lord gives you the bread of adversity and the water of affliction, your teachers will be hidden no more; with your own eyes you will see them." You see, all these troubles, these trials, the Lord says they're going to be like bread for us. And as we munch them up and speak God's word into the situation – then our faith is going to grow and grow.'

I didn't say anything for a while. I was coming to terms with what Melvin had said. He interrupted my thoughts.

'Most of us look at the impossible and think, "I wonder if I can do that for God?" But the scriptural way is to look at the impossible and cry, "It shall be done!" So you've got to be faithful, Hui, and stay close to the Lord and his word.'

There was adversity to be faced and encouragement to be enjoyed. Adversity in that two letters to Tracey were returned to me in February by the Malaysian Post Office. They were marked 'Gone away'. So now I had no clue to the whereabouts of Regina and Ryan. Since John Lee's visit the previous autumn I had heard nothing more. I was thinking about them a great deal, and also about my mother whom I had not seen for many years.

On the other hand there was great encouragement as people heard about my story and wrote to me. Annette sent a sample of my outpourings to a writer friend, who in turn sent it to Edward England, publisher of the Christian magazine *Renewal*. He invited me to contribute an article, and so I wrote a piece about my early life and my conversion. Annette corrected the English and helped me to make it the right length, and in March she wrote to say that it had been accepted. Then in April she wrote again with some very exciting news indeed.

> Where do you think I'm going now? You will never guess. I've just received an invitation from the church which I helped to found in Malaysia, to attend the dedication service of their new and enlarged church building . . . I may be able to get to Penang, and if I do, I will do my best to find Tracey's mother and the children. But don't raise your hopes too high. I don't want you to be disappointed. 'Trust in the Lord with all your heart' (Prov. 3:5) – and pray!

I wrote back immediately, asking Annette to try to obtain an address or telephone number so that I could contact my children when I returned home. In addition I asked if she could find a church or an organisation in Malaysia that might be willing to look after me for a while after my return. It seemed a lot to ask, and in any case conflicting reports were coming from Malaysia. The new laws permitted the police to detain me for up to sixty days as a Malaysian convicted abroad for a drug offence; but I heard of several people who returned with foreign drug convictions and were allowed to go free.

I tried not to think too much about the future. It was all in God's hands anyway, and I knew he loved me. In my prayers I made a conscious effort to hand over all my worries to him. I continued praying fervently for the gift of tongues, asking God to give me a new language, a new depth to my life, and a new power for telling others about him. And then I settled down to wait.

Annette was away from 18 April to 5 May, and I heard nothing from her until she wrote to me on the day she came home. However she was full of encouragement. She had been to my mother-in-law's address, and found her and the children still there. Tracey's mother had clearly decided that she wanted nothing to do with me, and that was why she had sent my letters back unopened. Annette had gone with a local pastor to see her, and she had poured out her anger at the sufferings she had endured because of my behaviour. Annette and the pastor spoke to her about Jesus, and described the change in my life, but she said again that she would only believe it if she saw it with her own eyes. Nevertheless Annette was encouraged by the meeting, and was able to report to me that the children were fine.

Her second news was that a Christian rehabilitation centre in Kuala Lumpur would be willing to accept me, and that she had met the director of another Christian organisation which offered help to people in my situation. He had offered to link me up with a Christian Malaysian who would help me through the first days of freedom. That was wonderful, but some of what she had to report was sobering:

> He told me what would actually happen to you when you are deported. You will be put on a British Airways flight to Kuala Lumpur. At the airport you will be met by the Anti-Narcotics Squad and put in Pudu Jail for interrogation. You will be questioned until they have extracted from you all the information relating to your former activities. This could take days,

weeks or months, depending on your co-operation.
It will be a dark tunnel for you to go through, and
you will need all our prayer support. Your faith, like
gold out of a quarry, will be tested and purified by
the experience . . .

The news reached me at a particularly distressing time. I
had requested early deportation, because I knew I would
face further interrogation when I got home and wanted to
get it over and done with. Now my application was being
investigated at The Verne in a series of interviews which
probed deeply into my past life and criminal activities. I had
the uncomfortable feeling that my claim to be reformed by
my Christian faith was not believed.

Annette's letter was none the less welcome; it reminded
me of how far I had come.

'I am like a caterpillar slowly turning into a butterfly,'
I wrote in reply, and was content to leave the matter in
God's hands.

One thing in particular Annette had emphasised. It
was very likely that I would have my Bible confiscated
when I returned to Malaysia. 'You must memorise some
Scriptures,' she urged me, not for the first time, and listed
some passages she particularly wanted me to learn by heart.
I began to memorise them. With the possibility of spiritual
trials and tribulations ahead, it was as well to be prepared.

26

THE DEEPER THINGS

It was well into June 1988 when my writing activities took another turn. David Porter wrote to say he had seen my article in *Renewal*. I knew who he was: he had written Rita Nightingale's book for her. I showed the letter to Derek in some excitement, and wrote to Annette about it. Her response was one of relief.

'I am really too old to be writing a book,' she told me. 'I have enjoyed helping you so far and would go on doing so, but the journey from Cardiff is a difficult one, and the writing is hard work too! I think you should talk to David Porter.'

David came to visit me at The Verne, and we agreed to work together.

'What will be involved?' I asked.

'Lots of conversations,' he replied, 'and you writing down for me as much as you can remember about your life so far.'

Edward England, the publisher of *Renewal*, told Hodder and Stoughton about the project, and they expressed interest in the book. We set to work.

My time was now very full. Besides the material for the book, which I was producing to a strict system, I was also working on further courses with the Emmaus Bible School. David Thompson had worked out a shorter timetable for me, and I aimed to complete one lesson every week. I was thinking over what I had learnt in one of the topics when I suddenly realised that, without drama or difficulty, I had

forgiven Paul for betraying me and my gang. All I knew
was that the bitterness inside me was removed and in its
place was acceptance and love for Paul. I could not have
managed it on my own: it was yet another example of the
Holy Spirit searching through my life, finding and changing
the things that displeased him.

The Holy Spirit was the focus of my interest. For weeks
and months I had devoted all my free time to praying for
the gift of tongues.

One night in August while praying for the friends and
fellowship God had given me at The Verne, I felt as if my
heart would burst with gratitude. As I remembered God's
goodness to me, more and more instances crowded into my
mind and I could hardly pray fast enough. It was as if a dam
was filling up in my head, and behind it a great pressure just
waiting to be released. I longed to praise and thank God
perfectly instead of fumbling for words and trying to put
things in the right order. Praying seemed such hard work
that night. I struggled, but couldn't get rid of the picture
of a dam blocking the flow of my words. I was perplexed:
usually I had no problem when I prayed. *Please help me,
God*, I pleaded as I struggled, *I don't know how to pray
any more*. And then the dam broke. Suddenly my mouth
was opening and closing, and words were pouring out that I
had never heard before. I knew I was not speaking nonsense.
The syllables roared and resounded like music. *It's my new
language*, I realised. *This is the gift of tongues! Thank you,
thank you Jesus!*

As I knelt in stupefied wonder, the unknown praises
ringing on my lips, I sensed the Lord Jesus in a way I had
never known before. The room was full of his presence, in
the way a room can be full of a sweet smell or a cloud of
fragrant smoke. Peace surrounded me like snowdrifts, and
tears ran down my cheeks.

'Praise the Lord, praise his name!' I shouted at the top
of my voice. 'All praise to Jesus!'

Chinese and English mixed with my new language as I lost all track of time.

In the morning the man in the next cell stopped me on the landing.

'What was going on last night?' he demanded. 'I couldn't get to sleep. You were singing your hymns and shouting in the middle of the night.'

I tried to look sorry but couldn't conceal my ecstatic grin.

'I'm sorry I kept you awake,' I said. 'Last night God gave me the gift of tongues. I was praying in a new language.'

He scratched his head doubtfully. 'Well next time it happens, would you mind keeping the noise down? Some of us need our sleep.'

All day I couldn't stop smiling, and collected a few bemused glances. I hugged my experience to myself, thinking, 'You don't deserve it, but the Lord is faithful! He answered your prayers and blessed you!'

I needed to tell somebody what had happened. Melvin listened, and then we prayed together. As the beautiful new language rose in praise once more, Melvin grasped my hands.

'You've been blessed by the Holy Spirit, Hui,' he assured me. 'You have been given the gift of tongues. Praise the Lord!'

Thereafter I was conscious of a deeper dimension to my praying, a sense of being controlled, so that when my own words were inadequate the Holy Spirit would take over and pray for me in tongues. And secondly I became aware of the reality of God the Father, God the Son and God the Holy Spirit, which I had never understood.

The turning point of my relationship with God had happened when I heard Annette speaking Chinese in my mother's voice. The turning point of my growth as a Christian was receiving the gift of tongues.

✤   ✤   ✤

I now knew that I would be deported to Malaysia on 8 September 1989 and my time in Britain would be over. With the realisation that there was only a year left of my sentence I decided my efforts must now be directed towards the arrangements for my return.

A primary concern was of course my family: I knew Ryan and Regina were all right, but I had lost touch with my mother and had had no news of her from any source; and so I had no idea whether she was healthy or ill, or even alive. I began to worry about her.

I sat bolt upright, suddenly wide awake. My cell was dark. Only the subdued light from the corridor cast a beam across the floor. I didn't know what had woken me but I couldn't get back to sleep. I decided to use the time praying, but couldn't concentrate. My mind was full of worries and fears about my mother. I could think of nothing else. In the quiet of the night I heard my voice screaming abuse at her, demanding money, jeering at her for loving me. I remembered how hard she had worked for us when we were children, and how little she had had for herself. Shame and grief for my behaviour almost overwhelmed me.

I'm going to write to her, I decided, and found pen and paper. Sitting in the light from the corridor I wrote her a letter, just saying briefly what had happened to me, about my conversion and baptism and my desire to serve God in some way when I returned to Malaysia. I said I was sorry I had hurt her, and asked her to forgive me. As I put my pen down I realised I was feeling sleepy again. *It was the Holy Spirit who woke me up*, I decided. *He wanted me to write this letter*.

The next day I photocopied my baptismal testimony and some of the articles about me, and put them with my letter in an envelope addressed to my mother. I gave it to Melvin to post for me. It was the first day of the 1988 postal strike. The letter would inevitably be delayed, but in any case I had no certainty of getting a reply.

*   *   *

When I had any free time from writing I spent it talking
to people in my cell. They came wanting to chat or to tell
me their problems: some had become Christians in The
Verne; others were interested in Christianity and wanted
to know more about it. There were so many visits in fact
that I had to pray to God for patience and understanding.
The fellowship group had dwindled as members completed
their sentences or were moved to other prisons; but I had
a growing fellowship with the cons who dropped in in the
evenings to pray or read the Bible with me. On Friday night,
a landmark in the week, groups from the local Christian
community visited the prison chapel to sing and share the
Gospel. I enjoyed these times, and especially the visit of a
duo called Pam and Joe. I remembered the sing-alongs at
Dartmoor, and smiled ruefully to think of my hard-bitten
cynicism. How much time I'd wasted!

So there was little time to sit about waiting for a letter
to arrive from my mother. The postal strike in fact was
over, but I had almost forgotten writing to her when
some three weeks later a blue aerogramme appeared in my
pigeon-hole.

I seized the letter and took it to my room. When I saw
the name on the back of the envelope, I had to sit down.
It was from Joseph, my son by my first wife Helen. My
hands were trembling as I opened it.

He had been visiting my mother when my letter came,
and offered to reply. He said he had often thought of me
and wondered where I was and what I was doing, 'After
so many years, Dad, now we know where you are!' He
gave me news of my mother, that she was well and sent her
love. She was pleased to hear that I was a changed person
but wouldn't be taken in until she saw me for herself.

I had hardly expected a reply, let alone one from my
son. I had neglected my first family for so long and Joseph
was now eighteen. He had not seen much of me during
his childhood.

'Whatever you have done, and even though you're in prison, you're still my father,' he wrote. 'I still love and respect you. Whatever you've done won't destroy that relationship. I will support you and be on your side for ever.'

Joy and shame struggled inside me. What a failure I had been as a father! How much grief I had caused my children and Helen; how much that was bad Joseph must have heard about me! And here he was promising to love me in spite of everything, saying things sons should say to their fathers, but which I didn't deserve.

I wanted to give something back, to share my happiness with my son and my mother. So I wrote explaining in more detail how I became a Christian and telling them they could have the same relationship with Jesus as I had found.

More letters arrived from the Malaysian Christian organisation that was to look after me on my return. They said I was certain to be detained on arrival, but they would be at the airport and would make sure the authorities knew there was an organisation in Malaysia taking an interest in my welfare. They promised to have a lawyer available to represent me if necessary, and to ring the prison regularly to find out what was happening to me. Having it spelt out like that made me realise I was truly going home; it was an answer to some very specific prayer that there would be people ready to receive me when I returned.

Then I received a letter from my sister Angela, a practising Buddhist who was sympathetic to any religious faith. Her response to my letter to my mother was jubilant:

It was a great relief, it was unbelievable. I'll give you full support, even though we're from different religions! It was my sincere hope and wish that only religion could change you – I'd hoped and prayed that the church members would help you to reform and my prayers were answered anyway.

'There is a lot of prayer work to do,' I wrote to Annette.

I began to write regularly to my mother, my son and my sister, explaining my new religion in the simplest terms I knew. Many letters were exchanged over the next few weeks. Joseph asked searching questions about the Bible, and I answered as best I could; Annette wrote to him also. A local pastor sent him a Chinese Bible, and I tried to help him understand what he was reading. I urged him to pray to God.

'The first thing you have to do is to make some sort of commitment,' I explained. 'Repentance is a commitment. Are you sorry for the things you have done that have caused God sorrow? Then speak to him, just talk to him and tell him you're sorry.'

Joseph wrote back. 'I tried it, Dad. I prayed. And when I did, something happened. I felt peaceful.'

'Now you must go on,' I told him. 'You must read the Bible, and ask God to help you understand it, and talk to him even more.'

He made astonishing progress. In mid-November he wrote to say that having carefully considered all that had been said, he had committed his life to Jesus.

I was stunned by the news. I had been praying for him and for my mother, but I had not imagined he would make a decision so quickly. I obtained permission to telephone Annette, and she was delighted. She wrote to me later:

> I have written to him in Chinese and sent him a copy of Mark's Gospel . . . How about taking on a new project and doing a correspondence course on Mark's Gospel in Chinese, you be the examiner and make up your own course? It will keep you busy until you go back!

So there was another task for me to undertake, and I set to with enthusiasm.

'What's this you're working on?'

Melvin picked up the lesson I was devising for Joseph. I explained Annette's suggestion. Melvin was impressed.

'That's a great idea.' He put the paper down. 'Hui, have you thought exactly what you will do when you go back to Malaysia?'

'I want to be in Christian work. I want to serve the Lord in my own country.'

'But have you thought in what way, specifically?'

I shook my head. 'No. Do you think I should be making plans?'

'Well, I believe that God has given you a gift,' said Melvin, pointing to the work on my desk. 'You have a skill as a teacher and a counsellor. I think you should be praying about work as an evangelist or a youth worker. You should be thinking about working in prisons in Malaysia.'

The Christian organisations at home were discussing the first stages of my rehabilitation, but I didn't tell them about the possibility of teaching and prison work. Everybody whose advice I sought at The Verne agreed that I had the necessary gifts to do such work, and I was willing to do anything I believed to be God's will. I knew, however, that the first days of my return would be a time of adjustment, and matters such as my long-term career would not be the most important priority.

But I was thrilled to think that God seemed to have plans for me not only for the next day and the next week, but for a long time ahead.

27

THE HOME STRAIGHT

Christmas 1988 was to be my last in England, and I was helping to organise a major sports competition in the gymnasium. The chaplain invited me to help with the carol concert also, and with other Christmas festivities. I enjoyed it all, but very little studying or writing was possible.

In the New Year I returned to my writing and planning for the future. I was now in contact by letter with my mother, my two sisters and my son Joseph; but I had no contact with Joseph's sister Eunis; and there was little news of Tracey, Ryan and Regina. I prayed for them constantly, and tried to be peaceful in my mind about them, but it was hard not to want God to move faster.

I urged Joseph to find a church he could go to, and local Christians who could answer his questions personally. To my joy, he told me in a letter that he had started to do so.

Both Joseph and my mother promised total support when I came home.

'We won't try to persuade you to live at home,' wrote my mother. 'We won't insist that you lead a nice quiet life!'

It must have cost her something to say that, because she knew I was corresponding in detail with Christian organisations in Malaysia about what I should do. It was generally agreed that if I was not detained on arrival I should stay with a Christian centre for several months.

A letter from just such an organisation in Malaysia had arrived on Christmas Eve. My name was given to them by a Bishop Chiu, who had read my article in *Renewal* and had written to me. The director wrote, 'I would like you to write to us concerning your plans, giving us some idea as to your skills and training, if any. We have ministry contacts throughout the country and would like very much to assist you in your integration and placement with a local church.'

I sent a copy of my reply to Annette, and also shared with her my mother's thankfulness for what God had done in my life. I wrote about my own 'gate fever', the almost painful anticipation of my deportation. Sometimes I despaired of ever managing to get through the coming months. Gate fever was a problem Rita Nightingale had experienced, and now I knew what she meant. My thoughts constantly strayed to Malaysia, to my family, to the sights and sounds I remembered so well. What made it worse for me was that I was the last one of my drug-smuggling band still in prison. When Paul was deported on 6 January it said a lot for the changes that had taken place in my life that we parted on reasonably friendly terms. But I couldn't help a pang of jealousy now as I thought of him back in Malaysia.

Annette's reply encouraged me:

> Lay your anxiety down at the feet of Jesus. When I get on a plane and it is about to take off, I say to myself 'My faith and trust are not in the airline, not in the plane and not in the pilot. My faith and trust are in God my Saviour and in him alone.'

There was certainly a lot to occupy my time. I had completed twenty-four Bible courses in 1988, and wanted to do as many more as possible before my release. I had more letters than ever to answer as my story circulated. And my free time continued to be spent with fellow-prisoners, either for Christian fellowship or trying to help them understand the Bible. My own understanding of Christianity deepened as I studied. My early confusion about the Trinity and other aspects had been carefully and expertly dealt with by my tutors, and by Melvin and Annette. I was gaining a solid grounding in the basic teaching of the Bible.

Wonderful things were happening in The Verne. Cons were being converted, and those who were Christians already were going strong. One example was Johnson, a Nigerian from another wing and a keen Christian who really loved Jesus. Some time after my first experience of speaking in tongues he came to my cell.

'I heard something wonderful happened to you,' he said.

I was always eager to talk about the new experience God had given me, and I told him all about it. He listened carefully.

'I want that too,' he said.

I shared with him my thoughts about what had happened, and suggested he followed the same principles, and then I showed him some Bible passages that had helped me. The next week when he came to see me he was radiant.

'I've been given the gift of tongues too!'

We didn't talk much about it; we prayed together instead, a wonderful time of praising God, speaking in tongues, and singing hymns.

Johnson was not the only prisoner in The Verne to be helped by what the Holy Spirit had done for me.

The early days of 1989 were brought to a climax by the letter I received in February from my daughter Eunis. I was almost afraid to open it as I didn't know her attitude to me; but it was a wonderful letter, honest and open. As I unfolded the pages a photograph fell out. Eunis was seventeen years old: my emotions as I studied her portrait were a mixture of pride that such a beautiful girl should be my daughter, and shame because she had had to grow up without me.

'I've come to understand you better since I read your letters,' she wrote. 'I'm willing to forgive you for all the suffering when you left us.'

I couldn't answer her for a few days. Every time I thought about her I found myself weeping. The Holy Spirit was showing me things from the past to which I had never faced up. When I did write I said very little about religion.

'I haven't witnessed to Eunis yet,' I told Annette. 'I will pray for God's timing to minister to her.'

But I told everybody I knew about my daughter Eunis, and showed them the photograph; and I recited the contents of the letter to anyone who would listen.

'Take this as encouragement,' I urged them. 'See how good God is!'

Joseph wrote later to tell me he was seeing Eunis and they had been to the Christian Centre in Kuala Lumpur to talk about what would happen when I returned. It reminded me that I would soon be able to greet my children face to face, that the long years of alienation had come to an end.

In March I received a visit from Bishop Chiu, formerly Bishop of Singapore, who had taken an interest in me.

'Tell me what has been happening to you recently,' he said.

This was always a dangerous invitation because I loved talking about the Lord Jesus and the amazing things that had happened to me; but I told the bishop about the Christian work in the prison, about my family, my plans for the future, and the things that were in my heart.

Then he said gently, 'I think there is more to do, Joshua. I think that the Holy Spirit has something he still wants to do in your life.'

'I was baptised in the Spirit. *And* I pray in tongues. It's fantastic what the Holy Spirit has done for me.'

My voice sounded defiant. How could there be more to do than that?

The bishop nodded, 'But I am sure there is still something binding you, from which God wants you to be delivered. Tell me again about the time you were initiated into the Triad.'

I explained the ritual, the solemnity, the pantomime costumes and the elaborate vows. As I remembered the thirty-six oaths I had sworn I was suddenly uncomfortable about them for the first time.

'Some of them were good vows – loyalty to my brothers, eternal friendship, that sort of thing,' I said haltingly.

'But who did you make the vows *to*?'

A shadowy, cramped memory of a hot night in a candle-lit pig-house came into my mind, more sharply focused than it had been for years; the picture that hung above the altar, the litany to the Chinese gods repeated by the painted Triad leader. The House of the Fragrant Blossoms, I remembered, paid homage in its proceedings to the Six Eternal Beings, the gods and goddesses to whom we gave our gifts and our vows. It had never seemed important before.

I told Bishop Chiu. He nodded.

'They were not gods, Joshua, but when you swore to serve them you opened a doorway for evil. An evil spirit still has a hold on you. I would like to pray for you to be delivered from it. May I do this?'

He prayed, and asked me to repeat the words after him. While we were praying, something inside me moved as if a door latch was being slid aside. My breathing became laboured, and I gulped for air in great gasps. Suddenly my mouth was wide open, as if to draw in as much air as possible. I could not have closed it even if I had wanted to. I was aware of my pulse drumming in my head. Then a wind from nowhere rushed out of my mouth like a balloon deflating, though it seemed to go on for several minutes. Gradually my breathing returned to normal, and my heart slowed down. A warm peacefulness spread all over me. The bishop was smiling.

'The holy command of the Lord has driven out the evil you embraced when you were initiated, Joshua.'

'I know,' I replied, and I really did know, with certainty. My strongest feeling was one of relief, of being freed from a burden I had scarcely known I was carrying.

*   *   *

In the weeks following the bishop's visit I was aware that the Holy Spirit was extending his activity in my life. Just as the evil I had embraced when I was initiated had penetrated deeper than I had realised, so I now discovered that accepting the Holy Spirit's demand to control my life meant allowing him to probe deeper and deeper. What I had regarded as minor problems – impatience, anger when provoked by other cons, being frustrated by small setbacks – I now saw as major hindrances to my spiritual growth; and at the same time as I recognised how big the problem really was I was given the help I needed to deal with it.

That help was needed when early in April I heard the bad news that Paul had been sentenced to a further four years imprisonment in Malaysia. That he had been re-arrested we knew, but the consequent sentence was a shock to all of us who knew him, and a great blow to me. I knew that my longer sentence in Britain indicated that my guilt was greater than his, and I could hardly expect better treatment for myself.

News of Paul's sentence spread quickly among the friends who corresponded with me, and I received many letters of support and encouragement including some from people writing for the first time.

One letter at this time was from my mother. She mentioned that it was her birthday the previous Saturday and she had refused invitations to a special meal to celebrate the occasion.

'I am waiting for your return,' she wrote. 'Next year when you're back, we'll celebrate my birthday. We'll have the special meal then.'

That night I hardly slept, thinking about the hurt I had caused her and the years of bitterness, and I got up at 5.30 and wrote to her. *Lord, let her live as long as possible, so I can repay all those wasted years*, I prayed as I closed the envelope.

Ten days later I received a letter from Joseph enclosing several photographs of my mother. She looked happy and healthy, just as I remembered her when I had last seen her eight years before. Seeing her relaxed and smiling in the garden of her home, I realised that God had given me the comfort for which I had been looking.

28

LEAVING

The Temple of the goddess of mercy in Pitt Street, Penang was thronged with market stalls, tourists, fortune-tellers and many others drawn by curiosity or the chance to make money out of the curious. I knew the market stalls best; during the festivals the gang visited them regularly to collect protection money. We used the temple backyard as a meeting place, lording it over the timid monks who scuttled past quickly, fearful of upsetting us. They didn't dare to stop us doing what we wanted. Sometimes we hid our knives and other weapons in the temple itself, knowing the monks would never reveal them to anybody. When we collected the money from the merchants we sat in cool corners counting it. My girlfriend, the daughter of one of the monks, used to carry it home so that nobody would steal it.

Such images from my past life came back to me as I studied Ephesians, my new Bible course for early May. Annette supplied fascinating background notes on what the city of Ephesus had been like in those days, full of idols and violence and wickedness. I recognised the same world I had made my own in Penang. And I compared my old life to the life I was now leading as I read the great truths of Paul's letter: the church, the fellowship of believers and the call for individual believers to follow the revelation of Scripture every day.

My spare time was fuller than ever with the visitors to my cell and my increasing correspondence; and I was now

writing to Eunis explaining how God had changed my
life.

Later in the month Bishop Chiu returned to The Verne at
the invitation of Derek Cordell to conduct a confirmation
service. He spent some time with me but the focus of his
visit was the service in the chapel, where he preached a
simple and powerful sermon about the fruit of the Spirit. He
was an unconventional preacher, sometimes bursting into
song and even speaking a little Chinese. There was a great
deal of laughter during the service, and many thoughtful
faces afterwards.

By the end of May I had moved on to study Philippians,
Colossians and Philemon. My time in England could now
be measured in weeks; and as I contemplated my return
to Malaysia, with all its uncertainty, I found Paul's words
to the Philippians especially comforting: 'Therefore . . .
continue to work out your salvation in fear and trembling,
for it is God who works in you to will and to act according
to his good purpose' (Phil. 2:12).

'Yes, God's promises are true and never fail,' I wrote
to Annette. 'I have claimed all those promises, to be with
me when I have to face any possible circumstances when
arriving in Malaysia.'

Circumstances in the prison were difficult temporarily:
the gymnasium was being redecorated and I was unable
to carry out my normal duties there as orderly. Instead
I was given various other tasks and found most of them
unfamiliar and tedious. Progress on the book was difficult
also, because it was noisy on my landing and I found it hard
to concentrate. To make matters even worse, relationships
with several of the prison staff became strained, and I didn't
handle the tensions very well. I discussed these problems
with Annette and Melvin and spent many hours in prayer,
until I began to see what changes I needed to make in myself
and what God wanted to teach me.

In June Derek Cordell left The Verne for Channings
Wood Prison. I was sorry to see him go. We had had

some misunderstandings, and it had often been his task to cope with my frustrations and anger when things did not go as I wanted; but Derek and the chapel in his care had both played an important part in my life at The Verne. As we said goodbye I reflected that without his enthusiasm I could not have been baptised by immersion, and one of the most precious memories of my life in prison would never have existed.

By 5 July I was able to write to Annette that 'Joseph is doing better than I ever expected'; he was attending a Baptist church and reading the Bible enthusiastically. He had a copy of the Living Bible, an easily readable modern version which had been given by one of my correspondents. I could also tell her the wonderful news that Eunis had joined a Pentecostal church and was taking part in the young people's activities. She had written to me about Bible passages she had been reading, and asked me to pray for her.

'When I read her letter,' I wrote, 'tears of joy kept running down my face. What a joy! I do not know how long I knelt there, thanking God for his love and mercy.'

I began to write the statement I would have to give to the Malaysian authorities when they detained me. I was going to plead guilty on my own account, and to say nothing about anybody who was involved with me. The result, I calculated, would be a sentence of four to six years – anything less would be a bonus. I would probably have got a shorter sentence if I informed on my colleagues, but I was determined to speak only about my own activities: I wasn't going to grass.

There was also the long task of writing thank-you letters to my numerous correspondents; and as I wrote each letter I reflected how important it had been for me to receive the encouragement and support of so many people. I thought of the members of St Austell Baptist Church, and their pastor Malcolm Thorpe; I only know them because of George and Mary, but how much a part of my family they had become!

I had a mountain of letters from them alone, and nobody knew how many hours of prayer they had undertaken for me. I wrote to my faithful visitors too: to Grace Walker who had visited me every fortnight at The Verne, often accompanied by her friend Rosemary, and with whom I had shared my deepest problems and joys; and to local Christians who had come regularly to see me.

The new chaplain John Bloomfield arrived. I found his sermons helpful, and he was interested in my story. When he heard that Bishop Chiu had visited me and that his sermon in chapel had been so successful, he asked for his address.

'We must ask him to speak here again,' he said.

In fact the bishop came to visit me on 3 August. He brought with him a letter from the Christian Centre in Kuala Lumpur, saying that they would do everything in their power to look after me when I returned. We had a wonderful time of prayer together.

'I'll come and see you again before you leave,' he promised.

There were lazy summer afternoons like the one I spent playing cricket after the Sunday morning service. As I enjoyed the warm sun I was full of happiness and praise to God. But there were also tense moments, and times of unbearable homesickness. Watching television one afternoon I saw scenes in Thailand, Malaysia, Singapore and Indonesia. The beautiful countryside with its swaying palm trees, wooded mountains and tranquil seas brought such a wave of emotion that I had to switch the set off. Afterwards I realised that it was not so much the scenery I was missing as my family. And how long would it be before I was free to be with them again?

'This is an emergency certificate for your return to Malaysia.'

The official from the Malaysian High Commission handed me a form. I looked at it. It stated that I was a deportee and had served a sentence for drug offences.

'Now, you've been working on a statement for the people at Kuala Lumpur, haven't you?' he said. 'Let me see it.'

He read it through carefully and made a few suggestions. 'I'll need a photocopy, by the way.' He sat back in his chair expectantly. 'Tell me more about this religious experience you've had.'

As I told him my story he made notes on a pad. He stopped me a few times and asked me to clarify what I'd said. When I'd finished he closed his notepad.

'Fine.' He stood up. 'Well, Mr Hui, we will give you what help we can. If you run into problems with the police at Kuala Lumpur you can suggest they contact us in London.'

As he left I reflected that I had not expected this: instead of being cross-examined about my offence I had been given the opportunity of saying how God had transformed my life.

I went to chapel on 13 August feeling rather sad. *In less than a month I'll be gone from here*, I thought. The Christian fellowship I had known here was centred on this building that I was soon to leave behind me.

As I entered I realised that the chapel was fuller than usual. Had a local church come in to join the service? That sometimes happened, but I was not aware that a visit was planned. Then I began to see faces I recognised, though for a moment I couldn't really place them. But suddenly I knew, and then warm smiles were greeting me and loving hands grasping mine. The entire church from St Austell had come to the service to say goodbye.

Afterwards Pastor Thorpe explained how they had managed it; the arrangements were made with the chaplain in secrecy, and I had been cleverly diverted until everybody was in place. It was a memorable farewell. I met again people who had come to my baptism, and others with whom I had shared by letter. Pastor Thorpe preached a sermon full of encouragement, challenging me to stand firm in my faith

and promising that the church in St Austell would continue
to pray for me and write to me when I was in Malaysia.

There were other goodbyes to be said. Bishop Chiu came
for a final visit, and spoke to me at length about Chapter 6
of Paul's letter to the Ephesians.

'When Paul talks about putting on the armour of God,' he
explained, 'he is describing a Roman soldier's uniform . . . '

I listened fascinated as he showed me how every part of
that armour was necessary for a Christian, and challenged
me to take it for myself for the rest of my life. It was hard
to say goodbye to him. I knew I would miss his guidance
and encouragement. In four meetings in just six months he
had taught me so much.

'We will keep in touch,' he assured me, and I determined to do so.

Annette came at the end of August. We took photographs
of each other and prayed together. After such a long
correspondence I found I didn't have very much to say
to her at our last meeting. All my love and appreciation
had been poured out in my letters, and now that the time
had come to say goodbye there was just an aching sense
of loss. We Chinese are not good at saying goodbye and
we find expressing our emotions difficult in public. When
she rose to go I stammered a few words of farewell, and
left quickly.

Grace Walker and the other local visitors came and
made their separate farewells, and I grieved as each left
for the last time.

I put off saying goodbye to my fellow-prisoners until the
last minute. During the final weeks my room was constantly
filled with people: Christian prisoners from Columbia,
Nigeria, Kenya, China, Hong Kong and Malaysia; Allen
Gay, who had been a companion in sport and had taught
me to play darts; Steve Spencer who had supported me
through bad times and shared good times with me. Not
all of them were Christians, but all were friends, and I
knew I would miss them. Some, such as Bob Campbell,

had known me for almost the whole of my Christian
life.

David Porter wrote to tell me when he was coming to
work on the book. 'Joshua, I'm going to give you a goodbye
present – I've arranged to bring Rita Nightingale with me
when I come next. She's coming down from Lancashire to
see you.' I could hardly believe my eyes.

The chaplain was away on the day they came. We met
in his office, with a deputy chaplain sitting in the corner.
Prison regulations had to be strictly enforced. Anything
we gave to each other had to be first given to the deputy
chaplain for examination, and we were not allowed to take
Rita to meet other prisoners. But after a while we forgot the
strange circumstances and were talking as if we had known
each other for years.

I looked at Rita sitting opposite me, and thought how
much had happened since our paths first crossed. In 1977
she had ruined my business and driven me to drunken
despair. In England, in a cold dirty cell in Exeter Prison,
the story of this woman I hated had been the means of
my finding God. Now she was sitting in The Verne, a
chaplain watchful in the corner, and we were talking as
brother and sister.

She signed a copy of her book for me – not the battered
copy I'd found in Exeter, which had been loaned out
until it was finally impossible to read, but a new copy
I'd bought since.

When she left we hugged each other. We said goodbye
in the bright, enthusiastic voices of people who are trying not to cry.

The last few official details were completed. David Porter
came once more to discuss the book, and told me he and
his wife Tricia were planning to come to Heathrow to see
me off. My friends came to my room to praise God for
my release and for the future, and to help me pack. I
was given presents, small gifts that cost weeks of prison

wages, and promises of prayer and support. In particular they promised, as many others had, to pray for me at 9 a.m. on 9 September, when my plane would arrive at Subang Airport, Kuala Lumpur.

One of my last tasks was to write to Annette to give her news of a prisoner on my landing who had recently become a Christian and had been coming to me regularly for help.

'I'm leaving you a new sheep to take care of,' I wrote.

On the morning of 8 September, my bags packed, I waited for the police to escort me to the prison van which was to take me to Heathrow. I was still a prisoner until the moment I stepped on to the plane. All my goodbyes were said except one.

Melvin Dunk appeared, to see me to the van as he had promised. We'd already had our last private meeting and had prayed together for one last time. Now he was brisk and businesslike.

'Have you got everything? You've put the things you need on the flight in your small bag?'

I showed him the shoulder bag, stuffed with my Bible, study materials, and pocket tape-recorder with a Songs of Fellowship praise tape.

'Fine. And your paperwork? Your statement?'

It was all in order. We knew it was in order. We'd checked it thoroughly the day before.

We made small talk until the police arrived. As they came through the door I looked at Melvin and he looked at me. I thought how like a father this brother had been to me, how thoroughly he had taught me and how much I owed to him. He had never bent a prison regulation, but he had become closer to me than any prisoner.

I blinked away a tear, and saw that Melvin was struggling with emotion too. I moved towards him hesitantly, unsure what to do and suddenly hampered by my Chinese reserve. In the end I held out my hand for him to shake.

'Goodbye, Brother Melvin,' I said. My voice was only just behaving itself.

Melvin looked at my hand in disbelief. There was a brief, tangible silence. Then he brushed my hand away with his own.

'Come here, Hui,' he said gruffly, and wrapped me in a huge bear hug.

When I finally pulled myself away, it was like leaving part of myself behind.

29

HOME

The Malay officer removed the limp cigarette from his lips and stabbed my papers with a forefinger.

'Deportee,' he grunted. He stared at me in distaste. 'Come with me,' he ordered.

I followed him to the Airport Immigration Department. Subang Airport, Kuala Lumpur, was crowded with Malaysians, Chinese and other Asians. I was home again.

The thick-set, burly Immigration Officer, cool and impressive in his uniform, pointed to a chair. I sat down.

'Where have you come from today?' He barked the question in the Malaysian Bahasa language, which I barely understood.

'London,' I replied.

'And your crime?'

'I've got a statement here,' I said, fumbling in my bag. He flushed angrily.

'Don't speak English. You are not in England now.'

I apologised in stumbling Bahasa. 'I don't understand your language. I don't speak it very well either.'

He grimaced. 'Big-time international crook, huh? But you don't speak good Malay. Uh-*huh*.' He laughed. 'OK, speak English.'

I gave him the statement I had written in England. It set out details of my arrest and imprisonment, my conversion and my desire to spend the rest of my life helping other people. He studied it in silence. Then he slid it into a cardboard folder. I didn't know whether he had been able to translate it or not. He motioned me to get up.

'Follow me.'

His colleague in the next office was a plump, courteous man who read my statement with care, nodding thoughtfully. Then he questioned me thoroughly. There were simple requests for name, address, age and so on; but there were also questions such as 'Do you love Malaysia?' and 'Are you planning to leave the country again?' The answers were carefully written down in immaculate Malay script.

After ten minutes interrogation he took me back to the other officer. They talked together in Bahasa. I buried my face in my hands and prayed, *Lord Jesus, take over this situation. Don't let me be arrested . . . But if that's your plan, I believe you're going to be with me in prison whatever happens.*

I opened my eyes. The Immigration Officer was staring at me.

'You can go.'

I was stunned. He said it again. I got to my feet. He handed me back my papers and told me to sign a form.

'Thank you,' I said.

On the way to the baggage carousel my mind was racing. Paul, James and Roger had all had a bad time on arrival in Malaysia. But I'd been questioned for only ten minutes. *I'm a free man*, I exulted. Bubbling with suppressed excitement I joined the crowd of passengers waiting for their baggage to appear. *I could go now.* The thought teased the back of my mind. *I could leave my bags and just walk out, not have to be checked through customs, get a taxi, disappear in the city.*

I prayed as I waited. I remembered the advice I had been given by some of the cons in The Verne.

'Jump the plane at Singapore,' they urged. 'If you go to Kuala Lumpur they'll arrest you, you might even hang. Get off at Singapore, you'd be crazy to go on to Malaysia.'

I'd resisted the temptation. I was sure God wanted me back home and that he had a plan for me there. And if I couldn't trust him to take care of me in Malaysia, how could I trust him for anything at all?

But this was different. I'd passed Immigration. The only thing left was to get my bags. If they were going to arrest me, that would be where they would do so. But did I need to collect my bags anyway? They held a few clothes, personal things, my file of lessons from Emmaus Bible School, a few Christian books – enough to guarantee me a further interrogation in the Customs Department, even without the statement I'd prepared for them. *God is giving me an opportunity*, I said to myself. *I can just walk out of here and bypass the rest of the controls altogether.*

Waiting in the airport, I knew, were friends from the Christian organisation that had undertaken to look after me. They would take care of me; they wouldn't even know I had made a run for it.

Then I realised I couldn't abandon the bags. There was too much in them that was precious. *How can I abandon God's word and everything I've been studying? Would Jesus forgive me if I did? And do I trust God anyway?* I decided to get my baggage.

A few minutes later I was loading my three bags on to a trolley when somebody tapped me on the shoulder. It was another officer. He thrust an identity card at me. With a sinking heart I saw that he was from the Anti-Narcotics Squad.

'Wait here,' he said.

Another officer arrived. They each took one of my bags, nodded to me to take the other, and escorted me through a side exit to a waiting car. During the brief drive I tried hard not to think about the signs in airport lounges, warning of the penalties for drug trafficking. I knew that my case could legally be reopened now that I was within Malaysian jurisdiction. The death penalty was still a possibility. I prayed quietly, and concentrated on remaining calm.

The Anti-Narcotics interrogation was conducted by a police officer who had a friendly face. But the size of the file in front of him bearing my name, and the fact that he was the first Malaysian officer I'd seen since my arrival who was tall, increased my worries.

My bags were carefully searched and I was asked to sign a paper stating that I had been detained for questioning under the 1985 Dangerous Drugs Act. Throughout the officers were firm but not unfriendly. There were no handcuffs or other measures, though there were plenty of officers around them, all armed. I knew there was no chance of escaping, even if I had tried.

I was given permission to telephone my mother in Penang.

'I've got here safely,' I said. 'I've been detained for questioning as we expected.'

My mother gasped at the other end of the line.

'Don't worry,' I said. 'Just keep on praying to the Lord Jesus, and I truly believe that everything's going to be all right.'

As I put the telephone down I sent up a quick prayer that both she and I would be able to hold on to that conviction.

Then the handcuffs were produced.

I was taken to a police van.

'Where are we going?' I asked.

'Police HQ,' I was told. 'Put these on.' I was handed a pair of spectacles with the lenses painted black. 'Get in.'

'I have friends meeting me,' I protested.

'They will be informed you are being detained. Get in.'

The spectacles were removed when we were inside a small room at the police station. Though it was late at night the room was crowded with men and women police officers, mostly young. Once again I was struck by how small we Malaysians are. Most of the screws in the English prisons were tall and powerful.

More forms were produced and filled in. The feeling of joyous freedom at the airport had completely evaporated. I was given an official number, 89. The younger officers began taunting me.

'Hey, white man!'

This is a big insult in my country. My skin is relatively fair.

'You made a lot of money in Europe. They didn't hang you there – but sorry, you're in our hands now! Ha!'

Only one of the young officers didn't join in. She was a Malay in her mid-twenties. She looked sympathetic as the others ridiculed me.

I didn't answer back.

'I'm tired,' I said quietly. 'I need to sleep.'

'Sure! Sleep – take him to the cell!'

There was no bed in the cell, only a few plywood slats on a thin cement floor. The bedding was an old wool blanket. A tap dripped stale water, and mosquitoes buzzed in an angry cloud. In a corner was the familiar squat-toilet, a hole in the floor with depressions on either side worn by many crouching feet. I didn't care. I pulled the blanket round me, said a brief prayer, and fell asleep.

It was a troubled sleep. At frequent intervals an officer kicked at the door to wake me up. He shouted my number and I had to answer 'Yes, *Tuan* (sir)'. There were obviously other prisoners. I heard them woken up in the same way.

The next day was Sunday and nobody wanted to interview me.

'May I have my books?' I asked the officer.

He laughed. 'Not allowed. No books.'

'May I have my Bible?'

'No Bible. Nothing.'

I thought about my friends in England. They would be attending church, worshipping God; I knew they would be praying for me. The thought cheered me up and I began to sing one of my favourite hymns. There was an immediate banging on the door.

'Quiet! Stop that noise!' It was the duty officer. 'No singing! Stop immediately.'

For the rest of the day I thought about each of my friends and family, and prayed about their needs in the situations they were in. The next morning the officer-in-charge came to my cell. I asked if I could have my Bible.

'You can't have it. That's the rule. No reading, no Bible. But you can pray to your God if you want to. Only keep your voice quiet.'

I spent the next five days locked in the cell. There were eight prisoners in the block, but we never saw each other, and calling out was not allowed. There were no exercise facilities. The remorseless heat was especially hard for me, having lived several years in England. After the first day the blanket reeked of my stale sweat. Apart from the duty police officers the only person I saw was the young policewoman I noticed on my first night, who came occasionally to see how I was. In our brief conversations I told her quite a lot of my story.

On the fifth day I was blindfolded, handcuffed and taken to a room in the police station. When the blindfold was removed there was a Chinese official sitting opposite me.

'Inspector Lee; Bukit Aman HQ. I am with the Anti-Narcotics Squad. I want you to co-operate with this investigation, Hui.'

A bulging file with my name on it lay on the desk in front of him.

'I'll co-operate.'

Lee nodded. He was in his early thirties, with a round, pleasant face and a large beer-belly. His manner was friendly.

'Let's start with the easy ones, then.'

He asked my name and personal details, but soon opened the file and began to ask much deeper questions.

'You seem to know a lot about me,' I ventured.

Lee grinned pleasantly.

'Dangerous Drugs Act became law in 1985. Since then you've been wanted by Interpol for one hundred per cent interrogation. A lot of people want to ask you questions, Hui.' He consulted the file. 'Now, about the young man you employed as courier—'

I interrupted him sharply, 'I'm not going to give you any information about anybody except myself. Only me.'

Lee sighed, his pleasant face creasing in a frown. 'Sure?'

'I'm definite on that. I'll take my punishment, but the others will have to answer for themselves. I won't answer questions about them.'

I wondered what the punishment would be, and whether they would try to beat me into doing what they wanted. I wondered how long I would be able to hold out. Under my breath I prayed for the strength to go through with my decision.

The Inspector exhaled thoughtfully. 'OK. Let's get on.' He moved his pen down the list of questions. 'It could well go against you when I submit my report, though.'

The interrogation took two days. Lee probed and sometimes dug painfully into my story. It was a bruising experience; his quiet manner and pleasant attitude sometimes slipped alarmingly and he banged the desk and raised his voice threateningly. I told him the truth in as much detail as I could remember; it had happened over five years before and I was unsure of many of the facts. But he went back over and over again, forcing me to dredge up every scrap of information I had.

When he had finished Inspector Lee gathered his papers together and prepared to leave. We waited for the duty officer to take me back to my cell.

'What will be your recommendation about my crime?' I asked nervously.

'My superior officer will be deciding that,' he replied.

Back in the cell I prayed all day. I prayed for a good outcome of the detention, for the friends I'd left in England, for my family, and for the strength to get through the present situation a day at a time. Sometimes I prayed in tongues, sometimes not, but all the time I prayed.

Conditions were becoming very hard. The food was unappetising and I was losing weight. The lack of exercise was making my body ache. The heat was oppressive, and at night I bit my lips until they bled as the mosquitoes stung the parts of my body the blanket didn't cover. Yet deep in my spirit the Lord Jesus comforted me. When I was close to despair I felt God's presence in the cell as clearly as I had felt it in England. When I was tempted to brood on the possibility of the death sentence – which I knew was fairly remote but could not help thinking about – the Holy Spirit reminded me of things that Melvin and Annette and others had taught me. And all the time I repeated to myself the passages of the Bible that Annette had made me learn.

Sometimes I was so moved by the reality of God that I sang hymns of praise at the top of my voice, and the duty officer came to the cell and shouted at me to keep my mouth shut. Even then I was full of hope. I began to mark the days on a calendar I invented, using rubber bands from the packets in which the food was brought.

My little calendar had recorded thirty days when I was asked if I wanted a half-an-hour visit from any of my family.

'My mother is seventy years old,' I told them, 'and she lives in Penang. It's impossible for her to come so far for half an hour.'

I gave them the address of the Christian organisation that had promised to look after me, and asked if 'I could have a visit from them. A week later I was taken under police escort to Kuala Lumpur Police Headquarters; two representatives of the organisation had been allowed to visit me there.

'It's not good news, Joshua,' the director told me. 'The police have told us that you will probably be sent to a detention camp for two years. Following that, you will be under police supervision for another two years.'

My face must have registered the shock I was feeling, though I had known that this was a likely outcome of the interrogation. The director went on talking, quietly and deliberately.

'You can be detained here legally for sixty days,' he said. 'The Home Affairs Office will issue their order on the fiftieth day. I'm afraid that this is the only visit you will be allowed to have until the sixty days are up.' He tapped a sheaf of papers lying on the table. 'This visit is to help you make arrangements in case you are detained further.'

'Arrangements?'

'It will be necessary for your luggage to be sent to your mother's home, for example.'

We talked and prayed together, and it was wonderful to be with Christians again, but the worry about what was going to happen cast a shadow over the visit.

Afterwards I wept for my mother. How would she be able to bear this new disappointment? She was seventy. What would she look like when I saw her again? I cried my heart out to God. I tried to cling to a hope that I would not be sent to a detention camp, but the prospect overwhelmed me. Did God really care for me? Had the police told the director the truth? Several days passed in a blur of misery. Gradually I pulled myself together. The Holy Spirit brought Bible passages to my mind, I began to pray again, and I remembered all the wonderful things that had happened in my life so far.

I decided I would fast as well as pray. For three days I ate no food and prayed almost continuously. On the fourth day I felt at peace again. I knew that God had something special for me in the future, and that he was just as able to make it happen inside a detention camp as outside one. All I had to do was to be patient and wait for him to do what he chose. In the days that followed I found, as had many other Christians in the same situation, that solitary confinement was a time when I grew as a Christian and deepened my relationship with

God in ways that I believe could never have been possible otherwise.

The fifty-day period would expire on 30 October. As the time drew near I became edgy and excited. The night before I only managed three hours sleep, but I was so excited I felt no tiredness. But it was a positive excitement; there was no hysteria or confusion in my mind. I had a sense that the Lord Jesus was planning some sort of a miracle.

Breakfast arrived. As I thanked God for the food I prayed that it would be the last food I ate in prison. An hour later my number was called. The duty officer sent me to have a shower. When I had finished he handcuffed me and put the dark spectacles on me. Then he led me down the long corridor to the waiting room. *I'm going to hear the decision*, I thought, *I'll know soon how much longer I'm going to be in prison. They've decided.* We reached the waiting room and the dark spectacles were taken off. My bags were standing in the middle of the floor. The policeman gestured at the crumpled shirt and pants I was wearing.

'Get some street clothes from your bag,' he said.

'What's happening?' I demanded. 'Where am I going?'

'Just get dressed,' he shouted.

I became angry and repeated my question, but before he could reply two police corporals came in. One spoke Chinese. He smiled at me.

'You are released, Mr Hui.'

I couldn't believe my ears.

'I didn't hear, please say that again.'

The corporal laughed. 'I think you heard me, Mr Hui. You are free to go.'

For a moment I was giddy with shock. There was a knock at the door. The young Malay officer who had visited me in my cell came in.

'Congratulations! All those prayers . . . It seems they have been answered!' She shook hands and patted me on the shoulder. 'Go and work with the people as you have wanted. Share your faith with them. Your God will help you.'

I realised I didn't even know her name.

By now I was weeping with happiness. I put on my clothes and said my goodbyes. A police van took me to another police station, where I recognised the officers who had interrogated me before Inspector Lee. They greeted me with smiles.

'Sign this form.'

I signed with a flourish. The document said that I had been released unconditionally. I began to pray aloud and praise God for what he had done for me. There were people standing round, but I didn't care. The officers looked on indulgently. People who were released unexpectedly often did crazy things.

I emerged from the police station. A sweltering heat haze shimmered over everything. It was the first time I had stood in a Malaysian street for over half a decade. I used to know the airport area well, but it was different; new skyscraper blocks and apartment buildings had gone up, and my old landmarks were gone. But the heavy traffic and the dark-skinned people were unfamiliar to me too, though I'd grown up among them.

I took a taxi and showed the driver the address of the Christian organisation. It was in Kuala Lumpur, and as we drove into the city I was amazed how that too had changed.

'What's that?' I asked the driver, pointing to a huge skyscraper.

'Offices . . . bank,' he said laconically.

'When was it built?'

'Last year – maybe this year.' He swerved into the slow lane. 'Lot of new buildings here. You been away?'

'For a while.'

I knew we were approaching our destination, but the new buildings and roads were confusing me. The driver was confused too.

'This is the road you want, but I can't find the place. You sure you got it right?'

I saw a telephone box.

'Let me out here,' I said. 'I'll ring them up.'

The director was astonished to hear my voice on the telephone.

'We had no idea. Praise God! Praise God!'

'What should I do? I can't find your office.' I told him where I was. 'It's all so different.'

'Don't go anywhere,' he said. 'We'll come and get you.'

The Christian Centre was only a few hundred yards from where I was, and within minutes I was being introduced to the staff. The director showed me the telephone.

'Would you like to make a call to anybody?'

'To Penang,' I said gratefully. 'I want to talk to my mother.'

She sounded frail and tired. 'Chan Hop? They let you make another call? Is there some news?' There was an edge of anxiety in her voice.

'I want you to sit down. It's good news.'

I told her what had happened. There was silence at the other end.

'Are you there? Are you all right?'

She replied in jerky sentences, between sobs. 'Thank God! Thank God! You're free, they let you go!'

We wept together, unable to say much. She was the first to pull herself together.

'Now, you stay in Kuala Lumpur for a little while. Take things easy, you need to settle yourself. Don't rush things. They are good people you're with. Don't come to Penang straight away. You need time to adjust.'

It was my mother's characteristic wisdom, familiar from my childhood. Whatever the situation, whatever the stress, life had to go on, and somebody had to be sensible. As a child I had often hated it. Now I gratefully accepted it. I knew it was good advice.

I stayed at the Centre for two days. During that time I met Christians who had been praying for me, and was introduced to the people who would be responsible for my rehabilitation. Both my sisters telephoned the Centre; my mother had told them my news. Angela was full of love and welcome. Joyce had set a date for a full family reunion before she finished her call.

When I went home to Penang I didn't tell my mother I was coming. I wanted to surprise her. I left Kuala Lumpur in the evening. The sun was setting behind familiar hills as I sped through the country, and when the taxi came to my mother's house it was four o'clock in the morning, just before dawn.

There was a slight chill in the air as I got out and paid the driver, but also the promise of another hot day to come. I picked up my bags, pushed open the gate, and knocked on the door. The early morning traffic was already on the roads, and in some houses lights were lit. I looked round the small garden and recognised my mother's favourite plants and some garden ornaments I'd grown up with. I knocked again. Inside the house a light came on and somebody fumbled at the door lock.

She looked older than I remembered. In the split second before either of us said anything many thoughts raced through my mind. I thought how many of the lines in her face had been written by my long absence and my anger and hostility to her in the past. How would she have looked if her eldest child had not been convicted of drug trafficking? Every careworn feature was a reminder of the destruction I had caused, not only to her but to countless people around the world who had been damaged by my drug dealing.

But as she opened her arms to me I saw too how wonderful God was. I had left Penang an underworld hero; I'd come back disgraced and punished. I wanted the world, and I had come back penniless. The Lord Jesus hadn't made the evil I had done disappear. But he had forgiven me. In my mother's incredulous, delighted smile I saw a picture of the whole of my life. Like the Prodigal Son, I had come home.

All this passed through my mind in seconds. Then she was hugging me. A forty-two-year-old man, I sobbed in my mother's arms like a baby.

'You look so *well*,' she said at last.

I thought of the weight I'd lost in the past few weeks and all the sleepless nights, and laughed.

'So do you,' I said.

'Come inside,' she said. 'You must be hungry. What time did you leave? And you won't have slept. Leave those bags, just come in and sit down.'

As I followed her into the house the new day was beginning, the sky was flushing a watery crimson.

At the time of printing, nine months after his deportation, Joshua has established a drug rehabilitation unit in Malaysia. He has called it the Annette Centre.

Hodder Christian Paperbacks: a tradition of excellence.

Great names and great books to enrich your life and meet your needs. Choose from such authors as:

Corrie ten Boom	**Jackie Pullinger**
Charles Colson	**David Pytches**
Richard Foster	**Mary Pytches**
Billy Graham	**Jennifer Rees Larcombe**
Michael Green	**Cliff Richard**
Michele Guinness	**John Stott**
Joyce Huggett	**Joni Eareckson Tada**
Francis MacNutt	**Colin Urquhart**
Catherine Marshall	**David Watson**
Jim Packer	**David Wilkerson**
Adrian Plass	**John Wimber**

The wide range of books on the Hodder Christian Paperback list include biography, personal testimony, devotional books, evangelistic books, Christian teaching, fiction, drama, poetry, books that give help for times of need — and many others.

Ask at your nearest Christian bookshop or at your church bookstall for the latest titles.

SOME BESTSELLERS IN HODDER CHRISTIAN PAPERBACK

THE HIDING PLACE by Corrie ten Boom

The triumphant story of Corrie ten Boom, heroine of the anti-Nazi underground.

"A brave and heartening story."

Baptist Times

GOD'S SMUGGLER by Brother Andrew

An international besteller. God's Smuggler carries contraband Bibles past armed border guards to bring the love of Christ to the people behind the Iron Curtain.

"A book you will not want to miss."

Catherine Marshall

DISCIPLESHIP by David Watson

" . . . breath-taking, block-busting, Bible-based simplicity on every page."

Jim Packer

LISTENING TO GOD by Joyce Huggett

A profound spiritual testimony, and practical help for discovering a new dimension of prayer.

"This is counselling at its best."

Leadership Today

CELEBRATION OF DISCIPLINE by Richard Foster

A classic on the Spiritual Disciplines.

"For any Christian hungry for teaching, I would recommend this as being one of the most challenging books to have been published."

Delia Smith

RUN BABY RUN by Nicky Cruz with Jamie Buckingham

A tough New York gang leader discovers Christ.

"It is a thrilling story. My hope is that it shall have a wide reading."

Billy Graham

CHASING THE DRAGON by Jackie Pullinger with Andrew Quicke

Life-changing miracles in Hong Kong's Walled City.

"A book to stop you in your tracks.'

Liverpool Daily Post

BORN AGAIN by Charles Colson

Disgraced by Watergate, Charles Colson finds a new life.

"An action packed story of real life drama and a revelation of modern history as well as a moving personal account."

Elim Evangel

KNOWING GOD by J I Packer

The biblical portrait that has become a classic.

"(The author) illumines every doctrine he touches and commends it with courage, logic, lucidity and warmth ... the truth he handles fires the heart. At least it fired mine, and compelled me to turn aside to worship and pray."

John Stott

THE HAPPIEST PEOPLE ON EARTH by Demos Shakarian with John and Elizabeth Sherrill

The extraordinary beginnings of the Full Gospel Business Men's Fellowship.